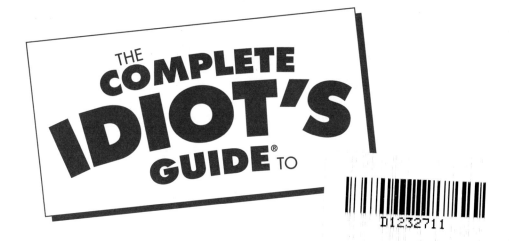

THE COMPLETE IDIOT'S GUIDE® TO

Asian Cooking

by Chef Annie Wong and Jeffrey Yarbrough

ALPHA

A Pearson Education Company

I would like to dedicate this book to my loving wife, Tara, and my beautiful triplets, Jackson, Garrett, and Mason. —Jeffrey Yarbrough

I would like to dedicate this book to the Liberty Noodles staff and patrons. Without them, we would never know how good our food really is. And to all the foodies, may you never keep good food a secret. —Annie Wong

International Standard Book Number: 0-02-864384-4
Library of Congress Catalog Card Number: 2002110194

04   03   02   8   7   6   5   4   3   2   1

Interpretation of the printing code: The rightmost number of the first series of numbers is the year of the book's printing; the rightmost number of the second series of numbers is the number of the book's printing. For example, a printing code of 02-1 shows that the first printing occurred in 2002.

Printed in the United States of America

For marketing and publicity, please call: 317-581-3722

The publisher offers discounts on this book when ordered in quantity for bulk purchases and special sales.

For sales within the United States, please contact: Corporate and Government Sales, 1-800-382-3419 or corpsales@pearsontechgroup.com

Outside the United States, please contact: International Sales, 317-581-3793 or international@pearsontechgroup.com

Publisher: *Marie Butler-Knight*
Product Manager: *Phil Kitchel*
Managing Editor: *Jennifer Chisholm*
Senior Acquisitions Editor: *Renee Wilmeth*
Development Editor: *Michael Thomas*
Copy Editor: *Michael Dietsch*
Illustrator: *Chris Eliopoulos*
Cover/Book Designer: *Trina Wurst*
Indexer: *Julie Bess*
Layout/Proofreading: *Angela Calvert, Megan Douglass, Mary Hunt*

Cover and insert photos © Dick Patrick, Dick Patrick Studios, Dallas, Texas

Contents at a Glance

Contents

Foreword

Much has been made of the contemporary buzzword *fusion*, whether it's in music, painting, fashion, or food. But at least in this last context, the word has a deeper, longstanding resonance in American gastronomy. Even in the pre-Colombian era the diet of Native Americans was a fusion of ingredients and cooking techniques that overlapped as nomadic, hunter, and farming tribes coalesced. The European settlers brought their own foods—pigs, chickens, steers, rice, sugar, and much more; in return, America exported tomatoes, potatoes, strawberries, corn, turkey, and chili peppers to the rest of the world. The valleys, bayous, and Great Plains flourished, and the cities embraced millions of immigrants who came with their own recipes and taste memories.

With each wave of immigrants—the Germans, Irish, Italians, Scandinavians, Chinese, and Spanish—American food fused with other cultures, creating cognate cooking: Italian American, African American, Cuban American, and so on. This is no less true of the most recent foreign arrivals—Thais, Cambodians, Vietnamese, Koreans, Filipinos, and so many others—who have come to dominate certain food sectors, like green grocers and seafood.

Traditionalists, who include myself, might inveigh against the compromises sometimes made in the name of fusing one cuisine to another (sashimi pizza leaps to mind), but that is what makes American food culture the most fascinating, exciting, and accessible in the world.

There is no better example of this accessibility, along with the engaging element of novelty, than Jeffrey Yarbrough and Chef Annie Wong's achievement at the appropriately named Liberty Noodles—a brazen Lone Star State name that only hints at the scores of dishes prepared here by Annie, who was born Arunee Wongchingchai in Northern Thailand. Following the hard path of so many immigrants before her, Annie went from being an underpaid sweatshop worker to a restaurant owner, finally making the move to Dallas in 1982, hooking up with Yarbrough in 1997 to open Liberty Noodles.

On one hand, the two couldn't seem more dissimilar, yet on the other, they shared a passion for food and a belief that they could bring something new to the diverse Dallas dining scene. Yarbrough's unbridled Texan exuberance and business sense along with Wong's feisty struggle to make a success from her culinary talents is a story as American as they come; indeed, their professional and personal fusion (he and everyone else at Liberty Noodles call her "Mommy") makes the whole thing work, from the strong design statement of the restaurant, with its rich colors, use of paper and metal, and outdoor patio and koi pond, to the sizzle of a kitchen capable of producing tantalizing dishes with names like Red Sea, The Royal Typhoon, People's Noodle, and La Mer du Vert. Wong serves food that begs for family-style eating—big platters of spring rolls and skewers, noodles and grilled items, lemongrass soup with plenty of crab and American corn, a bowl of egg noodles spiked with yellow curry and moderated by coconut milk, a salad made with Asian pears with goat's cheese and a sesame-ginger vinaigrette.

The flavors all make perfect sense. Cilantro, rife in Mexican cooking, is just as important under another name, coriander, to the Thai kitchen, and chili peppers—which did not arrive in the Far East from America until well into the seventeenth century—are the backbone of the cooking of Korea, Thailand, Burma, Singapore, and Laos. Nothing on the menu seems strained, and nothing ever tastes like a wide-eyed chef's experiment at the guest's expense. It is seamless, yet unquestionably a fusion of ideas as much as it is of ingredients.

The book you hold in your hands allows you inside the world of Chef Annie Wong and Jeffrey Yarbrough. The recipes are a form of Texas-Asian soul food, not difficult to produce unless the home cook is too lazy to gather the right ingredients—at which point fusion cooking becomes confusion. This is food you put in bowls and on platters. Offer everyone a canister of chopsticks, forks, and spoons, and plenty of paper napkins. The menu at Liberty Noodles reads "Eat Drink and Be Happy," which to me is the best fusion of all.

John Mariani

John Mariani is a food and travel columnist for *Esquire*, restaurant columnist for *Wine Spectator*, and food columnist for *Diversion*. He is author of the award-winning *Encyclopedia of American Food and Drink*, *The Dictionary of Italian Food and Drink*, and, with his wife, Galina, *The Italian-American Cookbook*.

Introduction

"I love to teach Westerners to cook Asian food!" says Chef Annie. She's found that Westerners' willingness to follow directions, experiment with new flavors, and in general get with the program make us a delight to teach. This is a new way of cooking for most of us. We arrive as blank slates and let Chef Annie color us in. And she's grateful for that, for, as she says, "Sometimes when I'm teaching in Thailand, I spend a lot of time arguing with students who say 'Well, that's not the way my grandmother taught me!' That never happens when I'm teaching Westerners."

Because she can't come to your kitchen without airfare, travel expenses, and a stay at a five-star hotel, look upon this book as a teaching guide to help you develop the artistic style that is Annie's way of cooking. We'll help you build a true pan-Asian palate by starting with traditional recipes, then borrowing and blending cooking methods and ingredients from all over Asia to create new dishes. As Chef Annie says, "The food is in my head and in my soul, not in a country."

The recipes in this book have been developed over decades as Annie has traveled and taught throughout Asia and the United States and cooked in the dozens of restaurants she's owned. Some will be familiar from visits to Asian restaurants; others will be completely new to you.

Though our recipes are written in a traditional Western style, calling for a cup of this and a tablespoon of that, it's helpful to remember that when Chef Annie teaches, every recipe begins with "Roughly, you use about a cup or so of …." Our pan-Asian cooking isn't like cooking French pastry, where if you substitute one ingredient for another or your measurements are off by just a little, you've created a mess instead of a masterpiece.

Annie always wants you to taste as you cook, adjust seasonings as you go along, look for what's available and fresh, and cook accordingly. As you become comfortable with new ingredients, it's mandatory that you experiment on your own. Look on our pan-Asian cooking as a journey through 5,000 years of revisions, amendments, and innovations that are only a starting point for the next 5,000 years.

Relax, enjoy, experiment, and have fun with this book. Cooking is nourishment for the body and the soul.

Extras

Throughout the book, you'll run across the following helpful sidebars:

Lucky Treasures

Our "Lucky Treasures" sidebars are chock-full of interesting tidbits about Asian history, culture, and cuisine.

Recipes for Success

These are tidbits of advice to make your culinary endeavor a great one. Be sure to read each one—from buying the ingredients to cooking a multi-course meal—to prevent fires in the kitchen or an excursion to the store for Mylanta.

Orient Expressions

The Orient Express railway quickly gets passengers from one destination to another in a clear, simple path. Our "Orient Expressions" will take you from the beginning to the end of this Asian culinary journey with quick and simple definitions of vocabulary terms and jargon so you can prepare the recipes and "chew, chew" your way to Asian cooking success.

Fortune Cookies

Just as a fortune cookie provides words of wisdom about life, our "Fortune Cookies" sidebars provide words of wisdom about cooking in the kitchen. These boxes contain helpful hints to make your cooking experience easy and fun.

Acknowledgments

The first group of folks we would like to acknowledge is very special, and it would have been very hard to do this book without them. I compare them to a sandwich. James "Fletch" Fletcher is the mayo that enhances what you know you really got up off the couch to eat. Fletch's creative genius gave us the roadmap for this book. His sense of humor is contagious, and I hope everyone who reads the introduction catches the bug that makes us foodies. Susan Friedman is like the bread that kept everything held together. She spent countless hours playing the air traffic controller between all the parts of this book flying in. Christine Carbone is the fresh veggies that kept the book crisp. Her expertise on food and editing recipes far surpassed all our expectations, while Louise Owens is the meat that helped fill the pages with her amazing knowledge of Asia. And Greg O'Neill is the toothpick that held everything in place. Greg's technical skills at writing recipes and brainstorming ideas were no easy tasks. Greg is a master technician with a gift for breaking down and documenting recipes.

We would like to acknowledge the management team of Todd Eckardt, Cindy Pippin, Raul Herrera, and Greg Watson for keeping the wheels on the bus while we took time out of the restaurants to write this book.

To DHS, David Hale Smith Literary, for bringing us a deal. To Paul Wong for the endless translations and transportation.

To Lillie, Allison Ford, Shelly Drought, and Larry North for the special ideas and recipes to help round out the book.

To my "Granny" Billie Henderson for always taking the time to cook for me and tell me how to do it. To my mother, Dorothy Yarbrough, for always allowing me to have so many irons in the fire. And to God for giving me the passion and strength to complete this project in order to share this information with those who want to learn more about food and entertaining.

Special Thanks to the Technical Reviewer

The Complete Idiot's Guide to Asian Cooking was reviewed by Karen Berman, a Connecticut-based writer and editor who specializes in food and culture. She is a contributing editor to *Wine Enthusiast* magazine, and her work has appeared in magazines, newspapers, and newsletters. She is the author of *American Indian Traditions and Ceremonies* and has worked in various editorial capacities on numerous cookbooks.

Trademarks

All terms mentioned in this book that are known to be or are suspected of being trademarks or service marks have been appropriately capitalized. Alpha Books and Pearson Education, Inc., cannot attest to the accuracy of this information. Use of a term in this book should not be regarded as affecting the validity of any trademark or service mark.

Part 1

Getting Started

"Good chefs are smart shoppers," says Chef Annie. Shopping for the ingredients for our new Asian recipes is a much easier task than it was 30 years ago when Chef Annie first arrived in the United States. Back then, the hunt for lemongrass or kaffir lime leaves could mean an all-day expedition. Today, cities large and small have strong Asian communities that support great Asian markets where the everyday necessities for Asian cooking are there for the asking. And many non-Asian grocery stores carry an array of Asian staples unheard of even 10 years ago.

In this part, we'll take a look at many of the intriguing, frequently used ingredients of Asian cooking and decipher the aisles of rice and noodles that are the backbone of every Asian market. We'll also talk a bit about how things came to be the way they are in the Asian kitchen, with a look at the history of Asian cooking.

Intro to New Asian Cooking

In This Chapter

- ◆ The fusion misconception
- ◆ Choosing and seasoning a wok
- ◆ Your steamer, your friend
- ◆ Utensil town—knives, gadgets, and gizmos
- ◆ Learn to use chopsticks—really!

Welcome to the tasty world of Asian cooking. Get your chopsticks ready: You're about to take a culinary journey through Asia. And if you don't know how to use chopsticks, don't worry. This guide will have you wielding them like an expert in no time at all!

More Flavors Than You Can Shake a Chopstick At

The continent of Asia extends clear from within the nation of Turkey to Japan's Pacific coast and includes nations that are not particularly well known in the West. When we think of Asian cooking, however, we think of the culinary gems of Thailand, China, Japan, Korea, Vietnam, Laos, India, Mongolia, Malaysia, and Indonesia, and it's these cuisines that are the focus of this book. Mention Asia and you conjure images of idyllic beaches, lush tropical forests, and snow-capped mountains, bustling cities and remote villages, emerald green rice paddies and throngs of people on bicycles and motorbikes. Preparing the dishes found in this guide can take you on a mini-vacation without leaving your kitchen.

Lucky Treasures

What comes to mind with the thought of Asian food? Typically, it's the crisp vegetables and fresh seafood of the orient—China, Korea, Thailand, Vietnam, and the like. Although Asia geographically includes the middle eastern countries such as Pakistan, India, Uzbekistan, Malaysia, and Afghanistan, in the culinary world they are not addressed as being Asian. This is largely because these are two different groups of cuisine that have different points of philosophical reference and flavor profiles.

Asian cooking is a very forgiving cuisine. You don't have to attend culinary school or be a chef at a trendy restaurant to succeed in the new Asian kitchen. The food is simple compared to other cuisines, but the flavors are intense and exotic. Whether it's rich Thai-inspired coconut milk soup or the refreshing tanginess of a green papaya salad from Laos, you'll be amazed at what you can create.

A Guide to the Guide

Just as breaking open a coconut reveals the sweet fruit inside, opening this guide unlocks the treasures of new Asian cooking. If you want to impress a date, these recipes can fuel your passion and make you look like a gourmet. If you want to spice up your family's dinner table with some new flavors, this guide is all you need.

Fortune Cookies

The recipes in this book are incredibly easy to make. The secret is to prepare all the ingredients ahead of time. Cut, shred, dice, and julienne before you ever turn on the heat and you'll have enough time to clean up the mess. Actually, the mess factor is minimal, too.

To create these exciting new dishes, you first need to learn a few things about traditional recipes and preparations from each cuisine. For example, stir-frying is a core lesson learned in Chinese cooking that will translate to any cuisine.

The most important concept you should get out of this guide is the spirit of experimentation. Part of the fun of Asian cooking is creating new dishes. Once you learn some basics, you can mix and match ingredients and styles with little fear of consequence. Asian cooking is perfect for culinary exploration. If you're looking for some adventure, the recipes in this book will help get you started!

Fusion: When Two Foods Collide

In the late 1980s, the term *fusion* saturated menus in restaurants of every cuisine. In culinary usage, fusion basically means that one region's food is combined with that of another, completely different, region. For example, a chef might take a traditional French dish and spruce it up with Asian ingredients or preparations. Because Asian cooking combines related flavors found across Asia, a better term would be *pan-Asian* cooking. Pan-Asian is the foundation upon which we will build delicious, new Asian meals.

Orient Expressions
Pan-Asian describes anything that derives its source from selected countries or areas of Asia.

But first let's get familiar with the tools you'll need to create wonderful pan-Asian cuisine.

Utensils, Gadgets, and Cookware

From woks and skimmers to chopsticks and bamboo steamers, Asian cookware and utensils are unique. They are also integral in the preparation of the food. If you've ever scrambled eggs, you know it doesn't matter whether you use an 8-inch omelet pan or a 10-inch skillet. But if you try to go wok-less and make stir-fry in a regular frying pan, the results could be hazardous to your palate.

Some of the items we're about to discuss can be replaced by gadgets that are probably already in your home. You'll soon know what you can substitute and what you need to buy—and have your equipment shopping list ready to go.

Wok 'n' Roll

The wok is the cornerstone in any Asian kitchen. Whether it's the classic cast-iron Chinese wok or the deeper Indian version known as a kadai, the wok gives life to the Asian kitchen. You can fry, steam, and even bake using your wok.

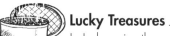

Lucky Treasures
In Indonesia, the wok is known as kuali; in Thailand, it's called kratha (pronounced *krah-tah*).

Choosing a Wok

The wok started as a solution to the limited resources of the region. Because fuel sources were rare and valuable, the Chinese needed to develop a fuel-saving cooking method that would cook their food fast. They developed a bowl-shape pan that distributed heat quickly and evenly. Because the pan was rounded, the sides helped keep the food in the pan and aided in the cooking process.

The wok has come a long way, baby. In addition to the cast-iron woks from long ago, carbon steel, Stainless-steel, aluminum, copper, nonstick surface, and even electric woks are available today.

Based on our experience, cast-iron and carbon steel woks are the best overall. However, the type of wok you choose depends on your needs. For example, college students might prefer an electric wok over a hot plate for their dorm rooms. It's more versatile and the pan and heating element are one and the same. Two things to keep in mind: Stainless-steel does not conduct heat as well as carbon steel and cast-iron. Also, the surfaces of nonstick pans were not designed to take the heat that accompanies wok cooking.

We use carbon steel at the restaurant because of the heat conduction factor and we have a very strong source of heat, which works well for this type of wok. Most homes don't have the raging gas burners needed to obtain the degree of heat necessary for carbon steel. Cast-iron is perfect for home use. If you have a gas kitchen, you're in great shape—just heat the wok for about 5 minutes before putting any food in it; if your kitchen is electric, you will need to heat the wok for at least 15 minutes.

A wok will have either two small, rounded handles across from each other or one long handle like a conventional frying pan. Again, whatever best suits your needs should dictate your decision. If you have arthritis, it may be difficult for you to lift the wok and its ingredients using one handle. A two-handle version might be better.

One-handled wok.

Two-handled wok.

Another factor you'll want to keep in mind when choosing a wok is size. Just like Goldilocks, you don't want a wok too large or too small—it must be just right for you.

If you're constantly cooking for a large number of people, you might want to look at a larger wok. Typically, a medium-size wok will be just right for most occasions.

The last thing to consider is wok accessories. Most woks today come in a "kit" form. You get a wok brush, various spoons or strainers, long cooking chopsticks, and a wok stand. The wok stand is very important if you have an electric stove. Because the coils on an electric stove are flat and the wok is curved, you need a round wok stand to keep the wok from toppling. If you choose a wok that does not include a stand, you might need to purchase one separately.

Fortune Cookies

When it comes to woks, size does matter. If you try to prepare too much food in a wok, it will not cook properly. If you put in too little food, it might overcook. If you choose a medium-size wok and follow the recipes, you will be fine.

Seasoning Your Wok

When you get a new wok, you must "season" it. Seasoning the wok prevents food from sticking to it and contributes some flavor. Seasoning it after washing it prevents it from rusting, too. If you bought a nonstick surface wok, a stainless-steel wok, or an electric wok, you can skip the seasoning because those surfaces are not affected by soap. (Soap strips the wok, leaving just cold, flavorless metal.) However, if you purchased a carbon steel or cast-iron wok, you'll need to pay attention to this section.

When you first get a carbon steel or cast-iron wok, the manufacturer will often ship it with a protective coat of wax or oil that covers the inside surface. The first time you wash your wok, use soap to remove this coating. When you dry it, rub oil over the inside of the wok with a paper towel. You will notice that the paper towel has some black on it. Rinse the wok with warm water and rub the inside surface with oil again. Repeat the rinsing and rubbing until the paper towel comes away with only the oil on it.

Fortune Cookies

Woks are best cleaned using only hot water and paper towels. If you do use soap, never use a scouring pad. In any case, after cleaning your wok, you should dry it immediately and rub a very thin coating of vegetable oil over the cooking surface to prevent rusting. Re-season your wok every time you wash it with soap.

Your wok is seasoned and ready to fire up.

Full Steam Ahead: The Right Steamer for You

Steamers are another important tool in the Asian kitchen. With your steamer, you can make succulent dumplings or any number of other Asian favorites.

The steamer consists of stackable trays and a lid. The trays are perforated with holes or slits. When the steamer is placed over boiling water, the perforations allow steam to rise through the contraption, cooking the food placed in the trays to perfection. Items that need more steaming are placed on the lower trays while items that require less steaming are placed on the upper trays. The curvature of the wok makes a perfect base upon which to rest the steamer.

Steamers come in two basic types: bamboo and metal. Which one you choose is up to you. For some people, a bamboo steamer is elegant and has an authentic look about it. Others take delight in watching the chrome of the metal steamer spouting out smoke like a shiny locomotive perched on the stove top. Items steamed in bamboo turn out more flavorful. However, the downside to bamboo is that the lid often warps because of wetness.

When steaming, select a large pot that is about a half inch smaller than the diameter of your steamer. To steam, you simply place the covered steamer on top of the uncovered pot. You can add enough water and not have to worry about refilling the pot. Traditionally, the steamer will rest in a wok with water that comes to just within the bottom rack of the steamer. Either way you want as much water as possible (to create the steam), but you don't want the water to touch the bottom rack of the steamer.

Recipes for Success
When steaming, remember to open the lid carefully. Always use a dry towel or potholder and keep your face away from that first rush of hot steam.

Lucky Treasures
Are you steamerless? If you can't find a steamer, a metal colander is a good substitute. Put the items to be steamed in the colander and place the colander in a boiling pot of water. Make sure the water level is low enough that it doesn't touch the items in your makeshift steamer. Cover with a lid and wait for that steamin' magic!

Fortune Cookies
Cleavers range in weight from heavy carbon steel to lightweight stainless-steel. Because of its ease of sharpening, a carbon steel cleaver is preferred. However, carbon steel rusts easily, so always dry your cleaver immediately after washing it.

Slicers, Dicers, and Other Fun Kitchen Gadgets

Part of the fun of learning a new cuisine is acquiring new gadgets for the kitchen. Most of the equipment used in Asian cooking should be familiar to you. In fact, some of the items may already have a home in your kitchen. With the popularity of Asian cooking on the rise, any items you don't have should be readily available at a local retailer or on the Internet.

◆ A cleaver is a heavy, rectangular-shape cutting instrument used for cutting through tough elements such as bone. It's also handy for shredding meat and mincing, slicing, and chopping vegetables.

- An elongated knife is razor sharp and used a lot in Japanese cooking. You can substitute a well-sharpened chef's knife.

- A boning knife is used to filet fish and makes quick work of those tricky moves necessary to bone poultry.

- A honing steel should be used just about every day. Running the full length of the knife against the steel helps keep the blade's edge straight.

Lucky Treasures

If you don't have a honing steel at your fingertips and need to straighten a blade, impress your friends with a quick fix: a ceramic bowl (don't use china for this). Any ceramic bowl will do as long as the round foot of it is unglazed. Hold the blade of the knife at a $22^1/_2$-degree angle and drag it along the raw edge. Repeat on the other side. Do this about five times. *Et voilà*, you will have a reasonably sharper edge. Be sure to buy the honing steel though, or soon you'll have a bunch of wobbly bowls!

- The chopping block is used primarily to withstand the heavy, aggressive blade of the cleaver. A chopping block should be several inches thick, more than a foot in length, and made of wood. For lighter slicing and mincing jobs, a regular, plastic chopping board is appropriate.

Fortune Cookies

Whether you buy a wooden chopping block or make one using hardwood lumber from your local home improvement store, you will need to season it much like a wok. Rub vegetable or peanut oil all over the surface of the block, cover with foil or waxed paper, and let it sit for a couple of days. Turn the block over and repeat the process. After seasoning and each subsequent use, lightly rinse with soap and water and dry the block immediately.

- Ladles, deep-bowled long-handled spoons, have dozens of uses, from stirring items in a wok to serving soups.

- A wok spatula is the single most important tool you will use when stir-frying. You can't do without it. The wok spatula is what is used to move the food, tossing and tumbling, for even, quick cooking and is curved to match the curve of the wok, which makes moving the food in the pan easier.

- The skimmer is basically a small to medium wire-mesh basket on a stick. Sometimes, they are even made of wood. They are best for removing deep-fried or boiled items from a wok. A large slotted spoon can be used in place of a skimmer.

Skimmer.

♦ Rice cookers, a more modern innovation, are the most convenient gadget in a new Asian kitchen. The alternative is of course the boiling pot of water in which you have to worry about consistent temperature and cook time. With rice being so important in Asian dishes, it's imperative that it be perfect. Rice cookers are inexpensive and remove the guesswork. (See Chapter 4 for more information about rice and cooking it.)

♦ Used extensively in Japanese cuisine, the bamboo rolling mat is the vehicle for perfectly rolled sushi.

Bamboo rolling mat.

♦ The familiar mortar and pestle is an ancient food processor invaluable in making pastes. You might recognize it from a visit to the pharmacy. The mortar is the bowl in which small amounts of herbs or spices are ground together using the pestle.

♦ A food processor is great for mixing or grinding large amounts of ingredients that are too large for the mortar and pestle. It's also a great way to chop and slice vegetables.

♦ Set aside a separate coffee grinder to use specifically for spices.

♦ Small graters are good for finely grating ginger and other roots. If you have a regular, multi-faced grater that has a "fine" side, feel free to use that.

♦ When draining noodles, a colander or other strainer is irreplaceable. The boiling water drains out of the hole-filled bowl, leaving behind the succulent noodles. Colanders can also double as part of a makeshift steamer. In Japan, bamboo baskets are used to drain noodles.

Colander.

Fork Be Gone: Learn to Use Chopsticks, Today

Too many people give up on using chopsticks before they even give the handy little items a chance. It can seem a daunting task, to be sure. How can one possibly be expected to feed oneself using two oversize toothpicks? Students of the chopsticks are intimidated by the image of Mr. Miyagi catching flies with his chopsticks in *Karate Kid.* If you noticed, it took Ralph Macchio almost the whole film to master the art.

The first step is to lose all preconceived notions about chopsticks. This one step will do the most for your chopsticks usage. The last step is to pick up the chopsticks and get a feel for them. Become one with the chopsticks as if they were a natural extension of your fingers. How? Practice, practice—take them to work with you, name them, use them to pick up paper clips or lint off your sweater. In no time you will become a master in the art of the kuai-zi (*kwi-zee*), or "quick little fellows" as they are called in China.

Now, extend your hand flat, rest the thicker end of the bottom chopstick in the web of your dominant hand, between thumb and index finger. Right-handed folk will use their right hands and southpaws will use their left hands.

Use your two middle fingers to keep the chopstick steady. Hold it firmly but not too rigidly. This bottom chopstick will remain fairly stationary while you eat.

Hold the top chopstick like a pencil between your thumb and index finger. This one does most of the moving.

And that's all there is to using chopsticks. Practice a while on chunks of food before you try ice cubes like Ralph!

 **Lucky Treasures**

Asian rice is easier to eat with chopsticks than it appears. Hold the chopsticks closely parallel to each other and gently press down on the rice. Insert the chopsticks into the pressed rice and lift a clump. Easy!

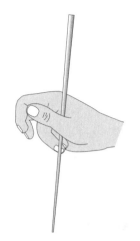

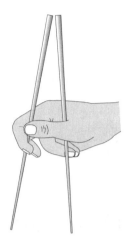

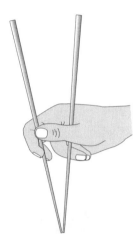

Place the bottom chopstick in the web of your dominant hand between thumb and index finger.

Hold the top chopstick like a pencil between your thumb and index finger.

The top chopstick does most of the moving. The bottom chopstick remains fairly stationary.

Although people have been eating Asian food for thousands of years, we have seen a renaissance in Asian cuisine in our restaurant. Sometimes it's called "pan-Asian," sometimes it's called "New Asian," or even "Asian Fusion," but it's always called Asian. Like the Italian cuisine has experienced resurgence in pasta, we reflect society's view of ages-old Asian cuisine. It's healthy and with the proper preparation can be very quick to make.

The Least You Need to Know

- New Asian cooking combines the flavors from many of the countries of Asia—Thailand, China, Japan, Korea, Vietnam, Laos, India, Mongolia, Malaysia, and Indonesia.
- Experimentation is a key ingredient in Asian cooking.
- Woks are the epicenter of the new Asian kitchen. When purchasing a wok, remember that cast-iron and carbon steel woks are what we find best overall. However, the type of wok you choose depends on your needs.
- Season your wok to make everything taste better, to prevent food from sticking to it, and to keep it from rusting.
- Steamers come in two basic types: bamboo and metal. Items steamed in bamboo turn out more flavorful, but the downside is that bamboo lids often warp because of wetness.
- Sharp knives make for sharp meals.
- Chopsticks aren't hard to learn to use if you first lose your preconceived notions about them.

Chapter 2

Navigating the Asian Market

In This Chapter

- The Asian supermarket, aisle by aisle
- Picking produce in any language
- Meat me at the butcher
- Stock, drop, and roll

Now that you've learned about the tools of the trade in Chapter 1, it's time to look at the ingredients used in Asian cooking.

Mentally prepare yourself for a trip to the Asian market. Nontraditional smells and sights will surround you like birds fluttering about a tree.

Proliferation of Flavors

As more Asians and Asian Americans share their culture, Asian groceries and supermarkets are popping up in neighborhoods all over America. Even conventional grocers are expanding their offerings in the Asian aisle. Whereas in the past, a regular supermarket's Asian section might have included only packaged chow mein noodles, water chestnuts, and soy sauce,

Fortune Cookies

No matter what market you are in, talk to the seafood and produce managers. Find out when shipments come in. If seafood comes in on Mondays, don't buy on Sunday; if Chinese long beans come in every Thursday, buy them on Friday.

Lucky Treasures

An ancient remedy for a familiar dilemma: motion sickness. Ginger capsules or tea can work wonders to calm an upset stomach, whether in planes, trains, or automobiles.

today their shelves are packed with Thai sauces, curry pastes, sushi ingredients, and dozens of noodles, rice vinegars, and gourmet spice blends. (Even though noodles and rice are big in the Asian supermarket, we will be discussing those two staples in-depth in Chapter 3.)

Your first trip to the Asian market might be a little intimidating. Your senses will be overloaded with new sights, sounds, and smells. Due to their popularity and segmentation, most Asian markets are crowded. Don't let that ruffle your feathers. Pretend you're at a regular grocery store, practice neighborly manners, and your experience will be fine. A little defensive driving with the shopping cart can only help.

If you have Asian friends or neighbors, enlist them to guide you on your first field trip to an Asian market.

Look to the glossary in the back of the book for definitions of Asian produce, spices, condiments, and sauces.

Produce

The produce section is one of the most exciting areas in the Asian market. You will recognize some of the fruits and vegetables there, but there are probably some exotic strangers lurking in the produce aisle. The following list goes beyond regular tomatoes and onions.

Baby corn	Chrysanthemums
Bamboo shoot	Coconut
Banana leaf	Cucumber, Asian/Japanese/Chinese
Bean curd (tofu)	Daikon
Bean sprout	Durian
Bitter melon	Eggplant, Asian/Japanese/Chinese
Bok choy (also called Chinese cabbage)	Galangal (Thai ginger)
Celery	Garlic
Chayote	Ginger
Chinese broccoli	Green onions (also called scallions)
Chinese cabbage (also called bok choy)	Guava

Horseradish, Japanese (called *wasabi*)

Jicama

Kaffir lime

Kohlrabi

Leek

Lentils

Lichee/litchi

Lime

Long beans

Loquat

Lotus root

Mango

Mung bean

Mushroom

Nori (see seaweed)

Papaya

Scallions (also called green onions)

Seaweed

Shallot

Squash

Soy beans

Star fruit

Sugar cane

Tapioca starch

Taro root

Tofu

Water chestnut

Water spinach

Winter melon

Lucky Treasures

Greens are a staple of many Asian cuisines, and you'll find many that don't exist in the Western kitchen. Chinese varieties typically have two names, one in the Cantonese dialect, and the other in Mandarin. The same variety may also be used in Japan, and if so, will have a Japanese name as well. The names used in each market will likely depend on the national origin of the market's owner and the market's clientele. (The owner might be, say, Cambodian, but might cater to your area's Laotian, Vietnamese, and Thai residents as well as culinary adventurers like you.) If you can't figure it out, the store staff and, quite often, fellow shoppers, will be happy to help you pick your way through the garden.

Meat Beat Manifesto

Arguably, the meat and seafood department can be the most intimidating section of an Asian market. You will see things you are accustomed to—cuts of beef and pork, chicken, and selections from the sea. However you will also find frogs, eels, and whole prepared ducks hanging from hooks.

Displays of exotic seafood, both fresh and dried, are a feast for the eyes and nose, though your nose may take a while to adjust to the unusual aromas. As with buying seafood anywhere, you'll want to make sure it's fresh, so follow these guidelines for choosing fresh fish:

- **Seafood test #1:** If it smells fishy, then it is not so freshy. The fishier the smell, the less fresh the seafood. A piece of fish should smell like the ocean or the sea, not the dock.

- **Seafood test #2:** It's time for the staring contest. A not-so-fresh fish will have cloudy eyes.

- **Seafood test #3:** Press the skin of the fish. If it springs back into shape, the fish should be fresh.

If your fish fails any of these tests, toss it back for someone else to catch.

Remember, your new Asian cooking experience should be fun and low-stress. If you prefer to stick with your regular haunts for meat and seafood, feel free to do so, because most of the recipes in this book call for meat and seafood that are available in most major markets.

Under the Sea

The Little Mermaid has the life, swimming and devouring the wonderful bounty of the sea. These are some of the most common things you will find in the seafood section of an Asian market:

Abalone	Oyster
Blue crab	Salmon
Carp	Scallop
Catfish	Shrimp (also called prawns, rock, pud, or come specifically sized)
Clam	
Crab	Shrimp, dried
Eel	Snapper
Flounder	Squid
Halibut	Swordfish
Lobster	Trout
Mussel	Tuna

Poul-try Position

Chicken is a worldwide favorite. Easy to raise even under difficult conditions, it's versatile, mild flavored, and easy to cook. Plus, if you've got a chicken, you've also got eggs! Take off the skin and you've got a low-fat source of protein. And from an economic viewpoint, it's cheap compared to other meats, especially if you buy it whole. For convenience, though, most of us prefer to buy our parts precut. Spicy and tangy Asian spices, sauces, and vegetables provide a flavor burst for chicken.

No wonder ducks float in water—they have an amazingly high fat content compared to other birds! When cooked, the dark meat has a much bolder flavor than chicken and, when properly done, the crispy, brown skin is a true delicacy. Because they are water birds, they have a huge chest cavity and a bone structure that makes their size deceptive. A four- or five-pound duck will probably only serve two to three people. Buy duck fresh or frozen at regular grocers or try the precooked Peking Ducks available at some Asian markets.

Quail has a slightly gamey taste but the dark, lean meat has a powerful, luxurious flavor. Quail can be found frozen in many supermarkets and is sometimes available fresh. Because the bones of these tiny birds are so small, look for ones that have had the chest cavity boned for easier cooking, serving, and eating.

Beef, Pork, and Lamb: The Big Meats

Where not prohibited by religious convictions, beef, pork, and lamb are widely used in Asian cooking. Because they are relatively expensive throughout Asia, if a cook is going to spring for meat, he or she often uses the most inexpensive cuts or parts of the animal. Some of these, like pig knuckles, tripe, and brains have almost disappeared from our stores.

For the recipes in this book, we've chosen cuts of meat available at both Asian markets and your local grocery.

One thing you will want to seek out at an Asian market is the various Asian sausages, especially the fiery Thai sausages and sweet/savory Chinese sausages. These are usually sold fresh and must be cooked before eating. A quick turn in a steamer, in a pot of boiling water, or in the wok should do the trick.

Fortune Cookies

When cutting any meat on the diagonal, look at the grain first, which is the way the strands of muscle tissue run. Hold your knife across the grain (or perpendicular) and angle it slightly. This is cutting on the diagonal, which creates odd shapes when cooked that create slight indentations that hold the sauce better than if you just "cut" the food.

The Spice Squad and the Herbal Heroes

Spices are like culinary diamonds. They have the ability to take an ordinary dish and make it sparkle. They are also addictive. The world is full of garlic junkies and chili-heads that live for their chosen spice. Like any vice, spices should be used responsibly. Moderation is the key to successful spice usage. This is especially important when dealing with the exotic spices that can be found at an Asian grocer.

Following is a list of the most common herbs and spices used in Asian cooking. Some of them will be familiar, as spices like chili peppers, cinnamon, and curry powder have found their way into kitchens the world over.

Orient Expressions

For the purposes of this book, we refer to **cilantro** as the green, lacy-leaved aromatic herb that is used fresh, and we refer to **coriander** as the tiny tan seeds that come from the cilantro plant. In some older Chinese cookbooks, for example, both are referred to as coriander, so remember that here cilantro is the herb and coriander is the seed.

Fortune Cookies

Hot things come in tiny packages. As a general rule, the smaller, pointy chili peppers are the spiciest. The larger peppers are the tamest. To defuse a spicy pepper, remove the seeds and the fleshy piths inside the pepper. For some peppers, this is a futile exercise. However, in most peppers it will soften the heat a notch or two.

Asian basil—also called Thai basil	Kaffir lime leaf
Bay leaf	Kari leaf
Cardamom	Lemongrass
Cayenne pepper	Mace
Chili pepper	Mint
Chinese five-spice powder	Mustard seed
Cilantro	Nutmeg
Cinnamon	Paprika
Clove	Peppercorn
Coriander	Poppy seed
Cumin	Saffron
Curry powder	Sesame seed
Fennel	Star anise
Fenugreek	Tamarind
Gingko nut	Tumeric
	Wasabi

Liquidity: Sauces, Oils, Pastes, Condiments, and Others

Just like herbs and spices, liquids—sauces, oils, pastes, and condiments—can add zing to any recipe. Oils can serve as both a cooking medium and a flavoring. Different oils have different smoking points and lend different degrees of flavor to a dish depending on how you use them. Sauces and pastes are also added during cooking to enhance flavor. Condiments are generally added at the table, to the individual diner's taste. Whichever—the liquids used in Asian cooking are bold and flavorful.

Here are some of the more common liquids:

Bean paste	Peanut sauce
Black bean sauce	Plum sauce (also called duck sauce)
Chili oil	
Chili paste	Rice vinegars
Chili sauce	Satay sauce
Coconut milk	Sesame oil
Curry paste	Shrimp paste
Fish sauce	Soy sauce
Hoisin sauce	Soya sauce
Mayonnaise	Sriracha
Miso paste	Teriyaki
Mustard oil	Yogurt
Oyster sauce	

Fortune Cookies

Soy sauce can be a rewarding addition to many Asian meals. If you are watching your sodium intake, make sure you go for the low-sodium soy sauce. Several soy sauce manufacturers designate low-sodium with a green lid on the bottle. Regular soy sauce usually has a red top and 900 mg of sodium per serving. The low-sodium versions taste virtually the same, with half the sodium.

Many sauces and stocks can easily be purchased at the supermarket, but for a true homemade taste and culinary kick, make them from scratch! The following recipes are used frequently throughout the cookbook and have been highlighted for a quick reference.

The Least You Need to Know

◆ The Asian market is a high-energy and high-sensory shopping experience.

◆ When choosing seafood, perform simple tests to determine freshness.

◆ Experiment with spices and sauces, but use in moderation in the beginning.

◆ Make some sauces and stocks yourself, and you will be pleased with the delicious flavors that come out of your kitchen.

Peanut Sauce

Prep time: 15 minutes • Cook time: 10 minutes • Portion: 1 pint

1 cup crunchy peanut butter	1 tsp. paprika
1 cup coconut milk	1 tsp. salt
¼ cup granulated sugar	

Heat peanut butter in the microwave at half power (50 percent) until softened.

Heat wok over low heat. Place warm peanut butter, coconut milk, sugar, paprika, and salt in the wok and whisk slowly for four minutes.

Turn off the heat and cool to room temperature before serving.

Fortune Cookies

Store peanut sauce in the refrigerator for up to one week. Each time it is refrigerated, the sauce will harden. To soften, heat in the microwave for a few seconds or add coconut milk and whisk until sauce reaches desired consistency.

Chicken Broth

Prep time: 5 minutes • Cook time: 30 minutes

2 gallons water	1 medium yellow onion, roughly chopped
Salt to taste	1 carrot, roughly chopped
½ lb. chicken fat and skin	1 stalk celery, roughly chopped

Bring the water to a boil in a 3-gallon stock pot. Lightly salt it and add chicken fat, onion, carrot, and celery. Return to a boil and reduce the heat to a strong simmer. Simmer the broth for 30 minutes.

Fortune Cookies

When trimming chicken, save the fat and skin by storing it in a container and freezing it. The simple flavor that comes from a chicken broth made with these two ingredients is far superior to any canned variety.

Chicken Stock

Prep time: 15 minutes • Cook time: 2 hours

1 lb. chicken bones (or 1 lb. chicken carcass)

2 gallons water

1 cup roughly chopped celery

2 cups roughly chopped carrot

2 cups roughly chopped white onion

Rinse chicken bones under cold running water and place in a 3-gallon stockpot. Pour in water; stir in celery, carrot, and onion and bring to a boil. Lower the heat and simmer for two hours, uncovered.

Remove the stockpot from the heat and allow fat to rise to the top. Skim fat from the surface of the stock with a large, flattish spoon and discard. Strain remaining stock through a fine colander lined with cheesecloth into another container. Discard bones and vegetables.

Cover and refrigerate. After stock is chilled, remaining fat will rise to the surface, making it easy to remove.

Fish Stock

Prep time: 20 minutes • Cook time: 1 hour, 5 minutes

$\frac{1}{4}$ cup vegetable oil for frying

2 lb. fish bones, chopped

1 cup celery, chopped

2 cups onion, chopped

1 gallon water

1 cup fresh mushroom, chopped

1 cup white wine

1 TB. salt

$\frac{1}{2}$ cup cilantro, chopped

2 bay leaves

Heat a wok over medium heat and add oil and fish bones. Stir-fry for one minute. Add celery and onion. Stir-fry for two minutes. Add water, mushroom, wine, salt, cilantro, and bay leaves. Bring to a boil, immediately reduce the heat to a simmer, and cook for one hour. If any scum should appear on the surface, skim it off and discard. Strain stock through a sieve and cool to room temperature. Pour stock into a container and chill.

Dashi

Prep time: 5 minutes • Cook time: 15 minutes

1 oz. kelp

1 oz. bonito flakes, dried

1¹/₂ quarts water (divided use)

Add kelp to 1 quart water in a pot and simmer for 10 to 12 minutes. Avoid boiling kelp or it might impart a strong odor to stock. Right before water boils, remove kelp.

Bring water to a full boil. Add remaining ¹/₂ quart water and bonito flakes. Return to a boil and immediately remove from heat. Once again, do not allow bonito to boil or it might impart a bitter taste to the stock.

Let flakes steep in stock for one minute. Skim foam from surface. Strain through cheesecloth and cool.

Noodles, Rice, and Everything Nice

In This Chapter

- ◆ Noodles and rice—staples of Asian cooking
- ◆ Noodles from A to Z
- ◆ Rice, rice, baby!

An Asian meal without noodles or rice is like a hamburger without the bun—doable but not much fun. In fact, in most of Asia, noodles and rice—not animal protein—has long made up the bulk of the meal, serving as a neutral contrast to the bold flavors served with them. This chapter will look at these quintessential parts of the Asian table.

Noodles Make the World Go 'Round

If you remember nothing else about China's Han dynasty (206 B.C.E. to 220 C.E.), remember it as the era when the Chinese started milling grains and making noodles. And they haven't stopped since.

Whether made from grain, or from grain and eggs, or from rice or beans, noodles are second only to rice as an indispensable part of Asian cooking.

Noodles 101

There are two basic styles of noodles: fresh and dried. Both are made in widths ranging from hairlike threads to thick ribbons. They're eaten hot or cold, alone or in soups, with fish, fowl, and meat, in an endless combination of meals.

Orient Expressions

In China, long noodles symbolize longevity and are always served at birthday and anniversary parties. But don't cut a celebratory noodle—the longer the noodle, the longer your life!

Hand-pulled noodles are the most famous of the Chinese noodles. Chefs train for years to learn the magic of whacking, tossing, stretching, and pulling noodle paste into delicate noodle threads. Even in China, hand-pulled noodles have become rarer as chefs' hands have been replaced by machines.

Oodles of Noodles

Check out the noodle section of an Asian market, and you'll find dozens of packages of noodles. No two are alike and most of the writing on the package is in Japanese, Chinese, Korean, or Vietnamese, with little in English to help you sort it all out. It's enough to give you brain freeze and make you want to try your luck using spaghetti—which is always an option, but then you miss the fun of experimenting with new noodles.

Orient Expressions

In Chinese, noodles are called *mein,* a term you no doubt know from eating American versions of chow mein and lo mein. Keep your meins in order by remembering that in chow mein the noodles are cooked separately from the rest of the dish and in lo mein the noodles are cooked with the dish.

Fortune Cookies

Asian noodles don't reheat well. They don't have oil or egg added to the dough, which is an advantage or disadvantage depending on how you look at it. If you must reheat, stir in a little extra sauce or water before refrigerating and reheat the dish in the microwave using the defrost setting or power level 3 until warm. This way the heat is introduced slowly and you can keep the noodles from being overcooked.

Oodles of Noodles

Noodle	Other Names	Sizes Available	Substitutes	Pre-Cooking Instructions	Cooking Methods	Shelf Life
Rice stick dry	Chantaboun or Pad Thai noodle	Measured in S M L XL flat	Dry fettuccine	Pre-soak in water for 20 minutes	Fried, broiled, and stir-fry	One year
Rice flake dry	Typhoon	One size (small triangular)	Penne	Pre-soak in water for 20 minutes	Boil and stir-fry	One year
Vermicelli dry	Wai Wai	1/8 inch round	Angel hair		Fry, stir-fry, and boil	One year
Vermicelli fresh	Chow Fun or rice roll noodles	Large sheets flat 12 × 12 inches	Rice flake	Soak 15 minutes	Stir-fry	Four days
Egg noodle fresh	Kanada	1/4 inch and 1/2 inch flat	Fettuccine		Stir-fry, boiled, and fried	Two weeks
Egg noodle fresh/dry	Chow mein	1/4 inch round	Spaghetti		Boil and stir-fry	Ten days/ one year
Spinach noodle	Green noodle	1/8 inch flat	Spinach or linguine		Boil and stir-fry	Ten days/ one year
Soba noodle fresh/dry	Buckwheat	1/8 inch round	Wheat pasta		Boil and stir-fry	One year
Bean thread dry	Cellophone, glass noodle, or Chinese Vermicelli	1/8 inch round	Angel hair	Soak 15 minutes	Fried, uncooked, boiled, and stir-fry	One year
Somen dry	Toshima	1/8 inch round	Angel hair		Boil and fry	One year
Udon fresh/dry	Japanese udon	1/4 inch round	Spaghetti		Boil and stir-fry	Three months in package
Rice paper dry	Spring roll wrapper	8 × 8 inch flat			Boil	One year

Here are a few kinds of noodles that are most often used and easily found:

♦ Wheat noodles, usually packed in round or square blocks, are the work-horse of Asian noodles. First made in the northern region of China, they are thin, pale white, and elastic, easy to work with and often called for in stir-frys.

♦ Egg noodles come in many forms, but the most common are a little thinner than spaghetti, have a yellow hue, and are sold folded into a ball.

♦ Udon noodles from Japan are thick, slippery, tummy-filling noodles made from flour and salt water. Perfect for slurping out of the soup bowl.

♦ Soba noodles from Japan are robust strands made with buckwheat, which gives them an earthy, nutty flavor. Though they're usually served in soup, you'll also find them served on their own with a dipping sauce on the side.

♦ Rice vermicelli are wispy, almost colorless strands of crisp noodles, used in stir fries, soups, and spring rolls.

♦ Rice sticks are similar to rice vermicelli but are a thicker, more substantial noodle and are occasionally referred to as chantaboun noodles. Very popular in Vietnam, where they are used in the country's favorite soup, phô, and in Thailand, where they are the main ingredient in the flavorful pad Thai.

♦ Rice papers are thin sheets of rice pasta. Used for wrapping spring rolls in Vietnam, they look like very thin tortillas.

♦ Hmm, what to call these things? Bean thread noodles, glass noodles, cellophane noodles, jelly noodles? They're all the same thing, an opaque white noodle made from mung beans and tapioca that turns almost clear when cooked. Great for soaking up flavor.

Fortune Cookies

Don't let packaging confuse you. It's not unusual to find the exact same noodles packaged under different names sitting side by side on the grocery shelf. Check the list of ingredients, which has to be in English in order to be sold in the United States, to help you figure out what's what.

History of Rice

To say that rice is a staple in Asian life is a bit like saying oxygen is somewhat useful. Asia produces 90 percent of the world's rice, more than 300 million tons a year, and rice makes up more than half the diet of most Asians.

Technically rice is just a type of grass with an edible grain. But it has been regarded as a divine gift since it was first domesticated in Southeast Asia more than 6,000 years ago.

In Bali, the legend is that Lord Vishnu created the world in order for rice to grow. In China, rice was a gift from the animals to save the humans after a great flood. Shintos in Japan believed that the emperor was the living embodiment of Ninigo-no-mikoto, the god of the ripened rice plant. And rice is still routinely placed on altars as an offering to the gods.

Healthy, hearty, and versatile, rice is the bond in the bowl of Asian life.

The Long and the Short of It: Types of Rice

Rice is broadly split into two major types: Japonica and Indica, with countless variations of each.

Japonica is short grained and tends to stick together when cooked. It is primarily grown in the temperate climate of northeastern China, Korea, and Japan.

Indica rice is medium to long grained and is grown in the hot climates of India, Thailand, and southern China.

Here are a few of the most commonly used types of rice:

- Basmati is a long-grain, beautifully aromatic rice from India, where it is considered king. You might find rice called Tex-Mati or Cal-Mati or Bob-mati or whatever; they are all versions of basmati rice that have been cultivated in different parts of the world and are acceptable substitutes for Indian basmati.

Lucky Treasures ___
Don't throw away leftover sushi rice. Save the lightly seasoned rice for soups and casseroles. Small balls of sushi rice can even be tossed in salads as croutons.

- Jasmine is a long-grain, aromatic rice used extensively in Thailand. It's sometimes called Thai basmati.

- Sticky rice, sweet rice, and glutinous rice are all names for the same short-grain rice that's very sticky and requires a lot of rinsing. It is almost exclusively used in desserts.

Recipes for Success ___
Rinse your rice before cooking to remove excess starch and debris. The Asian way is to cover the rice in cold water, slosh it around a bit, drain, and repeat at least three times or until the draining water runs clear. This is particularly important when cooking basmati and jasmine rice.

- Sushi rice is a short-grain rice that is used solely for sushi. Labeling for this rice can be somewhat confusing; if the bag doesn't specifically say *sushi rice* look for the word *new* or *Japanese rice* on the package.

- Pearl or short-grain is a round, rather sticky rice and can be used in sushi or desserts.

◆ Brown rice is not a type of rice but refers to rice that is unprocessed. With more than twice the fiber of white, processed rice and a rich, nutty texture and hearty flavor, many people prefer it to white rice. Except in sushi, brown rice may be substituted for white in almost any recipe. Natural food stores carry a wide variety of brown rice including basmati, sweet, short-, medium-, and long-grain rice.

Recipes for Success

Avoid the temptation to peek at or stir rice while cooking. If time is up and there is still liquid in the pot, just put the top back on and let simmer for a few minutes. If the liquid is all gone but your rice is still crunchy, add a little hot water and simmer for a few more minutes.

◆ On one hand, instant rice is quick to cook, foolproof, and readily available. On the other, it lacks the texture and flavor of long-cooking rice. Use it in a pinch, but once you've tried "real" rice, you might find it hard to go back.

The Rice Table

Properly cooked rice is crucial in Asian cooking. Luckily, it's not hard to do. Following is a table of the main types of rice along with the proper water-to-rice ratios and yields. Cooking times vary depending on whether you are using a rice cooker or cooking by the stove top method. If you prefer your rice a little on the chewy side, use a little less water; if you like it very moist, add a little more water.

Type	Rice	Water	Yield	Cooking Time
Basmati	1 cup	$1\frac{1}{2}$ cups	3 cups	25 minutes
Long-grain	1 cup	$1\frac{1}{2}$ cups	3 cups	30 minutes
Short-grain/pearl	1 cup	$1\frac{3}{4}$ cup	3 cups	20 minutes
Brown rice	1 cup	$2\frac{1}{2}$ cups	4 cups	35 minutes
Jasmine	1 cup	1 cup	$2\frac{1}{2}$ cups	30 minutes
Sticky rice	1 cup	As needed	$1\frac{1}{2}$ cups	30 minutes

Cooking Rice in a Rice Cooker

For all types except sticky rice, place rice and water in the rice cooker and turn on the machine. The machine will turn off when the rice is cooked regardless of what type of rice it is.

Stove-Top Cooking

For all types except sticky rice, place rice and water in a pot and bring to a boil. Cover, reduce heat, and simmer until all liquid is absorbed.

Sticky Rice: An Overnight Journey

Rinse rice in cold water until water runs clear. Cover the rice in water and let stand overnight. The next day, drain the rice dry. Line a bamboo or metal steamer with cheesecloth, add rice, and steam over water for 30 minutes.

Get out the pots and put on the water, you're now ready to make delicious rice and noodles that are an essential ingredient for almost every recipe in this book. And you might want to bookmark the rice and noodle charts for quick reference.

Recipes for Success

Steam your food, not your face. When opening a steamer, open toward the wall, not your body. Under no circumstances should you pop off the top and stick your nose in for a quick sniff—you might get a serious and painful burn.

Fortune Cookies

Don't throw away left-over steamed rice. Spread it on a cookie sheet, loosely cover it with plastic wrap, and refrigerate overnight. Use this "aged" rice for fried rice recipes.

The Least You Need to Know

- If Marco Polo could find China, you can find your way around the noodle aisle of an Asian market.
- The Chinese started milling grains and figured out how to make noodles during the Han dynasty (206 B.C.E. to 220 C.E.).
- Check the noodle or rice chart before you start cooking either.
- Rice is broadly split into two major types: Japonica (short grained) and Indica (medium to long grained).
- In a pinch, it's okay to substitute regular pasta for Asian noodles or instant rice for something more exotic.

Chapter 4

Kitchen History of Asia

In This Chapter

- ◆ From the Stone Age to the Space Age
- ◆ Invading food forces
- ◆ The merging modern

Summing up the history of Asian food in less than a few thousand pages is no easy task. In this chapter, we'll take you on a quick stroll through the last 10,000 years, stopping for major highlights along the way. In Part 2, we'll take a closer look at the history and traditions of several countries.

This is also a good time for a quick geography lesson. When we say Asia, we mean everywhere from Mongolia in the north, India in the west, Japan in the east, and south through Indonesia.

Asia is an enormous continent, where the climates and terrain run from the freezing tops of the Himalayas to the balmy beaches of Bali. It's easiest to think of it in five major groups: Mongolia, China, Korea, and Japan as the northern part; India and its neighbors Pakistan, Bangladesh, Bhutan, Nepal, and Sri Lanka as the south; the Middle East as western Asia, and Afghanistan and the former Soviet Republics that border it are known as Central Asia. The rest of the countries fall into Southeast Asia.

The Beginnings

First there was fire and then there was Chinese food. Well, not exactly, but it was only a couple thousand years after folks learned to make fire, sometime around 8000 B.C.E., that the Chinese began to cultivate rice, and small farming communities sprang up along the Yangtze River around 5000 B.C.E. (Then along came the wheel and no doubt with it came the first traffic jam.)

From then until around 200 B.C.E., not much of import happened in the world, except for the comings and goings of people like Confucius and Buddha, Alexander the Great, Cleopatra, the Queen of Sheba, and Helen of Troy, and the building of the Great Wall of China. Then a couple really huge things happened—the Chinese figured out how to stir-fry and they invented noodles during the Han dynasty (206 B.C.E. to 220 C.E.).

Orient Expressions

The **Silk Road** linked Europe and Asia by trade. More than 7,000 miles long, this route was forged by silk traders in a supreme effort to move their wares toward the Mediterranean Sea. Unfortunately, traveling by camel, yak, and horse did nothing for the traders' frequent flier miles or their safety, so they took to sailing the seas, leaving the Silk Road to the yaks.

By the year 1 C.E., the Silk Road was open for business; trade between the Far East, the Middle East, and the Mediterranean was rocking. The Greeks had been hopping over to India to pick up exotic spices like black pepper and cinnamon for 300 years. Rice cultivation was happening all over Asia and was spreading to the rest of the world.

It's hard for us to imagine, but even that long ago you could walk from the China Sea to the Mediterranean Sea on a road well traveled.

The Middle Centuries

Over the next few centuries, cooking throughout Asia was becoming, in addition to being a means to stave off hunger, an art form with elaborate presentations and customs evolving in the palaces of khans, emperors, and warlords. Some palaces were said to have as many as 5,000 people living in them, with half those folks being assigned kitchen duty.

What we call traditional Chinese or Asian medicine was developing. Spices, herbs, and fungi were being used for their medicinal value to heal the sick and ward off illness among the healthy. Many of these remedies are still in use today in Asia, and Western medical practitioners are beginning to take note of them. Some have become so mainstream that they have nestled into our food culture, like ginseng, chrysanthemum, ginger, and green tea.

Speaking of khans, emperors, and warlords, now that the wheel was firmly entrenched in everyday life, it was much easier to go about invading each other's countries for the next few centuries. One by-product of all this invading was that dining customs and cooking styles from one region were introduced to others.

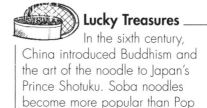 **Lucky Treasures**
In the sixth century, China introduced Buddhism and the art of the noodle to Japan's Prince Shotuku. Soba noodles become more popular than Pop Rocks of the 1980s.

Marco Polo and Other Water Games

Some legends never die, but this is one that must be laid to rest: Marco Polo brought noodles to Italy from China in the late 1200s.

Marco surely ate plenty of noodles during his travels, but he didn't get back home until 1297, and by that time Italians were making plenty of pasta without his help. Most likely, pasta was brought to Italy courtesy of German invaders of the fifth century. Sailor, writer, and raconteur were Marco Polo, but pasta king was not his thing.

How Hunan Got Hot

Searing Hunan peppers, tear-inducing Thai dishes, vindaloo from India so hot your lips refuse to let the next bite in. It's impossible to think of Asian food without thinking heat. But before the 1530s, Asians had to make do with black pepper to pump up the heat.

Then everything changed. The Portuguese invaded northern India, occupying Sri Lanka and bringing with them their stash of chili peppers picked up while exploring South America. Five hundred years later, chili peppers are so ingrained in every corner of Asia it's hard not to think of them as indigenous to the region.

Colonial Times

From 1600 to the end of the Second World War, it wasn't just Asian countries invading each other. The Europeans had also gotten into the act.

At the beginning of the 1600s, the Portuguese, Dutch, British, and French were all trying to colonize Asia. Soon, the Dutch would oust the Portuguese from India and the Spice Islands, and then spend the next 200 years fighting with Britain for control of the Asian spice, tea, and textile trade.

In 1824, the Dutch and British signed the Treaty of London, which gave the British everything above the Straits of Malacca, including Singapore, and the Dutch everything below. Now the British had a secure route to send tea from China back to England.

This was the beginning of the high period of European colonization of Asia—the British in India, the French in Vietnam, and the Dutch throughout Indonesia, most of which would last until after the Second World War.

The colonizers had a profound effect on the food of the colonies, the colonies changed the way the rest of the world ate in turn. Curries from India took Britain by storm and are considered the national dish of Britain today. The Dutch created their *rijstafel* (rice table) from the Indonesian-style feast of dozens of small dishes served with rice. Today, Indonesian restaurants in Amsterdam serve glorious rijstafel to tourists and locals alike.

But neither of those developments compares with the biggest thing to come out of Asia since white rice: tea. In 1610, the Dutch brought tea to Europe, but not until 1664 did it show up in London. One hundred nine years later, tea was such a mighty commodity that it provoked American colonist Samuel Adams to lead the Boston Tea Party when the British started fooling around with the fledgling country's tea supply. And we all know how *that* ended.

Asian Cooking Today

What makes Thai *Thai* or Chinese, well, *Chinese?* Historically, the biggest influence on a country's cuisine is geography. As you journey through this book, you'll find that recipes from regions where people live by the sea feature seafood. Head toward the fertile valleys, and meat and dairy products from domesticated animals show up, along with an array of fresh vegetables and fruit. Up in the mountains, whatever is edible is eaten; mushrooms, root vegetables, game, and domesticated animals are on the menu.

In Southeast Asia and India, you've got coconuts; therefore, you get lots of recipes with coconut milk. In Korea, most of the country is rugged mountains and the climate can be harsh and cold; preserved vegetables and meats rule. On the island of Japan, fresh fish and seafood, including seaweed, show up in everything from soup to sushi. But wherever you go, you can count on rice or noodles to be the center of attention.

In a large Asian city today, as in large cities the world over, you'll find restaurants and markets that offer foods from all over the world. But for those living in the countryside, where transportation, refrigeration, and fuel are at a premium, traditional, geographically centered meals are the norm.

Asian dishes lend themselves to experimentation and spur-of-the-moment adaptations depending on what's fresh at the market that day. Having the confidence to play it by ear and throw a dish together is the hardest thing for most of us to learn about Asian cooking. Develop your skills by making a recipe the first time just as it's written, and then add a little personal touch to it each time you make it.

East Meets West

From the first groups of Chinese immigrants who came to the United States in the 1800s, to the Little Vietnams and Little Indias that are a vibrant part of every major metropolitan area today, Asian Americans have become a vibrant and vital part of our everyday eating habits.

Sushi is sold in supermarkets, soy sauce has become as American as apple pie, curry in a hurry is a lunch staple, and little white boxes of take-out Chinese food are such common sights that no one would consider them exotic.

Of course we, as in mainstream America, managed to muck up a few things. Visit a Thai restaurant in the United States and you'll surely be given chopsticks to eat with. Unless you were in a Chinese restaurant in Thailand, you'd get a fork and spoon to eat with. But because we've decided that all Asian food should be eaten with chopsticks, the Thai restaurant owners indulge us in our little fantasy.

Even sillier is our penchant for plopping a beautifully prepared piece of nigiri sushi rice side down in a saucer full of soy sauce. Rice is like a sponge and soaks up so much soy sauce so fast that it hides the taste of the fish and the delicately seasoned rice. Briefly dip your nigiri sushi fish side down to add a drop of soy sauce as a complement to the sushi and a compliment to the chef.

Oh well, we can't do everything right. The important thing is that you feel free to explore the fascinating flavors and enticing dishes that make up the new Asian experience.

> **Lucky Treasures**
> *Ramen* is the Japanese word for noodles, a word that morphed out of the Chinese word for noodles "lo mein." Thanks to the Nissan Food Company, legions of American college students know how to pop a package of Top Ramen noodles in the microwave, add the flavor packet, and, voilà, they have dinner.

The Least You Need to Know

◆ Asian cuisine has been influencing the world for centuries.

◆ The Chinese began to cultivate rice in small farming communities that sprang up along the Yangtze River around 5000 B.C.E.

◆ Chili peppers were introduced to India by Portuguese invaders, who occupied Ceylon in the 1530s. They subsequently spread all over the continent.

◆ Contrary to popular belief, Marco Polo didn't introduce pasta to Europe. Most likely, pasta was brought to Italy by German invaders of the fifth century.

◆ The high period of European colonization of Asia—the British in India, the French in Vietnam, and the Dutch throughout Indonesia—was also a time of Asian influence on European cooking.

◆ Climate and geography is the major influence in Asian cooking and in all cooking.

Part 2

Cuisine by Country

Pan-Asian cuisine may be a modern term, but Asian countries have been panning themselves for ages. Whether invading each other or being invaded from countries far away, each invasion left some sort of culinary mark on the invadees. If the Portuguese hadn't brought chili peppers from Peru to India in the 1500s, Asian food might be very different today. In the north of Vietnam, you still see the effect of Mongol invaders of the thirteenth century in the use of beef in many dishes, while the use of soy sauce was picked up from neighboring China.

And on it goes, with everyone borrowing from everyone else but also creating distinctive regional dishes. In this part, we'll go panning around Asia with recipes from India to Japan.

Chapter 5

Thai One on: Thailand

In This Chapter

- ◆ The five Thai cooking styles
- ◆ Basic elements of Thai cooking
- ◆ Traditional Thai recipes from land and sea

Put together a steamer, a wok, and noodles from China; toss in some curry, ginger, chilies, and coconut milk from India; add the Thai penchant for lemongrass; simmer for centuries; and you've got modern Thai cooking.

Thai Cooking Styles

Thai food seeks a balance between spicy and bland, sweet and sour. Curries, lemongrass, and chili peppers are the unifying theme of Thai cuisine. From there you can break down Thai cooking styles by the five major regions of the country: Northeast, North, Central, South, and Gulf Coast.

The Northeast's style is popular all over the country. Lots of grilled meats, hot dipping sauces, sticky rice, and salads made with beef and pork are standards.

In Northern Thailand, bound by Laos and Burma, sticky rice shows up at every meal along with a variety of dipping sauces heavy on the chilies, ginger, onions, and tomatoes.

Orient Expressions
Lemongrass stalks are for seasoning, not for eating. A stalk peels apart in layers, the outer of which is serrated and rough. Once you peel down to the soft inner core, its ready to be used according to recipe directions. It will also impart lemony citronella-like aroma that will fill your work area.

Lucky Treasures
Palace cuisine is known for its abundance and penchant for going over the top. Oddly enough, His Majesty the King Bhumibol Adulyadej of Thailand was born in the United States, and his Majestic bride was born in Thailand.

Central Thailand is home to Palace cuisine. As its name implies, this intricately decorated style of presentation was created for the nobility. It's not what folks make at home, so don't feel bad if you can't whip out a dozen pineapple boats for your party.

In the South, they love to combine fiery chili peppers with sour or bitter herbs for intensely flavored dishes, then cleverly top them off with cool, crisp sprouts and beans to mellow the fire in their mouths.

Crab, prawn, lobster, and fish seasoned with lots of lime, chilies, cilantro, ginger, and garlic are regulars on the menu along the Thai Gulf Coast.

Thailand is Chef Annie's home, where she learned to cook as a child in her parents' kitchen. Using leftover odds and ends that didn't make it to the big folks' table, she would create her own mini versions of the adults' meals. Keep this childlike sense of adventure in mind as you begin to explore Thai cooking. As Chef Annie says, "The most important thing is to develop your palate. A strict adherence to measurements is not as important as learning to cook by taste."

The Least You Need to Know

- Lemongrass is the key to many things Thai.
- You can break down Thai cooking styles by the five major regions of the country: Northeast, North, Central, South, and Gulf Coast.
- Thai food seeks a balance between spicy and bland, sweet and sour.

Bar-B-Que Chicken

Prep time: 20 minutes • Marination time: 2 hours • Cook time: 40 minutes •
Serves 2 to 3

1 whole (2¹/₂- to 3¹/₂-lb.) chicken, cut in half

¹/₄ bunch cilantro

1 TB. minced garlic

1 tsp. freshly ground pepper, black

¹/₃ cup oyster sauce

¹/₄ cup soy sauce

³/₄ cup pineapple chili sauce

Wash chicken (especially the cavity) well with cold water. Pat dry with paper towels and cut in half down the middle. Remove excess pockets of fat and save for chicken broth.

Combine cilantro, garlic, black pepper, oyster sauce, and soy sauce in a nonreactive bowl. Coat chicken halves well with marinade and marinate for two hours in the refrigerator.

Heat a grill to medium high and place chicken halves on the grill. Cook for five minutes on each side. Lower the heat or move chicken to a cooler side of the grill and continue to cook for 20 minutes or until done. Serve chicken with pineapple chili sauce that has been poured in a small bowl for dipping.

Fortune Cookies

If chicken isn't finger-lickin' good to you, try substituting five quail that have been cut in half. Cut the cooking time down to 10 minutes or at least until a thermometer carefully inserted into the tiny side registers 165°F. Serve five halves per person for dinner or two halves for a nibbler.

Recipes for Success

There are several ways to check the chicken for doneness. The breast will always cook faster than the dark meat, which has bones, so check the meat between the bones by piercing with the tip of a paring knife. If the juices run clear, it's done. (A meat thermometer should read 165°F when the chicken is done.)

Coconut Chicken Soup

Prep time: 15 minutes • Cook time: 10 minutes • Serves 2

2 whole boneless, skinless chicken breasts, sliced diagonally, ¼-inch thick

4 kaffir lime leaves

2 lemongrass stalks, trimmed to 6 inches and peeled to the soft core

2 cups chicken stock

2 cups chicken broth

2 cups canned coconut milk

¼ cup fish sauce

2 tsp. chili paste made with soya oil

1 tsp. Thai chili powder

¼ cup fresh lime juice

2 roma tomatoes, quartered

½ cup fresh pineapple chunks

6 oz. chantaboun noodles, soaked in water

2 TB. chopped fresh cilantro

2 TB. chopped green onion

Heat a wok over high heat and add chicken, lime leaves, lemongrass, chicken stock, and chicken broth. Bring to a boil and cook for three minutes.

Stir in coconut milk, fish sauce, chili paste, chili powder, and lime juice. Cook for three more minutes.

Add tomatoes and pineapple and bring to a boil. Immediately turn off the heat.

Place noodles in boiling salted water and cook for three minutes; drain.

Using tongs or two forks, place noodles into two serving bowls, ladle soup in, and garnish with cilantro and green onions. Serve hot.

Orient Expressions

Not to be confused with the middle eastern yogurt drink, kaffir, a **kaffir lime** looks like a lime and smells like a lime, but its leaves are strangely demented looking and hauntingly flavorful. Each leaf consists of two lobes that are placed in such a way that they resemble a figure eight along the stem. There really is no substitute for kaffir lime leaves. If you can't locate these highly prized leaves, a grating of lime zest will do, but just barely.

Green Curry Chicken

Prep time: 15 minutes • Cook time: 7 minutes • Serves 2

2 TB. canola oil

2 whole boneless, skinless chicken breasts, diagonally sliced into $^1/_4$-inch thick pieces

4 kaffir lime leaves

2 tsp. green curry paste

1 Chinese eggplant, cut into matchstick julienne

$^1/_2$ red bell pepper, cut into matchstick julienne

1 jalapeño chili pepper, quartered

$^1/_2$ cup chicken stock

$^1/_2$ cup chicken broth

$1^1/_2$ cups canned coconut milk

$^1/_4$ cup fish sauce

1 tsp. granulated sugar

10 sprigs Asian basil or sweet basil

2 cups cooked rice

Heat a wok until very hot and add oil. When oil is smoking, add chicken, lime leaves, and curry paste. Sear chicken. Add eggplant, red pepper, and jalapeño chili; *sweat* for a minute until the vegetables are tender.

Once vegetables and chicken have mixed well with curry, add chicken stock, chicken broth, coconut milk, and fish sauce. Bring to boil and continue to cook until chicken is no longer pink and cooked through, about four to five minutes. Stir in sugar and basil. Place 1 cup rice into each soup bowl and ladle curry chicken over rice. Serve hot.

Orient Expressions
Don't run for the deodorant when we say "sweat." To **sweat** is a professional term that means to sauté whatever you are cooking in a little oil until it gives off its moisture.

Khao Soi

Prep time: 15 minutes • Cook time: 12 minutes • Serves 2

1 gallon + 1 TB. canola oil

2 whole boneless, skinless chicken breasts, diagonally sliced into $1/4$-inch thick pieces

2 tsp. yellow curry paste

2 cups chicken stock

2 cups chicken broth

2 cups canned coconut milk

1 TB. granulated sugar

$1/4$ cup fish sauce

14 oz. fresh egg noodles (divided use for fried noodles)

$1/4$ cup pickled mustard cabbage

1 lime, thinly sliced or wedged

2 TB. fried onion

1 jalapeño pepper, sliced

2 sprigs fresh sweet basil

$1/2$ cup chopped red onion

Heat 1 gallon canola oil in a heavy-duty 2-gallon pot to 350°F. While oil is warming, heat a wok until very hot and add 1 TB. canola oil. When oil smokes in the wok, add chicken and curry paste. Tossing and stirring, quickly sauté for one minute. Stir in chicken stock, chicken broth, and coconut milk. Bring to a boil. Add sugar and fish sauce, stirring until sugar is dissolved. Continue to cook until chicken is just cooked, about two to three minutes.

In a 4-quart pot, bring 3 quarts of water to a boil. Place half the noodles in the water and cook for four minutes. Drain well. Divide noodles between two soup bowls. Ladle chicken soup over noodles. Garnish the soup bowls with pickled cabbage, lime, fried onion, jalapeño, basil, and red onion by placing them on the surface of soup with a large spoon.

To make fried noodles: Divide the rest of the noodles in half. Place one batch uncooked noodles into hot oil and fry until puffed and crispy, about 20 seconds. Repeat with remaining noodles. Place a nest of fried noodles on the rim of each bowl; they should emerge from the surface of the soup like a giant boulder.

Serve immediately.

Masman Chicken

Prep time: 15 minutes • Cook time: 12 minutes • Serves 2

$^1/_2$ cup diced Idaho potatoes

2 TB. canola oil

2 TB. masman curry paste

2 whole boneless, skinless chicken breasts, cut into 1-inch chunks

$^1/_2$ cup diced red bell peppers

$^1/_2$ cup diced green bell peppers

$^1/_2$ cup diced white onion

$1^1/_2$ cups chicken stock

$1^1/_2$ cups canned coconut milk

$^1/_4$ cup fish sauce

2 TB. paprika

2 TB. granulated sugar

$^1/_4$ cup unsalted dry-roasted peanuts

1 tsp. tapioca starch

2 TB. water

Place potatoes in a 1-quart pot filled with cold water. Bring to a boil and cook four minutes; drain and reserve. Potatoes shouldn't be fully cooked through, but slightly al dente.

Heat a wok until very hot and add oil. When oil is smoking, add curry paste and cook for one minute, stirring constantly. Add chicken and stir, coating well with curry. Add red and green bell peppers and onions. Sauté for one minute more. Add chicken stock and coconut milk; bring to a boil.

Add potatoes, fish sauce, paprika, sugar, and peanuts and cook together until chicken is no longer pink and cooked through, about four to five minutes. Mix tapioca starch with water and add to mixture. Bring to a boil to thicken properly. Sauce should coat the back of a spoon. Ladle into two warm soup bowls.

Pad Thai with Shrimp and Squid

Prep time: 15 minutes • Cook time: 10 minutes • Serves 2

16 oz. chantaboun noodles, presoaked

2 TB. canola oil

8 oz. shrimp (16 to 20 count), peeled and deveined

4 oz. squid, cleaned and cut into 1-inch pieces

2 large eggs, lightly whisked

³/₄ cup pad Thai sauce

2 TB. fish sauce

2 TB. paprika

¹/₄ cup chicken stock

²/₃ cup fried tofu, shredded

¹/₄ cup green onion, thinly sliced diagonally

¹/₄ cup unsalted dry-roasted peanuts, chopped (divided use)

¹/₂ cup fresh bean sprouts

2 TB. shredded red cabbage

¹/₄ cup shredded carrot

¹/₂ lime, cut into wedges

Boil 3 quarts lightly salted water in a 4-quart pot. Add presoaked noodles, blanching for two minutes. Drain noodles and set aside.

Heat a wok until very hot and add oil. When oil is smoking, add shrimp, squid, and egg. Sauté for one minute, shaking the pan frequently.

Fortune Cookies
Blanching the noodles will put them on a level playing field with the other ingredients so everything will finish at the same time. The blanched noodles will definitely be al dente and become silky limp after the final cooking.

Add blanched noodles. While moving noodles around in the wok, add pad Thai sauce, fish sauce, and paprika. Stir until noodles are coated with sauce. Add chicken stock, tofu, green onions, and half the peanuts. Keep moving noodles until liquid reduces in volume by half. Add half the bean sprouts and turn off the heat.

Place noodles on one side of each of two serving plates. Garnish the other half with piles of fresh cabbage, carrot, lime wedges, and remaining peanuts and bean sprouts. Serve hot.

Pork Panang

Prep time: 15 minutes   •   Cook time: 10 minutes   •   Serves 2

2 TB. canola oil

12 oz. pork butt, sliced $^1/_4$-inch thick

4 kaffir lime leaves

2 tsp. panang curry paste

$^1/_2$ cup green bell peppers, roughly chopped

$^1/_2$ cup red bell peppers, roughly chopped

$^3/_4$ cup bamboo shoots, sliced

$^1/_2$ cup chicken stock

$^1/_2$ cup chicken broth

$1^1/_2$ cups canned coconut milk

$^1/_4$ cup fish sauce

2 tsp. granulated sugar

2 tsp. paprika

2 cups steamed jasmine rice

Heat a wok until very hot and add oil. When oil is smoking, add pork, lime leaves, and curry paste. Sauté for two minutes. Add green and red peppers and bamboo shoots.

When all vegetables and pork have picked up curry color, add chicken stock and chicken broth. Bring to a boil. Add coconut milk, fish sauce, and sugar. When pork is almost cooked through, stir in paprika. Remove wok from heat. Divide rice between two soup bowls and ladle pork mixture over rice. Serve hot.

Spicy Noodles with Chicken

Prep time: 15 minutes • Cook time: 10 minutes • Serves 2

2 TB. canola oil

2 tsp. minced garlic

2 tsp. chili paste

2 whole boneless, skinless chicken breasts, sliced diagonally into $1/4$-inch thick pieces

$1/2$ cup diced green bell peppers

$1/2$ cup diced red bell peppers

$1/4$ cup green onions, sliced

$1/2$ cup jalapeño chili peppers, sliced

2 roma tomatoes, thickly sliced

$1/2$ cup chicken stock

12 oz. fresh chow fun noodles, cut into 1-inch strips

$1/2$ cup oyster sauce

$1/4$ cup sweet soy sauce

4 sprigs fresh basil

1 jalapeño pepper, halved lengthwise, for garnish

Heat a wok until very hot and add oil. When oil is smoking, add garlic, chili paste, and chicken. Sauté for two minutes. Add green and red bell peppers, onions, jalapeños, and tomatoes. Sauté all together for two or three more minutes. Add chicken stock. Bring to a boil. Add chow fun noodles. Once noodles are hot, add oyster sauce and sweet soy sauce.

Continue to cook until chicken is cooked through and is no longer pink and noodles have absorbed sauce. Remove from heat and toss in basil. Spoon mixture onto two serving plates. Garnish center of each plate with half a jalapeño. Serve hot.

Spicy Shrimp Soup with Lemongrass

Prep time: 15 minutes   •   Cook time: 12 minutes   •   Serves 2

2 TB. canola oil

12 oz. shrimp (16 to 20 count), peeled and deveined

1 stalk lemongrass, trimmed and peeled

6 kaffir lime leaves

2 cups chicken stock

2 cups chicken broth

8 dried red Thai chilies

¼ cup fish sauce

2 cups canned coconut milk

½ cup straw mushroom

¼ cup fresh lime juice

½ cup bamboo shoots

2 tsp. chili paste

2 cups steamed jasmine rice

¼ cup loosely packed fresh cilantro leaves

Heat a wok until very hot and add oil. When oil is smoking, add shrimp, lemongrass, lime leaves, chicken stock, chicken broth, and chilies. Bring to a boil and cook for four minutes. Add fish sauce, coconut milk, mushrooms, lime juice, bamboo shoots, and chili paste. Bring back to a boil and cook for three more minutes. Shrimp should have a nice firm texture and be solid white with red streaks running through meat.

Divide rice into two soup bowls and ladle soup over rice. Garnish with cilantro. Serve hot.

Steamed Mussels

Prep time: 15 minutes   •   Cook time: 15 minutes   •   Serves 2

2 TB. canola oil

2 shallots, chopped

1 tsp. minced garlic

1 lb. black mussels, cleaned

4 kaffir lime leaves

1 stalk lemongrass, peeled, trimmed, and chopped

1 cup chicken stock

1 TB. fish sauce

$^{1}/_{2}$ cup chopped Asian basil

$^{1}/_{2}$ cup green onion, sliced

1 tsp. Thai chili powder

$^{1}/_{4}$ cup fresh lime juice

2 basil sprigs, for garnish

Heat a wok until very hot and add oil. When oil is smoking, add shallots and garlic. Cook for one minute. Add mussels, lime leaves, lemongrass, and chicken stock. Bring to a boil. Add fish sauce, basil, green onion, chili powder, and lime juice.

Cover the wok with a lid and steam mussels until shells open completely, about four minutes. Once they have opened, turn off the heat. Discard any that do not open. Divide mixture between two warmed soup bowls. Garnish with basil. Serve hot.

Whole Fried Fish

Prep time: 15 minutes • Cook time: 15 minutes • Serves 2

1 whole (1- to 2-lb.) dressed whitefish, such as snapper or catfish

1 gallon plus 4 TB. canola oil

2 TB. minced garlic

$^1/_2$ cups pickled ginger

2 TB. black bean sauce

2 TB. chili mix

12 fresh shiitake mushroom caps

1 cup thinly sliced red onions

$^1/_2$ cup chopped green onions

$^1/_2$ green bell pepper, thinly sliced lengthwise

$^1/_2$ red bell pepper, thinly sliced lengthwise

1 cup chicken stock

1 cup chicken broth

2 TB. granulated sugar

$^1/_4$ cup soy sauce

$^1/_2$ cup tamarind sauce

Take a sharp knife and score fish on both sides every two inches. Heat 1 gallon oil in a heavy 2-gallon pot to 350°F. Submerge fish in hot oil. Cook fish for six to eight minutes, or until golden brown.

While fish is cooking, heat a wok over high heat with 2 tablespoons oil. When oil has begun to smoke, add garlic, ginger, black bean sauce, and chili mix into the wok. Sauté for one minute. Add mushrooms, red onions, green onions, and green and red bell peppers. Sauté for two minutes. Add chicken stock and chicken broth and reduce by half. Toss in sugar, soy sauce, and tamarind sauce. Bring to a boil.

Remove fish from oil. Drain well on paper towels. Place fish on a serving platter and ladle vegetable mixture and sauce over top. Serve hot.

Orient Expressions

Most whole fish you buy at mainstream American markets are already gutted and cleaned. In an Asian market, it pays to ask if your fish has been cleaned. If it hasn't, ask the fishmonger to do it for you. This is called **dressing a fish.**

Chapter 6

The Raw and the Cooked: Japan

In This Chapter

- ◆ Sushi secrets revealed
- ◆ Fine-tuning teriyaki
- ◆ Souper troopers
- ◆ Some great Japanese recipes

Japan is home to some of the most delicious, exotic, and dangerous foods in the world. Where else do people eat fugu (the infamous puffer fish), a fish with a poison in its organs that is so deadly that one bite can kill you; that is, unless it is prepared by a specially educated and licensed chef. Then there's sashimi, exquisite colorful strips of utterly fresh seafood the flavor of which will take you directly to the exotic islands. Although it can't kill you, improperly prepared sashimi can make you sick. In this chapter, you'll learn to prepare many of the Japan's treasured dishes. We won't address puffer fish here, but armed with a little common sense and good food safety habits, you won't need the intense, adrenaline-packed training of a fugu chef to make sashimi or sushi.

Clearing Sushi's Good Taste

The common misconception about sushi is that it is just raw fish; however, some sushi is vegetarian and some is cooked. The word *sushi* means "flavored rice," and as you will learn, the flavoring is subtle. Nonetheless, the essence of sushi is rice.

Lucky Treasures

Wasabi is an above-ground root similar to horseradish. It is the green stuff served with sushi that looks like guacamole. Its pungent aroma is balanced by its slightly sweet, but intense, spicy flavor. Because only 10 percent of the plant is used to make the condiment, real wasabi is typically hard to find. Horseradish mixed with food coloring is a tasty substitute.

Orient Expressions

Daikon is the long Japanese radish that can grow in excess of a foot. The simplest way to serve it is to julienne it.

Sushi can be classified into four categories. The most common sushi that novices start out with is the *maki*, or roll. Veggies, seafood, and rice are rolled into pressed seaweed sheets, or *nori*, to form a tube. The tube is then cut into pieces and served on a decorative plate with wasabi and ginger.

The second category—and the easiest sushi to make—is the hand roll. The nori is formed into a cone shape and then stuffed with rice, veggies, and seafood.

What is typically called sushi, or *nigiri*, is a semi-flattened ball of rice with a slice of seafood on top. The rice is formed in the chef's hand and before the seafood is placed on top, the chef rubs a small amount of wasabi on the rice. Nigiri is prepared by the piece and mostly served in pairs.

The fourth and last type of sushi is called *sashimi*. To get sashimi, you lose the rice and add a few more pieces of seafood. Often, sashimi is served with shreds of *daikon*.

The rice and the freshness and quality of the fish are the most important elements of preparing sushi. When serving sushi, appearance is all-important. Sushi is about harmony and balance. The dishes should look and smell as good as they taste. The color, shape, and layout of the sushi on the plate add so much to the experience. Decorative plates of varying sizes and shapes can spark a dinner.

Tools of the Trade

To make sushi, you need the help of some valuable tools. Sushi is tool-intensive, but not overwhelming. To make the rice, you need a rice paddle, a rice cooker or pot, a wooden or glass bowl, and a wet cloth. To cut your seafood and veggies and rolls, you need a sharp, sharp, *sharp* knife. To roll the rolls, you need a bamboo rolling mat and some plastic wrap.

Number-One Ingredient: Rice

You can tell the importance of rice in sushi by the meaning of the word. The rice can make or break the sushi. The flavoring added to the sushi is rice vinegar. It is not the tart vinegar found in vinaigrette, but a little sweeter. It does not flavor the rice that much, but it covers up the starch and gives the rice a nice foundation of flavor.

It is best to use short-grain rice. Some packages, especially in an Asian grocery, will have "sushi rice" written on them. It's hard to find short-grain rice at a regular supermarket. Medium-grain is a reasonable substitute, but try to stay away from long-grain rice. The longer the grain, the less it tends to stick together.

The first thing you have to do is wash the rice. The rice gets a white powder on it from the milling process. To wash the rice, the easiest thing to do is place it in a sieve and set it under running water. You will notice the water runs cloudy at first. Once the water runs clear, the rice is clean.

If you have a rice cooker, you're on easy street. However, rice can be made just as easily with a pot and some boiling water. If you have a rice cooker, you put an equal amount of rice and water, about 3 cups, depending on your cooker, into the machine and press start. Most machines will "ding" or let you know in some other way when the rice is finished. Read the instructions that came with your machine for proper usage. You might want to check on the rice after about 15 to 20 minutes. If the surface of the rice looks like it is hardening, just take a large spoon and stir it. Again, check with the operating manual.

If you don't have a rice cooker, you will place equal amounts of water and rice into a pot. Let the rice soak for about 15 minutes and then turn on the heat and bring to a boil. Cook until the rice has zero crunch to it, around 10 minutes.

Whether you use a pot or a cooker, once the rice is cooked, you want to let it steam off some heat for about 15 minutes. When you actually start making the sushi, the rice should be at room temperature. If it is too hot, it could start cooking the fish. Once the rice starts getting cold, it starts to harden.

After the rice steams, add the rice vinegar. Rice vinegar can easily be found at an Asian market and in a lot of ethnic sections at regular grocers. If you can't find rice vinegar, you'll have to make your own. To do this, mix together and heat 5 tablespoons vinegar, 3 tablespoons sugar, and 1 tablespoon salt. Right before the mixture comes to a boil, remove it from the heat.

Dump the rice into your wooden or glass bowl and pour the rice vinegar or your mixture onto the rice evenly. Next take your rice paddle, or spatula, and separate the rice using a slicing

Fortune Cookies

Make sure the bowl you use to hold the cooked rice is glass or preferably wooden. If you use a metal bowl, the rice will pick up a metallic taste. Although it sounds like a good name for a hard rock band, no one wants to eat "metallic sushi."

motion. Once you separate the rice, gather it together again using your paddle. Again, separate the rice by using a slicing motion. This helps cool the rice and mixes in the vinegar. Gather it one more time. This time, cover with a wet cloth and let cool to body temperature. The wet cloth will help keep the rice moist.

Roll Out the Sushi

The basic sushi roll is one of the most difficult maneuvers in Asian cooking, but it is fairly easy to master. Basically, you take all the ingredients that you are going to put into the roll, place them onto the cut piece of pressed seaweed that is resting on the rolling mat, and then you roll.

To roll sushi, the first thing you do is take a bamboo rolling mat, or *makisu*, and wrap it in plastic wrap. It is best to place the mat down on the plastic wrap and then fold the wrap over to cover both sides of the entire mat. The side that you had face down will become your rolling surface. The wrap will protect the mat and also, when you learn to make inverse rolls (with rice on the outside), you will be able to keep the rice from sticking to the mat.

The next step is to lay a bamboo sushi mat on the counter with the longest side toward the edge of the counter. Place a nori sheet glossy side down on the mat about 1 inch from the mat edge closest to you. With damp fingers, spread the rice about $1/2$-inch thick onto the nori evenly, a row at a time, leaving a $1/4$-inch margin on the opposite side. At this point, you can take a little wasabi or mustard paste and run a line of it down the center of the rice with your finger. Cover with a damp paper towel to keep it moist if you need to.

Place the stuffing on the rice and run a finger dipped in a little water along exposed edge of nori. Lift the bamboo mat slightly, hold the stuffing in place with the fingers, and roll the mat over the nori sheet halfway. Lift the top portion of the mat to keep it from getting caught up in the roll. Keep it as tight as possible while rolling.

When completely rolled over, make sure nori is sealed by pressing lightly where it was moistened earlier. Remove any unsightly lumps by rolling one more time (like you were using a rolling pin) in the bamboo mat. Cut into two-inch pieces and serve cold.

Orient Expressions
Mustard paste is a little-known secret of sushi chefs. An interesting alternative to the mound of wasabi in a dipping dish of soy sauce or colorful swipe in a sushi roll, it is available in most Asian markets right next to the tubes of wasabi. Mustard paste is similar to Chinese mustard, only thicker and way hotter.

Lucky Treasures
Something we can all get behind is the etiquette of eating sushi. Eat with your fingers—not with your chopsticks.

Place stuffing (fish or other ingredients) on rice near center.

Gently roll mat up, holding stuffing in place with your fingers. Roll leading edge of nori into middle of roll. Lift top portion of mat to keep it from getting caught up in roll.

Gently cut roll into two-inch pieces and turn on ends to serve.

Tuning Teriyaki

Announcing the marriage of the lustrous Teri to the hot head Yaki, henceforth to be called Teriyaki.

Teriyaki, from *teri*, which means "luster" in Japanese, and *yaki*, which means "grilled" or "broiled," is a Japanese style of cooking as well as the name of the sauce used in the same preparation. Made from *mirin* and soy sauce, teriyaki

Orient Expressions

Mirin is a rice wine made specifically for cooking that's low in alcohol, and slightly sweet, used mainly to add flavor to sauces and glazes. Don't confuse mirin with American mainstream cooking wines; they can't be substituted.

sauce is used as a marinade for fish, meat, and poultry before grilling, roasting, or broiling. When finished, teriyaki dishes have a shiny, taut, lustrous look to them.

Japanese Souper Trouper

Think clear and elegant, a simple broth with a few perfect slices of seafood and/or vegetables served in a lacquered bowl: This is the *suimono* ("something to drink") style of Japanese soup, named so because it is typically drunk straight from the bowl; pesky spoon not required.

Think of a hearty mix of tofu, vegetables, eggs, meat, and seafood, the broth thickened with miso, and you've got a *shirumono* (thick) soup.

The most popular soup in Japan by far is miso soup. Rich in minerals, amino acids, and protein, miso is one of the most wisely used staples in Japan today. Made from soybeans and grains (usually rice or barley), its blend and age determines the type. Among its many recipe applications, miso can be a key ingredient in soups, dipping sauces, and marinades. Miso in the USA is available in three main types, although there are an infinite number of regional variations in Japan:

♦ **Yellow miso.** Briefly aged; usually made with rice; sweeter than dark (or red) miso; mellow and savory; used in traditional miso soup. The most versatile, this miso is the one to have if you don't want to invest in all three types.

♦ **Red (or dark) miso.** Medium strength; aged up to three years; most popular in Japan; used for hearty soups, sauces, and marinades.

♦ **Blonde miso.** Very briefly aged; a little harder to find; less salty than the other types; used in lighter soups, dressings, and marinating fish.

And don't forget the ever-popular noodle soups made with ramen, soba, udon, or whatever noodle strikes your fancy. They're sold in soba houses or by street-corner vendors, and instant versions are popped into the microwave by busy folks everywhere.

> **Lucky Treasures**
> Slurping your noodles is common in Japan. Do it with abandon and your host will love you, or better yet, offer you more.

What they all share is *dashi*, a unique soup stock made with *kombu* (dried kelp) and *katsuobushi* (dried bonito flakes), both of which can be bought at any Asian market.

Whatever Japanese food you are interested in trying, be it cooked or raw, obscure or mainstream, don't be afraid to eat it, share it, or cook it. The key to Japanese cuisine is simplicity; so keep it simple, pay attention to the rules, and you can't go wrong.

The Least You Need to Know

- Sushi means something made with rice that's seasoned with rice vinegar.
- Eat sushi with clean fingers, not with chopsticks.
- Japanese soups, whether suimono, shirumono, or noodle style, contain dashi, a stock made with kombu (dried kelp) and katsuobushi (dried bonito fish).
- Teriyaki is marinating and grilling or broiling fish, fowl, or meat. It is also the name of the marinade.

California Roll

Prep time: 10 minutes • Cook time: 10 minutes • Serves 2

2 sheets nori seaweed

1 cup steamed sushi rice, seasoned with rice vinegar

4 oz. shrimp (16 to 20 count), peeled and deveined

1/2 avocado, sliced 1/4-inch thick

1 seedless cucumber, sliced into 3 × 1/4-inch thick strips

Soy sauce, wasabi, and pickled ginger for serving

To roll sushi, the first thing you do is take a bamboo rolling mat, or *makisu*, and wrap it in plastic wrap. It is best to place the mat down on the plastic wrap and then fold the wrap over to cover both sides of the entire mat. The side you had face down will become your rolling surface. The wrap will protect the mat and also, when you learn to make inverse rolls (with rice on the outside), you will be able to keep rice from sticking to the mat.

The next step is to lay a bamboo sushi mat on the counter with the longest side toward the edge of the counter. Place a nori sheet glossy side down on the mat about one inch from the mat edge closest to you. With damp fingers, spread rice about 1/2-inch thick onto nori evenly, a row at a time, leaving a 1/4-inch margin on the opposite side. At this point, you can take a little wasabi or mustard paste and run a line of it down the center of rice with your finger. Cover with a damp paper towel to keep it moist if you need to.

Impale shrimp with a bamboo skewer, holding shrimp as straight as possible. Simmer shrimp in lightly salted water for five minutes or until they turn firm and opaque. Cool.

Recipes for Success

How clever the Japanese are! The notion that something as simple as tiny reeds held together by a little string can be so fundamental in the preparation of a dish that is made all over the world is pure genius in its simplicity. You simply cannot make any kind of roll without a mat.

Place avocado slice across the center of rice. Cut shrimp in half lengthwise and place on top of avocado. Lay cucumber on top of shrimp. Lift the bamboo mat slightly, hold the stuffing in place with your fingers, and roll the mat over the nori sheet halfway. Lift the top portion of the mat to keep it from getting caught up in the roll. Keep it as tight as possible while rolling.

When completely rolled over, make sure nori is sealed by pressing lightly where it was moistened earlier. Remove any unsightly lumps by rolling one more time (like you were using a rolling pin) in the bamboo mat. Cut into two-inch pieces and serve cold.

✂ ♉ ✂

Cucumber Roll

Prep time: 8 minutes • Cook time: 8 minutes • Serves 2

3 sheets nori seaweed

1 cup cooked sushi rice, seasoned with rice vinegar

1 seedless cucumber, sliced into $3 \times \frac{1}{4}$-inch thick strips

1 tsp. white sesame seeds

Soy sauce, wasabi, and pickled ginger for serving

To roll sushi, the first thing you do is take a bamboo rolling mat, or *makisu*, and wrap it in plastic wrap. It is best to place the mat down on the plastic wrap and then fold the wrap over to cover both sides of the entire mat. The side you had face down will become your rolling surface. The wrap will protect the mat and also, when you learn to make inverse rolls (with rice on the outside), you will be able to keep rice from sticking to the mat.

The next step is to lay a bamboo sushi mat on the counter with the longest side toward the edge of the counter. Place a nori sheet glossy side down on the mat about one inch from the mat edge closest to you. With damp fingers, spread rice about $\frac{1}{2}$-inch thick onto nori evenly, a row at a time, leaving a $\frac{1}{4}$-inch margin on the opposite side. Place cucumber in the center of rice and sprinkle on sesame seeds. Run a finger dipped in a little water along exposed edge of nori. Lift the bamboo mat slightly, hold cucumber in place with your fingers, and roll the mat over the nori sheet halfway. Keep nori as tight as possible while rolling.

Cover with a damp paper towel to keep it moist if you need to.

Place stuffing on rice and run a finger dipped in a little water along exposed edge of nori. Lift the bamboo mat slightly, hold stuffing in place with your fingers, and roll the mat over the nori sheet halfway. Lift the top portion of the mat to keep it from getting caught up in the roll. Keep it as tight as possible while rolling.

When completely rolled over, make sure nori is sealed by pressing lightly where it was moistened earlier. Remove any unsightly lumps by rolling one more time (like you were using a rolling pin) in the bamboo mat. Cut into two-inch pieces and serve cold.

Miso Soup

Prep time: 10 minutes • Cook time: 15 minutes

4 cups dashi

1/4 cup miso paste (all-purpose)

1 lb. tofu, cut into 1-inch pieces

2 oz. shiitake mushrooms, sliced

1 cup bean sprouts

1/2 tsp. black pepper

1/4 cup chopped cilantro leaves

Heat wok over medium heat. Whisk 1/2 cup dashi into miso paste, add this and the rest of the dashi to the pot, and whisk again. Bring to a simmer. Do not boil or the flavor will change. Add tofu, shiitake mushrooms, and bean sprouts and simmer for five minutes or until heated through. Ladle soup into a bowl and garnish with black pepper and cilantro.

Miso Pickled Mahi Mahi

Prep time: 10 minutes • Marination time: 24 hours • Cook time: 25 minutes • Serves 2

1/4 cup yellow miso paste

2 TB. sake

3 TB. mirin

2 TB. granulated sugar

1 lb. skinless mahi mahi filet, cut in 2 pieces

2 pieces cheesecloth

1 lemon, cut in half lengthwise

Fresh chives, for garnish

Steamed snow peas

Mix miso, sake, mirin, and sugar together. Spread the miso mixture over fish. Wrap each piece of fish in the cheesecloth, place in a nonreactive bowl, and refrigerate for 24 hours.

Heat the broiler to 400°F. Remove fish from the cheesecloth. Rinse in cold water, pat dry, and place on a broiling pan. Broil for eight minutes or until opaque and flaky.

Squeeze lemon over top, garnish with a couple blades of fresh chives, and serve with steamed snow peas.

Recipes for Success

Cutting a lemon lengthwise makes it easier to get more juice. Squeeze lemon into a tea strainer or your cupped hand to be sure the seeds don't get into the food.

Pan-Broiled Salmon

Prep time: 15 minutes • Cook time: 20 minutes • Serves 2

1 TB. canola oil

1 lb. salmon filet, cut into 2 (8-oz.) pieces

2 TB. unsalted butter

2 TB. rice vinegar

2 TB. mirin

$^1/_2$ cup green onions, finely sliced

1 tsp. fish sauce

1 TB. sweet soy sauce

1 lemon, quartered

Heat a sauté pan over medium heat and add oil. When oil begins to smoke, add salmon and sear on each side for five minutes.

Carefully remove remaining oil from the pan. Add butter. Coat fish with melted butter. Remove salmon from the pan. Add rice vinegar, mirin, green onion, fish sauce, and sweet soy sauce to the pan. Whisk sauce until butter has emulsified with other ingredients. Spoon sauce onto salmon and serve with lemon on the side.

Fortune Cookies

The best way to tell when fish filets are cooked is to check for a change in color. Fish such as sole, halibut, and bass will also become visibly flaky. Tuna, swordfish, and salmon are a little more difficult. Gently insert the point of a sharp knife into the flesh and pry open. Look for the desired doneness expressed in the recipe. Unless you are familiar with these fish and are used to judging their doneness, make a little dummy filet that you can poke at all you want and still have dinner that doesn't look like it came from *Nightmare on Elm Street*.

Recipes for Success

To skin or not to skin: Traditionally the skin is left on the salmon. It gives a crisp crunch and adds an equal amount of flavor. Think of it as the bacon on a filet mignon

Sake-Simmered Halibut

Prep time: 10 minutes • Cook time: 15 minutes • Serves 2

1 lb. skinless halibut filets

$^1/_2$ cup sake

2 TB. soy sauce

6 TB. sweet soy sauce

$^1/_2$ cup dashi

$^1/_2$ cup mirin

1 tsp. granulated sugar

Score fish every 2 inches, $^1/_4$-inch deep to allow liquid to penetrate fish.

Heat a sauté pan to high heat and add sake, soy sauce, sweet soy sauce, dashi, mirin, and sugar. Bring to a boil and add fish.

Lower the heat, cover with a lid, and cook over a strong simmer for about 12 minutes or until fish turns opaque and flaky. Keep the lid on the pan while fish is cooking.

Carefully place fish on warmed serving plates with a spatula and pour sauce over it.

Serve with steamed rice and steamed Asian broccoli.

Steak Teriyaki

Prep time: 12 minutes • Cook time: 10 minutes • Serves 2

2 TB. canola oil

1 lb. beef sirloin, cut into 2 (8-oz.) pieces

2 TB. sweet soy sauce

$^1/_2$ tsp. Japanese mustard paste

2 TB. sake

2 TB. mirin

Heat wok to very high heat and add oil. When oil begins to smoke, add sirloin steaks. Sear for three minutes on each side. Remove steaks from the wok and keep warm.

Add sweet soy sauce, mustard paste, sake, and mirin to the wok and bring to a boil. Cook until liquid reduces in volume by half and return steaks to the wok. Cook on each side for two minutes more, remove, and serve with remaining sauce on warmed serving plates. Serve with steamed rice.

Tempura Shrimp with Udon Noodles

Prep time: 20 minutes • Cook time: 15 minutes • Serves 2

1 cup ice water

1 medium egg yolk, lightly beaten

1 cup all-purpose flour, sifted

24 oz. shrimp (16 to 20 count), peeled and deveined

3 quarts canola oil

2 cups fresh udon noodles

$^1/_2$ cup soy sauce

1 tsp. shredded ginger

$^1/_4$ cup mirin

$^1/_2$ cup dashi

$^1/_2$ cup daikon radish, grated

Lightly beat ice water into egg until just barely mixed together. Add flour and mix lightly to incorporate.

Dry shrimp with a towel before coating with egg-flour batter. Heat a 6-quart heavy-duty saucepan half filled with oil to 350°F. Submerge shrimp in batter and immediately drop into oil. Fry shrimp for eight minutes, turning occasionally.

While shrimp are in oil, boil noodles in water for eight minutes. To make sauce for noodles, simmer soy sauce, ginger, mirin, and dashi for five minutes in a small saucepan.

Place noodles into a bowl and pour sauce over and toss together. Divide between two bowls. Place shrimp and daikon over noodles and serve.

Recipes for Success
    A light hand is the only trick to making tempura. Don't overwork the batter—just lightly whisk the ingredients together.

Tuna Roll

Prep time: 20 minutes • Cook time: 15 minutes • Serves 2

4 sheets nori seaweed

1 cup steamed sushi rice, seasoned with rice vinegar

$^1/_2$ tsp. wasabi paste

4 oz. sushi-grade ahi tuna, cut into $3 \times ^1/_2$-inch strips

Soy sauce, wasabi, and pickled ginger for serving

To roll sushi, the first thing you do is take a bamboo rolling mat, or *makisu*, and wrap it in plastic wrap. It is best to place the mat down on the plastic wrap and then fold the wrap over to cover both sides of the entire mat. The side you had face down will become your rolling surface. The wrap will protect the mat and also, when you learn to make inverse rolls (with rice on the outside), you will be able to keep rice from sticking to the mat.

The next step is to lay a bamboo sushi mat on the counter with the longest side toward the edge of the counter. Place a nori sheet glossy side down on the mat about one inch from the mat edge closest to you. With damp fingers, spread rice about $^1/_2$-inch thick onto nori evenly, a row at a time, leaving a $^1/_4$-inch margin on the opposite side. Cover with a damp paper towel to keep it moist if you need to.

With your thumb, spread wasabi down the center of rice. Place tuna in center of rice covering length of nori and run a finger dipped in a little water along exposed edge of nori. Lift the bamboo mat slightly, hold the stuffing in place with your fingers, and roll the mat over nori sheet halfway. Lift the top portion of the mat to keep it from being caught up in the roll. Keep it as tight as possible while rolling.

When completely rolled over, make sure nori is sealed by pressing lightly where it was moistened earlier. Remove any unsightly lumps by rolling one more time (like you were using a rolling pin) in the bamboo mat. Cut into two-inch pieces and serve cold.

Serve with soy sauce, wasabi, and pickled ginger.

Yakitori Chicken

Prep time: 20 minutes • Cook time: 20 minutes • Serves 2

1 tsp. minced garlic

$^1\!/_4$ cup sake

$^1\!/_2$ cup sweet soy sauce

2 TB. mirin

1 TB. granulated sugar

1 lb. chicken thighs, skinned, boned, and cut into 1-inch pieces

$^1\!/_2$ cup shiitake mushroom caps, cut into 1-inch pieces

1 medium white onion, cut into 1-inch chunks

$^1\!/_2$ cup green bell peppers, seeded and cut into 1-inch pieces

6 to 8 (9-inch) bamboo skewers, soaked in water for 1 hour

Place garlic, sake, sweet soy sauce, mirin, and sugar into a saucepan. Bring to a boil. Simmer for five minutes; remove from the heat and reserve.

Place chicken and vegetables on skewers, alternating chicken, mushroom, onion, and pepper onto a skewer. Start at the bottom, leaving some space to hold the skewer, and continue to the tip of the top.

Heat the grill to high. Place the skewers on the hottest side of the grill. (Old chef's trick: Soaking the skewers well in water will help to keep them from catching fire.) While basting lightly with a brush, grill for three to four minutes on each side. Serve as an appetizer.

Recipes for Success

When basting the chicken, don't let too much of the basting sauce drip down into the fire. The sauce will spike the flames and cover the food with soot. Good for Santa; bad for chicken.

The Mein Land: China

In This Chapter

- ◆ Snapshot of Chinese regions
- ◆ Stirring it up with stir-fry
- ◆ It's a saucy world out there
- ◆ Some terrific Chinese recipes

How often do you eat Chinese? Once a week? Once a month? Try almost every day. Noodles, rice, and tea are so ingrained in our everyday diet that it doesn't even occur to us that we are *indeed* eating Chinese every day.

And when we eat Chinese, we probably don't concern ourselves with whether we are eating Cantonese, Peking, or Szechuan. But each of these distinctive styles of cooking makes up one of the greatest cuisines in the world.

To get a handle on the dozens of styles of Chinese cooking, it's helpful to look at them in terms of the major styles and regions of the country.

Probably the most familiar to us in recent years are the hot, spicy dishes of the western provinces of Szechuan and Hunan.

The Southeast and its Cantonese cuisine are famous for the use of exotic ingredients (turtle, snake, and bat among others), and for their light touch with stir-fry, emphasizing fresh ingredients and mild flavors, fried

Lucky Treasures
Food is such an important part of the social fabric that the Chinese often greet each other with the question, "Have you eaten already?"

rice, and grilled meats. Cantonese food was the first of the regional cuisines to be exported from China.

From the Northeast's Peking/Shantung style comes the mighty Peking duck. Wheat, not rice, is the primary grain, and oodles of noodles and steamed pastries are mainstays on northern menus.

To the east, the province of Fukein lies along the sea. Lots of fish and seafood are typical of the region, as well as seaweed, along with an array of fresh vegetables that thrive in the subtropical climate.

Mandarin and Shanghai are states of mind, not sites on the map. Mandarin means "Chinese official" and Mandarin dishes are the aristocrats of Chinese cooking, incorporating the best of the provinces to create elaborate, refined dishes. Shanghai style, like the city, is a cosmopolitan combination of all things Chinese.

In this chapter, we'll look at recipes from around the country.

Sauces

Several sauces regularly show up in Chinese cooking. Luckily the biggies—hoisin, black bean, plum, sweet and sour, and chili—are readily available in most supermarkets. Though we usually think of a sauce as something that goes on top of a dish, in Chinese cooking these sauces are used both as an ingredient and as a condiment or dipping sauce to a finished dish.

Hoisin

Dark, thick, spicy, and sweet, hoisin sauce is a mix of soybeans, sesame seeds, chili peppers, and sugar. It's used in hundreds of recipes for meat, noodles, and vegetables and as a condiment.

Black Bean

Black bean sauce is made from fermented black beans and soy sauce. Closer to a paste in texture than a sauce, it's very salty and usually used in small quantities in cooking, often with a dab of sugar for balance.

Plum

Plum sauce is a jamlike combination of plums, vinegar, sugar, and chilies. This is that orange-hued sauce in the little plastic packet that comes with your egg rolls. Traditionally served as a condiment with roast duck and Peking duck, plum sauce is also called "duck sauce." This is probably because most Americans didn't know the name of the sauce and thinking it was too complicated to remember, renamed it duck sauce.

Fans for *Fan*

The essential ingredient of an everyday family-style Chinese meal is the *fan*, or grain (which is usually rice or noodles), and the bulk of the meal. *Ts'di* dishes are the smaller-size plates of meat, fish, fowl, and veggies that go along with the fan. Our "gimme the jumbo size" mentality thinks of it as miniscule, to be sure. Ts'di dishes are almost like condiments for the fan, central to the flavor of the dish, but not the bulk of it.

Soups are served at the end of the meal and are properly enjoyed by sipping from your spoon and breathing at the same time, making an almost musical sipping noise. While that might seem tacky to some, it serves two very useful purposes. First, it cools the soup before it hits your mouth. Second, breathing in allows the aromas of the soup to get up in the nose, which, as any wine geek will tell you, is key for enhancing the tasting experience.

Beverages, even water and tea, aren't usually served with everyday meals, with soup doing double duty as food and drink.

Fortune Cookies

Don't leave your fan on the table. Bring the bowl to your mouth and pop the noodles or rice into your mouth with your chopsticks. In the Chinese culture, eating from a bowl of fan on the table suggests that your are less than thrilled with the dish by "holding it at arm's length."

The Yin and Yang of It All

The Chinese include the idea of yin and yang into their diet to create harmony and good health. This philosophy originated in Canton, where the finest of Chinese cooking is created. The Cantonese divide the yin and yang into *methods* and *ingredients*.

Cooking methods such as steaming, boiling, and poaching are considered *yin* methods, while deep frying, stir-frying, and sautéing are yang. This idea is illustrated in the Chinese appetizer of "pot stickers," which are dumplings that are poached and then fried on one side.

Cabbage, watermelon, tofu, and soy beans are included in the yin ingredients, which are considered to have a *cooling* nature. Yang ingredients such as lamb, garlic, and ginger are warming. Besides the wonderful flavor, this is why you see so many dishes with ginger in them. Consider the dish Eggplant in Garlic Sauce, which creates balance on the plate and in the tum.

Now that you know that yin/yang isn't just a tattoo, but a philosophy of Chinese cooking, you're ready to create some wonderful Chinese dishes.

The Least You Need to Know

- The Chinese include the idea of yin and yang into their diets to create harmony and good health.
- Sauces may be used as an ingredient or for dipping in Chinese cuisine.

Chicken Bok Choy Lo Mein

Prep time: 15 to 20 minutes • Marination time: 1 hour • Cook time: 17 minutes • Serves 2

3 tsp. tapioca starch	2 TB. canola oil
1/4 cup shaoxing wine	1 TB. fresh garlic, thinly sliced
1 lb. chicken thighs, skinless	1 cup shiitake mushroom caps, quartered
1/2 cup oyster sauce	1 cup chicken stock
1/4 cup green onions, sliced	2 quarts water
1 TB. minced fresh ginger	2 cups lo mein noodles
1 TB. sambal	2 cups bok choy, roughly cut

Thoroughly mix tapioca and *shaoxing wine* in a nonreactive bowl. Add chicken, oyster sauce, green onions, ginger, and sambal. Mix well. Cover with plastic wrap and marinate in the refrigerator for at least one hour.

Heat a wok to high heat and add oil. When oil begins to smoke, add garlic and mushrooms. Stir-fry for two minutes and add chicken. Continue to cook for three minutes, or until browned. Add chicken stock. Bring to boil and simmer for seven to nine minutes.

While chicken and the sauce are cooking, boil 2 quarts water in a pot, add lo mein noodles, and cook until done, about six minutes. Drain and reserve.

When the time is up on chicken, add bok choy and cook three more minutes. Add noodles and toss well, making sure noodles are coated with the sauce. Serve hot.

Orient Expressions

More intensely flavored than sake, **shaoxing wine** is drunk more in China than just about any other liquor. Yellow in color and a little heavier than its sister sake, it works well in Chinese cuisine. If you find it too heavy for your taste, just cut back by half the quantity called for in the recipe (or to taste).

Chicken in Red Beer

Prep time: 15 minutes • Cook time: 1 hour • Serves 2

1 whole chicken, about 2 to 3 lb.

1/2 cup peanut oil

1 TB. sesame oil

2 green onions, sliced

1 tsp. granulated sugar

Kosher salt to taste

1 tsp. minced fresh garlic

1 TB. minced fresh ginger

2 cups beer

1/4 tsp. red food coloring (about 6 drops)

1 TB. tapioca starch

2 TB. water

Steamed rice for serving

Cut chicken into pieces, separating breasts, legs, wings, and thighs. Cut those parts into smaller bite-size pieces, leaving bone and skin intact.

Heat a wok over high heat. Add peanut oil. When it begins to smoke, add chicken pieces. Stir-fry for two minutes. Add sesame oil and sear all for one minute. (To sear, use less of a tossing motion than you do in the stir-frying technique.) Toss in green onion, sugar, salt, garlic, and ginger, and stir-fry for three minutes. Add beer and food coloring and bring to a boil. Immediately lower the heat and simmer for 20 minutes, uncovered.

Mix tapioca starch with water and then add to the wok. Bring to boil. Remove from heat at once and spoon onto warm serving plates. Ladle any extra sauce over all. Serve with steamed rice.

Chinese Fried Rice

Prep time: 15 minutes • Cook time: 10 minutes • Serves 2

8 oz. pork shoulder

Salt and freshly ground black pepper to taste

$1/4$ cup sesame oil (divided use)

2 eggs, lightly beaten

1 tsp. minced fresh garlic,

$1/2$ cup julienned shiitake mushroom caps

$1/2$ cup bean sprouts

$1/2$ tsp. Thai chili powder

$1/2$ cup diced carrot

2 cups steamed jasmine rice, left uncovered in the refrigerator overnight

2 TB. soy sauce

$1/2$ cup green peas

4 green onions, thinly sliced

Season pork with salt and pepper. Heat the wok over high heat. Add 1 tablespoon sesame oil and when oil begins to smoke, add pork, searing on all sides, cooking for a total of about six minutes. Remove pork from the wok, cut into small pieces, and set aside.

Wipe the wok clean and heat it over medium heat. Add remaining oil and pour in eggs, scrambling them just until done. Add garlic, mushrooms, bean sprouts, chili powder, and carrot. Stir-fry for two minutes. Add rice, pork, and soy sauce, mixing vegetables and pork thoroughly with rice. When rice is hot, toss in green peas and green onions.

Serve family-style on a warm serving platter or individually in big warm bowls.

Kung Pao Beef

Prep time: 20 minutes • Marination time: 1 hour • Cook time: 15 minutes • Serves 2

12 oz. top round of beef, cut into 1-inch cubes

2 TB. soy sauce (divided use)

2 TB. rice wine

3 TB. sesame oil

Salt to taste

1 egg white, whisked

2 TB. canola oil

1/2 tsp. minced fresh garlic

1/4 tsp. Thai chili powder

1 tsp. fresh ginger, minced

1/2 tsp. Szechuan peppercorns, toasted and ground

2 green onions, thinly sliced

1/2 cup red bell pepper, diced

2 TB. rice wine

1 tsp. granulated sugar

1 TB. Chinese black vinegar

1/4 cup chicken stock

1 tsp. tapioca starch

2 TB. water

1/4 cup unsalted, dry-roasted whole peanuts

Steamed rice for serving

In a nonreactive bowl, mix the beef with 1 tablespoon soy sauce, rice wine, and sesame oil. Lightly salt beef mixture to taste. Add egg white. Mix thoroughly, cover, and refrigerate for one hour.

Heat a wok over low heat and add oil. When oil is smoking, add remaining soy sauce, garlic, chili powder, ginger, and peppercorns. Allow flavors to infuse on low heat, watching so as not to burn spices, which will cause a bitter flavor.

Remove beef from marinade and discard marinade. Toss beef in the wok with green onions and red bell peppers. Turn heat to high and stir-fry until beef is golden brown, about four minutes. Add rice wine, sugar, Chinese black vinegar, and chicken stock and bring to boil. Dissolve tapioca starch in water, then incorporate into the wok. Bring to boil again and immediately remove from heat. Spoon onto warmed plates and sprinkle with peanuts. Serve with steamed rice.

Orient Expressions

Chinese black vinegar is used mainly in sauces and braises. Although it's not as thick, black vinegar imparts a rich, sweet flavor with a complexity that is comparable to balsamic vinegar.

Lobster in Black Bean Sauce

Prep time: 12 minutes • Cook time: 15 minutes • Serves 2

1 (1$\frac{1}{2}$- to 2$\frac{1}{2}$-lb.) live lobster

$\frac{1}{4}$ cup peanut oil

1 tsp. minced fresh garlic

2 TB. black bean sauce

1 tsp. minced fresh ginger

1 TB. dry sherry

1 oz. soy sauce

1 tsp. granulated sugar

1 cup chicken stock

1 TB. tapioca starch

$\frac{1}{4}$ cup cold water

2 green onions, sliced

Steamed rice, for serving

Using a cleaver, chop live lobster into one-inch pieces, removing head, gills, and legs. Pick out any pieces of splintered shell.

Heat the wok over high heat and add oil. When oil begins to smoke, add lobster, stir-frying for one minute. Add garlic, black bean sauce, and ginger. Cook for two minutes. Add sherry, soy sauce, and sugar and cook for two more minutes. Next, add chicken stock, cover, and simmer for seven more minutes. The lobster should be tender at this point.

Mix tapioca starch with cold water and incorporate into lobster mixture. Bring to a boil, toss in onions, and remove from heat. Spoon lobster into warmed serving dishes with steamed rice.

Recipes for Success

This recipe is not for the faint of heart. If you can't bring yourself to chop up a live lobster, ask your fishmonger to do it for you. If you like to suck on the legs, include them. Take your package, go straight home, and cook it. Don't stop at GO, have your nails done, or take a nap. Cook it at once. Why? For some odd reason, the flavor and texture of lobster diminishes after it's slain.

Mu Shu Pork

Prep time: 1 hour • Marination time: 30 minutes • Cook time: 30 minutes • Serves 2

12 oz. boneless pork shoulder, trimmed of fat	1 large egg, beaten
¼ cup soy sauce (divided use)	1 tsp. minced fresh garlic
⅓ cup hoisin sauce (divided use)	1 tsp. minced fresh ginger
¼ cup dry sherry (divided use)	1 cup napa cabbage, shredded
1½ cup all-purpose flour, sifted	¼ cup dried wood ear mushroom
2 large eggs	¼ cup julienned carrot
2 cups water	¼ cup sliced green onion
Salt to taste	½ cup bean sprouts
2 TB. canola oil	¼ cup chicken stock
3 TB. peanut oil (divided use)	1 tsp. granulated sugar

Slice pork as thinly as possible. Cut each slice into thin slivers. Place pork into a bowl and add 2 tablespoons soy sauce, 2 tablespoons hoisin sauce, and 1 tablespoon dry sherry. Mix well, cover with plastic wrap, and marinate in the refrigerator for 30 minutes.

While meat is marinating, make pancakes. Whisk together flour, eggs, and water in a medium bowl until mixture is smooth and lump-free. Add salt to taste. Heat a small, 6-inch nonstick sauté or crepe pan over medium heat. Put enough canola oil in the pan to just coat the bottom and wipe lightly with a paper towel to remove excess. Pour 1 tablespoon batter into the center of the pan. Quickly tilt the pan in a circular motion to coat the pan with batter on all sides. Cook until pancake sets or begins to dry on top (about 30 seconds). Flip and cook other side for about 20 seconds. Wipe out the pan with a paper towel and proceed to make as many pancakes as you like. You might need to add more oil every couple pancakes or so. Keep pancakes covered with a warm, barely moist towel to prevent them from drying out.

Heat a wok over medium heat and add 1 tablespoon peanut oil. When oil is hot but not smoking, pour in egg and spread it by tilting the wok, making a thin pancake. When egg is set, transfer it to a cutting board, cool, and cut it into ½- × 3-inch strips.

Recipes for Success

This recipe takes a little while to prep, so have fun with it. You might as well enjoy yourself. And don't sweat over making the egg cake—this isn't rocket science, and because it's going to be cut up later, it doesn't have to be pretty.

Wipe the wok out with a towel and turn heat to high. Add remaining oil. When oil begins to smoke, add garlic, ginger, and pork, stir-frying until pork is golden brown, about four minutes. Add cabbage, mushroom, carrot, green onion, and bean sprouts. Stir-fry for two minutes and add chicken stock. Bring to a boil, then add sugar and remaining soy sauce and sherry. Bring back to a boil and toss in egg strips. Remove from heat and reserve. To serve, spoon hoisin sauce in middle of each pancake and place Mu Shu Pork on top. Roll pancake and serve.

Orange Beef

Prep time: 20 minutes • Marination time: 1 hour • Cook time: 12 minutes • Serves 2

12 oz. beef flank steak	2 tsp. rice vinegar
2 egg whites, beaten with a fork	1/4 cup chicken stock
3 TB. peanut oil (divided use)	1 orange
2 tsp. dry sherry	2 tsp. minced fresh ginger
1 tsp. tapioca starch	2 tsp. minced fresh garlic
3 quarts canola oil	1 tsp. Thai chili powder
2 TB. sweet soy sauce	1/2 cup sliced green onions
2 TB. granulated sugar	Steamed rice, for serving

Slice beef into 1/2-inch strips. Place in a bowl with egg whites and mix until beef is coated. Toss in 1 tablespoon peanut oil, dry sherry, and tapioca starch. Mix well with beef and marinate in the refrigerator, covered, for one hour.

Heat a wok or deep-fryer filled with at least 3 quarts canola oil to 400°F. Remove beef from marinade and discard marinade. Separate beef with your fingers and slide half of it into hot oil; keep pieces separate by moving them around with tongs. Fry for one minute. Remove and place on paper towels to drain. Repeat with remaining beef.

Raise the temperature of oil to 425°F and fry beef (in two batches again) for two more minutes; this will give beef a crispy crust. Drain again. Whisk sweet soy sauce, sugar, 1 tablespoon peanut oil, rice vinegar, and chicken stock together. Set aside.

Zest half the orange with a zester and cut orange into segments.

Heat a wok over high heat. Add remaining peanut oil. When it begins to smoke, add ginger, garlic, and chili powder. Stir-fry for one minute, tossing constantly. Add orange zest, green onions, and beef. Cook for one more minute. Stir in sauce, bring to boil, and immediately remove from heat. Ladle onto a warm plate and garnish with fresh orange segments. Serve hot with lots of steamed rice.

Fortune Cookies

When you want a lighter, more delicate coating when deep-frying, use tapioca starch or tapioca flour.

Peking Duck

Prep time: 15 minutes • Cook time: 2 hours, 20 minutes • Serves 2

1 whole Peking duck

Kosher salt and freshly ground black pepper as needed

1¹/₂ cup all-purpose flour, sifted

2 large eggs

2 cups water

2 TB. canola oil

1 cup hoisin sauce

Steamed vegetables and steamed rice, for serving

Heat oven to 350°F.

Rinse duck well and pat dry. Season duck with salt and pepper inside and out. Place duck on a roasting pan fitted with a rack and place in the oven for two hours, uncovered, or until a meat thermometer inserted into the thigh reads 175°F to 180°F. Duck should have a nicely browned, crispy skin. Remove duck from the oven and let it rest for 20 minutes.

About 30 minutes before duck is done baking, whisk together flour, eggs, and water in a medium bowl until mixture is smooth and lump-free. Add salt to taste.

Heat a small, six-inch nonstick sauté or crepe pan over medium heat. Put enough oil in the pan to just coat the bottom and wipe lightly with a paper towel to remove excess. Pour 1 tablespoon batter into the center of the pan. Quickly tilt the pan in a circular motion to coat it with batter on all sides. Cook until pancake sets or begins to dry on top, about 30 seconds. Flip and cook other side for about 20 seconds. Wipe out the pan with a paper towel and proceed to make as many pancakes as you like. You might need to add more oil every couple pancakes or so. Keep pancakes covered with a warm, barely moist towel to prevent them from drying out. If pancakes are done before duck, wrap pancakes and towel in foil and keep in a warm spot.

To serve duck, cut out each whole breast piece, and slice thinly, keeping skin intact. Keep warm. Do the same for legs and thighs, carefully trimming meat from bone. Take one pancake and spread some hoisin sauce onto it. Place a few pieces of duck in center and roll pancake tightly. Place on a serving platter; serve with steamed vegetables and steamed rice.

Recipes for Success _____

When checking the temperature, insert the thermometer into the thickest part of the leg or thigh area away from the bone toward the upper part of the bird. If you melted your thermometer from the last duck you cooked, insert the tip of a paring knife into the lower portion of the thigh. If the juice runs clear, it's ready.

Sesame Chicken

Prep time: 25 minutes • Cook time: 10 minutes • Serves 2

3 cups water

$^1/_2$-inch piece fresh ginger, sliced

8 green onions, sliced

2 chicken breasts, skinless

1 TB. sesame oil

2 TB. soy sauce

2 tsp. white vinegar

2 tsp. dry sherry

$^1/_2$ tsp. granulated sugar

1 TB. black sesame seeds

$^1/_4$ cup chicken stock

2 tsp. tapioca starch

2 TB. water

Freshly ground black pepper to taste

Steamed rice for serving

Add water, ginger, and half the green onions to a 2-quart stockpot. Bring to a boil over high heat and add chicken. Immediately reduce heat to low and simmer for two minutes. Remove from heat and let chicken sit in cooking liquid to absorb flavor.

To make sauce, heat a wok over high heat, and add sesame oil, soy sauce, white vinegar, dry sherry, sugar, sesame seeds, and chicken stock. Bring to a boil and add remaining green onions and tapioca starch mixed with water. Bring to a boil, immediately remove from heat, and season with black pepper to taste.

Remove chicken from cooking liquid and place each breast onto a warm serving plate. Ladle sauce over chicken and serve hot with steamed rice.

Sweet and Sour Simmered Shrimp

Prep time: 15 minutes • Cook time: 15 minutes • Serves 2

2 TB. canola oil

1 lb. shrimp (16 to 20 count), peeled and deveined

¼ cup tomato paste

¼ cup water

2 TB. cider vinegar

2 TB. granulated sugar

2 tsp. minced fresh ginger

1 tsp. tapioca starch

1 tsp. salt

2 TB. thinly sliced green onions

Steamed rice, for serving

Heat wok to high heat and add oil. When oil begins to smoke, add shrimp. Cook for five minutes, keeping food constantly moving in the wok.

Mix together tomato paste, water, vinegar, sugar, ginger, starch, and salt in a small nonreactive bowl. Add this mixture to the wok, simmer for four minutes, and toss in onions. Serve hot with lots of steamed rice on the side.

Twice-Cooked Pork with Hoisin Sauce

Prep time: 15 minutes • Cook time: 1 hour, 15 minutes • Serves 2

1 lb. pork shoulder

Water as needed

2 TB. peanut or canola oil

¼ cup sliced green onions

½ cup julienne of red bell peppers (1 inch long)

½ cup julienne of green bell peppers (1 inch long)

½ cup hoisin sauce

¼ cup chicken stock

Steamed rice and kailan or Chinese broccoli for serving

Heat a wok over high heat. When hot, place pork into the wok and add water to cover. Bring water to a boil and immediately lower the heat. Simmer, uncovered, for one hour.

Place pork shoulder on a cutting board and slice it thinly across the grain. Wipe the wok clean and heat again over high heat. Add oil. When it begins to smoke, add green onions, red and green bell peppers, and sliced pork. Stir-fry for two minutes. Add hoisin sauce and chicken stock. Bring to a boil and remove from heat. Serve hot with kailan (or Chinese broccoli) and steamed rice.

Chapter 8

Next Stop: Vietnam

In This Chapter

◆ Chinese and French influences

◆ Soup's on!

◆ Aromatic recipes from Vietnam

Vietnamese describe their land as a long pole with a rice basket on each end. The northern rice basket of the Red River Delta is cooler, producing fewer varieties of vegetables and fruits than the southern rice basket of the Mekong Delta.

Northerners have a penchant for beef, soy sauce, and lots of black pepper in lieu of chili peppers. In the south, a fish sauce called nuoc mam replaces soy sauce, and more fresh fruits and vegetables and lots of fish and seafood come into play.

The Chinese ruled Vietnam for almost 1,000 years and their culinary stamp is on food throughout the country, especially in the North, which is closest to the China border where stir-frys and stews are popular. But the Vietnamese hold their own, particularly in the way they use rice papers in many dishes that is a refreshing twist in Asian cuisine. In the South, lots of chili peppers and lemongrass come in to play and fresh herbs and tropical flavors are added to the mix to create refreshingly flavorful dishes.

Throughout the country, decades of French colonization left a curiously edible mark. Lemongrass is referred to by its French name, *citronelle*, but paté refers to a paste of coriander, shrimp, and black pepper. Today, little Vietnams across America are dotted with storefronts marked as "French Bakeries," where you'll find baguettes and sausages for sale but little else with a French influence.

Another thing the Vietnamese didn't pick up from the French was butter and cream; Vietnamese cooking is very low fat with little oil in stir-frys and lots of fresh veggies and fruits.

Fee, Fi, Phô, Yum: Soups

Phô is an aromatic noodle soup that is as much a part of Vietnamese life as pasta is to Italians. Traditionally, phô was a breakfast food but is now served all day and has become a meaningful family ritual. Different cuts of beef, chicken, or seafood are added for variety. Virtually nothing is wasted; a lot of recipes call for beef tendon (not included in this book), which is actually pretty tasty and adds textural contrast.

Lucky Treasures ———
The holy trinity of Vietnamese flavors is basil, cilantro, and mint. These fresh herbs come alongside a lot of dishes as enhancements or *fresh* condiments, packing a unique wallop of flavor.

Lucky Treasures ———
Fresh condiment platters are found everywhere in Vietnamese cuisine. To enhance a contrast of hot and cold, a cold platter of leafy lettuce leaves and fresh herbs is served alongside hot appetizers such as Spring Rolls and Sugar Cane Shrimp.

The art of phô is using a palate of toppings served at the table to create your own work of phô art. Asian basil, a squeeze of fresh lime, chili peppers, and bean sprouts are served as fresh condiments to personalize each bowl to taste.

Eating a bowl of phô looks a little daunting, but it's not. Just follow these steps:

1. Eat it hot. Once it starts to cool, the noodles will start to expand and get mushy.

2. Add some bean sprouts, a little black pepper, and the juice of half a lime to your bowl.

3. Use your spoon to slurp the soup, while picking at the noodles and beef with a pair of chopsticks. A noodle hanging from the mouth is totally acceptable in Vietnamese etiquette. If your glasses fog up, remove them and press on.

4. Eat your way through the herbs by placing them in your soup as you slurp, whittling your way through them a little at a time.

5. Take an occasional bite from the fresh chili pepper as you slurp the soup, if you dare. The contrast between the slight pain of the pepper and the ingredients of the soup only heightens the flavors. Go ahead, you'll live.

6. You don't have to finish all the broth. It's there in such a large amount to keep the rest of the food warm.

7. Above all, serve with an icy cold beer.

Whether you are in the mood for a hearty grilled beef dinner or shrimp on a sugar cane stick, these Vietnamese recipes are a great place to look for flavorful and quick recipes—not to mention culinary adventure.

Orient Expressions

Don't make a phool of yourself. **Phô** is pronounced *foo* as in *foot*, which is a good thing to keep out of your mouth while eating phô.

The Least You Need to Know

- Phô is Vietnamese noodle soup in which you create your own work of art using such ingredients as Asian basil, a squeeze of fresh lime, chili peppers, and bean sprouts.
- Decades of French and Chinese colonization left an edible mark on Vietnamese cooking.
- Nuoc mam is in or served with almost everything.
- Vietnamese cooking is very low fat with little oil in stir-frys and lots of fresh veggies and fruits.

Phô

Prep time: 25 minutes • Cook time: 10 minutes • Serves 2

1 quart beef stock

2 TB. fish sauce

2 TB. light soy sauce

2 tsp. granulated sugar

1 TB. freshly ground black pepper

2 quarts salted water

4 oz. rice-stick noodles, soaked in hot water for 15 minutes

1/2 cup julienned carrot, cut about 1 inch long

1/2 cup bean sprouts

8 oz. sirloin, thinly sliced across the grain

1/4 cup green onion, sliced

2 whole serrano chilies

1/4 cup fresh cilantro leaves

1/4 cup Asian basil leaves

1/4 cup mint leaves

1 lime, quartered

Freshly ground black pepper to taste

Sriracha sauce (optional)

Hoisin sauce (optional)

Bring beef stock, fish sauce, soy sauce, sugar, and black pepper to a boil over high heat in a small stockpot. Turn heat to low and hold at a very low simmer.

Bring 2 quarts salted water to a strong rolling boil in a 3-quart pot and add softened noodles. Boil for 15 seconds and drain; keep warm.

When ready to serve, bring stock to a rolling boil. Add carrot and bean sprouts, and cook for 15 seconds or until stock returns to a boil. Stock must be as hot as possible when serving.

Divide hot noodles among two large, deep, warmed serving bowls. Ladle soup into each bowl. Place sliced sirloin into each bowl. Serve with a garnish platter of green onion, chilies, cilantro, basil, mint, lime, and a pile of black pepper. Serve sauces on the side in tiny bowls.

Orient Expressions

Sriracha sauce is a purée of fresh red chili peppers, garlic, a little sugar, and salt. With a decidedly garlic kick to it, sriracha is not so spicy hot, but imparts a nice fresh pepper flavor. If you really want a hot foot, add a little more than directed in the recipes.

Lucky Treasures

Like spaghetti to the Italians and butter sauce to the French, phô is probably one of the most significant dishes in Vietnam. Usually served family-style, phô is a nutritionally complete, deeply personal dish that has kept Vietnamese families together at the table since the French occupation.

Broiled Bass with Ginger Sauce

Prep time: 25 minutes • Marination time: 2 hours • Cook time: 30 minutes • Serves 2

1 lb. filet of bass, skin on	1 TB. nuoc mam
2 TB. fresh lime juice	2 TB. white vinegar
1 TB. sesame oil	$\frac{1}{2}$ cup plum wine
2 TB. grated fresh ginger	$\frac{1}{4}$ cup thinly sliced green onion
$\frac{1}{2}$ cup fresh mushroom, sliced thin	1 fresh red chili pepper, sliced thin
2 stalks lemongrass, trimmed and peeled to the soft core, sliced thin	1 tsp. tapioca starch
	2 TB. water

Score skin of fish four times and place in a nonreactive bowl. Pour lime juice over fish and marinate in the refrigerator for two hours.

Preheat oven to 450°F.

Brush bass on both sides with sesame oil and bake for about 10 to 12 minutes. Fish will turn opaque when it is ready. Do not place too close to the heat or fish will cook too fast on the outside and not in the middle. Place fish on a serving platter and keep warm.

To make sauce, heat a wok to medium hot and add ginger, mushrooms, lemongrass, nuoc mam, vinegar, and plum wine. Bring to a simmer, then add green onion and red chilies. Cook for three minutes.

Whisk tapioca starch and water together in a small bowl and pour into sauce. Bring to boil and immediately ladle over fish. Serve hot.

Chicken and Pork Noodles

Prep time: 25 minutes • Cook time: 20 minutes • Serves 2

$^1/_2$ tsp. vegetable oil

2 tsp. chopped garlic

$^1/_4$ cup fish sauce

2 tsp. sambal

2 tsp. granulated sugar

2 TB. water

2 TB. white vinegar

$^1/_4$ cup chopped unsalted peanuts

2 TB. Asian basil, chopped

2 TB. fresh cilantro leaves, chopped

8 oz. chicken breast, skinless

8 oz. pork butt

Salt and freshly ground black pepper

Canola oil for brushing meats

12 oz. rice vermicelli noodles, soaked in tap water for 20 minutes

$^1/_2$ cup julienned carrot

$^1/_2$ cup bean sprouts

$^1/_2$ cup julienned cucumber

Heat vegetable oil in a small pot over medium high heat. Add the garlic and quickly stir-fry until golden brown. Remove from the heat and reserve. Do not overcook, or garlic will be bitter.

Heat a small saucepan over medium heat. Combine fish sauce, sambal, sugar, water, and white vinegar and bring to a boil. Lower heat and simmer for five minutes. Stir in peanuts, basil, fried garlic, and cilantro. Set aside.

Heat the grill to medium-high heat. Season chicken and pork with salt and pepper, brush them with oil, and grill until fully cooked, about 10 to 12 minutes. Remove from the grill and cut into $^1/_4$-inch thick slices. Set aside.

Bring a 3-quart pot of lightly salted water to a boil. Add noodles and cook for one minute. Strain and divide noodles between two warmed serving bowls. Pour sauce over noodles, tossing lightly. Top with chicken and pork slices in the center of the bowl. Place carrot, bean sprouts, and cucumber in small piles around the bowl cold. Serve at once.

$\succ\ominus\prec$

Garlic Roasted Duck

Prep time: 25 minutes • Marination time: 4 to 6 hours • Cook time: 40 minutes • Serves 2

$^1/_2$ cup red wine vinegar

1 tsp. nuoc mam

1 tsp. juniper berries, ground

$^1/_2$ cup chopped white onion

$^1/_2$ tsp. minced fresh garlic

1 tsp. whole fennel seed

2 duck breasts

$^1/_2$ cup plain yogurt

Salt

Freshly ground black pepper

For marinade, mix together red wine vinegar, nuoc mam, juniper berries, onion, garlic, and fennel seed in a medium bowl. Rub marinade on duck. Reserve any leftover marinade. Cover and refrigerate for four to six hours.

Remove duck from marinade and place skin side down on a roasting pan. Reserve marinade. Preheat the oven to 425°F and roast duck for 15 minutes on each side.

Put remaining marinade into a saucepan and reduce in volume by half. Strain marinade into a bowl and whisk in yogurt, salt, and pepper. Slice duck breast into medallions by cutting against the grain, making $^1/_4$-inch thick slices. Pour sauce on the plate and top with duck slices. Serve warm.

Grilled Lemongrass Beef

Freeze time: 1 hour • Prep time: 15 minutes • Marination time: 2 hours • Cook time: 15 minutes • Serves 2

1 lb. sirloin

1 TB. fish sauce

2 TB. sesame oil

2 pieces lemongrass stalk, peeled to the soft core and chopped

1/4 tsp. freshly ground black pepper

1 TB. sesame seeds, toasted

1 tsp. shallots, chopped

1 tsp. garlic, chopped

1/2 tsp. red chili powder

1 TB. granulated sugar

Canola oil for brushing meat

2 sprigs fresh mint

Wrap sirloin tightly in plastic wrap and place in the freezer until meat is almost frozen, about one hour. This will make it easier to cut. Cut into thinnest slices possible against the grain and set aside on a plate to thaw out.

To make marinade, put fish sauce, sesame oil, lemongrass, black pepper, sesame seeds, shallots, garlic, chili powder, and sugar into a food processor fitted with a metal blade; process to a paste. Toss beef with paste, and marinate for at least two hours in the refrigerator.

Brush the grill lightly with canola oil. Heat the grill to medium-high. Place beef slices on the grill and cook for about one minute on each side or until medium rare. Cooking times can vary, depending on how thin the slices are. Transfer to a serving plate. Garnish with mint sprigs. Serve hot.

Roasted Spare Ribs with Lemongrass and Chili

Prep time: 3 hours, 15 minutes • Marination time: 3 hours • Cook time: 1 hour, 30 minutes • Serves 2

2 lb. pork spareribs

2 TB. honey

2 tsp. garlic purée

2 lemongrass stalks, trimmed, peeled to the soft core and sliced thinly

$^1/_2$ tsp. red chili powder

3 TB. nuoc mam

2 TB. sake

Steamed jasmine rice, for serving

Rinse ribs and pat dry. Combine honey, garlic, lemongrass, chili powder, nuoc mam, and sake in a bowl and mix well. Coat ribs with marinade, reserving some for basting later. Refrigerate for three hours.

Preheat oven to 350°F and roast ribs for about $1^1/_2$ hour, basting every 20 minutes until ribs are fully cooked.

Serve warm with rice or Wasabi Mashed Potatoes (see Chapter 11).

Spicy Barbecued Chicken Legs

Prep time: 30 minutes • Marination time: 2 hours • Cook time: 30 minutes • Serves 2

2 lb. chicken legs

3 TB. sesame oil (divided use)

1 tsp. minced fresh garlic

1 stalk lemongrass, trimmed and peeled to the soft core, finely chopped

$^1/_4$ cup chopped green onions

1 tsp. red chili powder

1 TB. nuoc mam

1 tsp. granulated sugar

$^1/_2$ tsp. kosher salt

$^1/_2$ tsp. freshly ground black pepper

Juice of 2 fresh lemons

Using a sharp knife, pierce some holes in chicken legs to better absorb marinade.

Heat a wok until medium hot and add 1 tablespoon sesame oil, garlic, lemongrass, and green onion. Stir-fry for three minutes, tossing with a spatula. Add chili powder, nuoc mam, and sugar. Remove marinade from heat and cool.

Rub marinade deep into skin of chicken legs and refrigerate for at least two hours. When ready to cook, brush chicken with remaining oil and broil for 20 minutes or until chicken is no longer pink and juices run clear. Mix salt, pepper, and lemon juice together, pour into a small serving bowl, and serve with chicken and steamed Chinese long beans.

Steamed Crab with Rice Wine

Prep time: 10 minutes • Cook time: 15 minutes • Serves 2

1 TB. sesame oil

1 tsp. fresh garlic, minced

1/4 cup green onions, chopped

2 stalks lemongrass, trimmed, peeled to the soft core and chopped

1 tsp. fresh ginger, minced

1 lb. fresh crab claws

1/2 cup sake or rice wine

1 TB. fish sauce

Heat a wok until medium hot and add oil. When oil is smoking, add garlic, green onion, lemongrass, and ginger. Stir-fry for two minutes, then add crab claws, sake, and fish sauce. Bring to a boil and then simmer for five minutes. Serve hot.

Stir-Fried Lamb with Mint and Chili

Prep time: 15 minutes • Cook time: 15 minutes • Serves 2

2 TB. canola oil

1 lb. lamb tenderloin, thinly sliced

1 tsp. garlic, minced

1/2 cup chicken stock

2 TB. oyster sauce

1 tsp. granulated sugar

1/2 tsp. red chili powder

1 TB. nuoc mam

1/4 cup mint leaves

Heat a wok until very hot and add oil. When oil is smoking, add lamb and garlic. Stir-fry until lamb is golden brown. Add chicken stock, oyster sauce, sugar, chili powder, and nuoc mam. Continue to cook for three minutes. Turn off heat and toss in fresh mint leaves. Serve at once.

Stuffed Chicken Thighs

Prep time: 30 minutes • Marination time: 20 minutes • Cook time: 1 hour 20 minutes • Serves 2

1 lb. chicken thighs	2 TB. oyster sauce
$\frac{1}{4}$ cup dried wood ear mushroom	$\frac{1}{4}$ cup green onions, chopped
2 oz. glass noodles	$\frac{1}{4}$ cup julienned carrot
2 TB. nuoc mam	$\frac{1}{4}$ tsp. chopped fresh cilantro leaves
1 large egg, beaten	Salt and freshly ground black pepper
8 oz. ground pork	

Bone chicken thighs by running tip of a paring knife along bone, starting at underside of thigh. Soak mushrooms and noodles in cold water for 15 minutes; remove and drain well. Quarter mushrooms and cut noodles into smaller pieces with three cuts of the knife.

In a nonreactive bowl, mix noodles and mushrooms with nuoc mam, egg, pork, oyster sauce, green onion, carrot, and cilantro. Season with salt and pepper to taste and marinate for 20 minutes. Spread open chicken thigh and spoon filling into center. Roll tight and secure with toothpick.

Preheat oven to 350°F and roast chicken thighs for 40 minutes or until center of pork filling is cooked, or 165°F on a meat thermometer. Serve hot.

Sugar Cane Shrimp

Prep time: 20 minutes • Cook time: 20 minutes • Serves 2

8 oz. shrimp (16 to 20 count), peeled, deveined and finely chopped

8 oz. ground pork

1 TB. fish sauce

1/2 cup white onion, diced

1 tsp. garlic, minced

1/4 cup fresh cilantro, chopped

1 tsp. freshly cracked black pepper

1 large egg, beaten

1/2 tsp. tapioca starch

4 (6-inch) sticks sugarcane

1 quart canola oil for frying

Mix shrimp, pork, fish sauce, onion, garlic, cilantro, and pepper in a large bowl. Add egg, mixing it in with your hands. Add tapioca starch and work mixture again until all is evenly mixed. If sugarcane still has its outer bark, peel it off with a paring knife.

Take a quarter of the mixture and mold it around each sugarcane stalk, leaving 1/2 inch cane visible on each end. Heat a heavy-duty pot with oil to 350°F and carefully place wrapped sugarcanes into it. Fry, turning frequently, for about five minutes or until brown. Serve hot with a platter of leaf lettuce leaves, mint, cilantro, and Asian basil. Add a dipping sauce of nuoc mam and finely shredded carrot.

Korea: Land of S(e)oul

In This Chapter

- ◆ Korea's food is reflected by its geography and weather
- ◆ Bulgogi is more popular in Korea than Swatches were in the 1980s
- ◆ Chili peppers and pastes make Korean dishes a spicy experience
- ◆ Some great dishes from Korea

Bound by the Sea of Japan to the east and the Yellow Sea to the west, Korea is a mountainous peninsula with icy winters and scarce farmland. To survive the winters, Koreans became the kings of pickling and preserving. *Kim chee*, dried cuttlefish, and dried sardines are always at hand.

People in the mountains rely heavily on the mushrooms, wild roots, and ferns found there. Those who can farm in the valleys have an abundance of fresh vegetables, rice, and beans to add to their meals. Though fish and rice are the mainstays of the Korean diet, when it's party time, or the money's there, it's beef that Koreans yearn for, especially *bulgogi*, a Korean-style barbecue made from thin strips of beef marinated in soy sauce, sesame oil, ginger, garlic, and onions prior to grilling.

> **Orient Expressions**
>
> **Kim chee** is a condiment of spicy hot, garlic pickled vegetables, usually cabbage and/or turnips. It is served as a side dish at almost every meal and occasionally shows up as an ingredient in recipes.
>
> There is so much garlic in kim chee that eating any more than a couple condimentlike nibbles will give you breath that is close to terminal. No matter how much you brush or gargle, you simply won't be able to get rid of the offending odor. Seems the sulphur in the fermented garlic lasts in the stomach for about two days. What can you do? Eat it on a Friday, of course.

Liberal use of chili peppers and pastes has inspired tales of Korean dishes so hot it takes a month for your mouth to cool down. But more often it's not how much chili pepper is used in cooking, but what you add at the table that brings out the dragon in you.

The Least You Need to Know

- Kim chee is a condiment of spicy pickled vegetables, usually cabbage and/or turnips.
- Bulgogi is a Korean barbecue made from thin strips of beef marinated in soy sauce, sesame, ginger, garlic, and onions prior to grilling.
- A glass of water on the side is recommended while eating spicy Korean food.

Baked Clams

Prep time: 20 minutes • Cook time: 20 minutes • Serves 2

2 lb. littleneck clams	$^1/_2$ tsp. red chili powder
$^1/_2$ cup sake	$^1/_2$ cup green onion, finely chopped
2 TB. mirin	1 TB. sesame oil
1 TB. garlic, minced	1 tsp. fish sauce
2 TB. soy sauce	1 tsp. sesame seeds, toasted

Rinse clams of all sand. Heat a skillet or saucepan over high heat and add clams, sake, mirin, garlic, and soy sauce. Cover and bring to a boil. When clams open, toss with chili powder, green onion, sesame oil, fish sauce, and sesame seeds. Discard any clams that do not open. Serve hot in large, warmed soup bowls.

Boiled Stuffed Chicken with Ginseng

Prep time: 15 minutes • Cook time: 2 hours, 15 minutes • Serves 2

1 whole (2 lb.) chicken	$^1/_2$ cup glutinous rice
1 (2- to 3-inch) piece fresh ginseng root	Water as needed
1 TB. garlic, minced	2 TB. fish sauce
$^1/_4$ cup green onion, chopped	1 tsp. freshly ground black pepper

Rinse chicken (especially the cavity) with cold water. Pat dry with paper towels.

Mix ginseng, garlic, green onion, and rice together in a small bowl. Stuff cavity with rice mixture.

Place chicken into a shallow pot and fill pot halfway with water. Add fish sauce and black pepper to water and bring to a boil. When boiling, reduce heat and cover, simmering chicken for two hours.

Spoon rice out of cavity and place into two large warmed soup bowls. Pick out and discard ginseng. Cut chicken into serving pieces and place atop rice. Serve immediately.

Lucky Treasures

Zap! You have just been hit with ginseng, which has been used for centuries for its medicinal properties to increase vitality and life span. It is common in today's pop culture in beverages, teas, and even as tablets and pills. As a recipe ingredient, there is no substitute.

Braised Short Ribs

Prep time: 25 minutes • Cook time: 1 hour, 20 minutes • Serves 2

1 lb. beef short ribs

1/4 cup wood ear mushroom

1/2 cup Asian pear, grated

2 TB. soy sauce

3 tsp. granulated sugar

4 TB. green onion, finely chopped

1 tsp. garlic, minced

2 TB. sesame oil

2 cups chicken stock

1 TB. sesame seeds

1 TB. dry sherry

Score meat with a knife to the bone without cutting meat off.

Soak mushroom in a little warm water for 15 minutes. Drain well and chop roughly.

Mix grated pear with soy sauce, sugar, green onion, garlic, sesame oil, chicken stock, and sesame seeds. Pour mixture into a 3-quart saucepan and bring to a boil. Reduce heat and add ribs, mushrooms, and sherry. Simmer for one hour or until rib meat is falling off the bone.

Spoon ribs onto warmed serving plates.

≻⌣≺

Grilled Sliced Beef

Prep time: 30 minutes • Cook time: 8 minutes • Marination time: 1 hour, 30 minutes • Serves 2

1 lb. sirloin, well chilled

1 large white onion, cut in thick slices

1 TB. sake

2 tsp. granulated sugar

2 TB. soy sauce

1 tsp. water

1 TB. garlic, minced

$^1/_2$ cup green onion, sliced

1 tsp. toasted sesame seeds

1 tsp. freshly cracked black pepper

1 TB. sesame oil

Cut beef into thin slices and place into a nonreactive pan. Mix onion, sake, and sugar, and pour over beef. Refrigerate for 30 minutes.

In another bowl, mix soy sauce, water, garlic, green onion, sesame seeds, black pepper, and sesame oil.

Pour beef mixture into marinade and refrigerate for one more hour.

Heat the grill to high heat. Remove beef from marinade along with white onions. Discard the rest of marinade. Grill onions and beef for five minutes. Place on warmed serving plates. Serve hot.

Pork Pancake

Prep time: 20 minutes • Cook time: 15 minutes • Serves 2

$^{1}/_{2}$ cup kim chee, rinsed and minced

8 oz. ground pork

$^{1}/_{4}$ cup sliced green onions

1 tsp. minced fresh garlic

1 TB. fish sauce

1 tsp. toasted sesame seeds

1 tsp. freshly ground black pepper

$^{1}/_{2}$ cup all-purpose flour

1 TB. canola oil

2 large eggs, beaten

Place kim chee into a medium-size stainless-steel bowl. Add ground pork, green onion, garlic, fish sauce, sesame seeds, and black pepper.

Shape 2 tablespoons mixture into a patty about $^{3}/_{8}$ inch thick. Dip each patty into flour, coating both sides; set aside.

Heat a sauté pan to medium heat and add oil. As oil heats, dip each patty into beaten egg and carefully place into the pan. Cook until patties are golden brown on both sides, about 8 to 10 minutes. Serve hot.

Potatoes and Beef

Prep time: 20 minutes • Cook time: 20 minutes • Serves 2

1 lb. potatoes

2 TB. canola oil

1 lb. sirloin, well chilled and thinly sliced

1 tsp. garlic, minced

$^{1}/_{4}$ cup jalapeño chili peppers, sliced

1 quart chicken stock

1 tsp. fish sauce

1 tsp. beef paste

1 TB. granulated sugar

2 TB. soy sauce

2 TB. sake

1 TB. sesame oil

1 TB. sesame seeds

2 TB. thinly sliced green onions

Peel and cut potatoes into $^{1}/_{4}$-inch slices. Rinse them in cold water to remove starch.

Heat a wok until very hot and add oil. When oil is smoking, add beef and potatoes, stir-frying for two minutes. Add garlic and jalapeños to the wok and stir-fry for one minute. Add chicken stock, fish sauce, and beef paste. Bring to a boil. Add sugar, soy sauce, and sake. Simmer until liquid reduces in volume by half. Potatoes should have a crisp texture.

After plating, drizzle with sesame oil and sprinkle with sesame seeds and green onion. Serve hot.

Seafood with Hot Mustard

Prep time: 20 minutes • Cook time: 15 minutes • Serves 2

1 quart water

Kosher salt to taste

8 oz. shrimp (16 to 20 count), peeled and deveined

8 oz. calamari tubes, cut into 1-inch rings

8 oz. sea scallops

3 TB. hot mustard powder

2 TB. granulated sugar

1 TB. fish sauce

2 TB. distilled white vinegar

3 TB. water

1 TB. pine nuts, chopped

2 Asian pears, sliced

$^1/_2$ cup cucumber, sliced

Boil 1 quart lightly salted water in a 3-quart saucepan. Lower heat to medium and cook shrimp, calamari, and scallops about four minutes or until white, opaque, and firm to the touch. Remove from heat, strain, and transfer to a bowl sunk into a large bowl of ice water to chill, tossing occasionally.

In another bowl, mix mustard powder, sugar, fish sauce, vinegar, and water. Add cooled sea-food, pine nuts, pears, and cucumber, tossing well. Spoon onto cooled serving plates. Serve cold.

Stir Fried Pork with Kim Chee

Prep time: 20 minutes • Cook time: 20 minutes • Serves 2

1 lb. boneless pork ribs

2 cups kim chee

2 TB. sesame oil

$^1/_2$ tsp. red chili powder

$^1/_4$ cup green onion, sliced

1 TB. fish sauce

1 tsp. garlic, minced

1 TB. toasted sesame seeds

$^1/_2$ tsp. salt or to taste

Cut pork and kim chee into 2-inch strips.

Heat a wok until very hot and add oil. When oil begins to smoke, add pork. Stir-fry each side for three minutes. Add kim chee, chili powder, green onion, fish sauce, and garlic. Stir-fry for three minutes more. Stir in sesame seeds and salt. Serve hot on warmed serving plates.

Beef and Mushroom Stir-Fry

Prep time: 20 minutes • Cook time: 15 minutes • Serves 2

1 TB. canola oil

$^1/_2$ cup shiitake mushroom caps, quartered

$^1/_2$ cup button mushrooms, quartered

$^1/_2$ tsp. garlic, minced

8 oz. beef sirloin, well chilled and thinly sliced

$^1/_2$ cup chicken stock

$^1/_4$ tsp. beef paste

1 TB. fish sauce

$^1/_2$ tsp. freshly ground black pepper

8 green onions, cut into 1-inch pieces

1 TB. sake

$^1/_2$ tsp. sesame seeds, toasted

Heat a wok until very hot and add oil. When oil begins to smoke, add shiitake and button mushrooms. Stir-fry until browned and add garlic and beef sirloin. Stir-fry for two minutes and add chicken stock and beef paste. Bring to a boil and add fish sauce, black pepper, green onions, and sake. Bring to a boil, then remove from heat. Serve on warmed plates and sprinkle with sesame seeds. Serve hot.

Fortune Cookies

Beef paste can be found in the soup aisle of most grocery stores next to the bouillon. Basically, it is concentrated soup stock. Annie uses it in concentrated form.

Stuffed Prawns

Prep time: 30 minutes • Cook time: 25 minutes • Serves 2

1 lb. fresh prawns (10 per pound), with heads and tails still on

1 lb. medium shrimp (16 to 20 count), peeled and deveined

¼ cup thinly sliced green onion

¼ cup finely chopped carrot

2 tsp. minced fresh garlic

1 (1-inch) piece ginger, minced

½ tsp. salt

1 tsp. freshly ground black pepper

1 TB. sesame oil

1 medium egg, beaten well

Clip underside of prawn tail where legs meet shell with a pair of kitchen shears or sharp paring knife making a long cut the length of the tail. Pull tail meat out of the shell of each prawn with a side-to-side tugging motion, leaving head and tail intact. Mince prawn meat.

In a bowl, mix prawns and shrimp with green onion, carrot, garlic, ginger, salt, and black pepper. Stuff prawn shells with seafood mixture and close the tail around the stuffing so it looks like a pristine prawn.

Pour about 2 inches water into the bottom of a large pot that will accommodate a bamboo steamer. Bring to a boil. Fit the steamer into the pot and place prawns on a plate on the rack of the steamer. Cover with a lid and steam for 12 to 14 minutes.

Meanwhile, heat the wok over medium heat and add the sesame oil. Pour in the egg and cook until set, about 2 minutes. Remove the "omelet" from the wok and cut into thin strips. When prawns are done, garnish with egg.

Tofu Steaks with Ground Beef

Prep time: 15 minutes • Cook time: 15 minutes • Serves 2

8 oz. firm tofu

6 oz. lean ground beef

2 TB. soy sauce (divided use)

3 TB. sesame oil (divided use)

1 TB. green onion, chopped

$\frac{1}{2}$ tsp. red chili powder

1 tsp. sesame seeds

1 tsp. garlic, minced

1 tsp. granulated sugar

2 TB. water

Cut tofu into $\frac{1}{2}$-inch slices. Pat tofu dry with paper towels and set aside.

Mix ground beef with 1 tablespoon soy sauce, 1 tablespoon sesame oil, green onion, chili powder, sesame seeds, and garlic.

Heat a sauté pan over medium heat, add 1 tablespoon sesame oil, and sear tofu on each side for two minutes. Remove tofu from the pan. Top each tofu slice with ground beef mixture, pressing firmly so it will adhere to tofu.

Heat the sauté pan over medium heat, and add remaining sesame oil. Sear tofu with beef side down for two minutes. Add remaining soy sauce, sugar, and water. Simmer until beef is done, five more minutes more. Flip tofu over, beef side up, and place on warm serving plates. Serve immediately.

Chapter **10**

Orient Express: Singapore, Malaysia, Indonesia, and India

In This Chapter

- ◆ Island-hopping in Southeast Asia
- ◆ Curry without the hurry in India
- ◆ A selection of dishes from Southeast Asia and India

Hop on the express train and we'll take a whirlwind tour of Southeast Asia and India.

Southeast Asia

Malaysia begins at the Malay Peninsula on the southernmost bit of mainland Asia, ending in the island city-state of Singapore. It picks up again across the South China Sea on the island of Borneo. Hop back west a bit toward the Indian Ocean and you're at the top of Indonesia's chain of 13,000 islands, stretching almost to Australia. In all these areas you'll find a healthy mix of Chinese/Indian food with a strong tropical punch. Satay, which is grilled meat, tofu, or chicken on a stick, and dishes made with coconut milk and peanuts are popular throughout these countries.

India

India anchors central Asia, spreading its spice-laden tentacles to the entire continent. Cinnamon, cardamom, nutmeg, cloves, coriander, and nutmeg are just a few of the spices routinely used in Indian cooking that have found their way to the rest of Asia and in kitchens worldwide.

There are dozens of regional styles of cooking on the Indian subcontinent, but at its most basic, you can divide Indian food into the northern, wheat-growing region, and the southern, rice-growing region, with lentils, called daal, unifying the whole.

Lucky Treasures

Where the word *curry* originated is a subject of some debate. Most believe it came from the Tamil word *kari*, meaning spiced sauce. But others claim it might well have English roots, referring to *The Forme of Cury*, an English cookbook compiled at the behest of Richard II in the late 1300s. We'll let the experts debate and enjoy our curry before it gets cold!

Recipes for Success

Masala literally means a mixture. In cooking, it's an Indian term for a mixture of spices. Traditionally, Indian cooks made their masala from scratch, but these days there are plenty of good-quality prepackaged masalas. Garam Masala is the one most frequently called for in Indian cooking.

Chili peppers brought long ago by the Portuguese, saffron and pistachios from the Middle East, tandoori ovens, and chicken and lamb are key elements in northern dishes. In the south, seafood, coconut milk, garbanzo beans, and vegetables in every variety and form come into play.

And then there's *curry*, which means many things to many people. In modern Indian terminology, curry refers to any dish with a gravy-style sauce. And in the sauce is that divine blend, called a masala, of spices and herbs that we get a mere hint of when we buy packaged curry powder at the grocers. Almost all Indian homes have a spice grinder and every family its own variation of spices for creating curry dishes.

Mixing it up with masala is a major part of Indian cooking. There are hundreds of variations of masalas, including wet and dry masalas. Depending on the dish, the masala is added during the cooking or after.

All aboard, the train is leaving the station! We've gathered a few of our favorite recipes from India, Singapore, Malaysia, and Indonesia to feed you on your journey.

The Least You Need to Know

- Curry is a dish with gravy or the gravy itself, not the powder in the jar.
- Satay is grilled meat on a stick, extra yummy with peanut dipping sauce.
- Masalas, wet or dry, are mixtures of spices.

Chicken with Green Tomatoes (India)

Prep time: 20 minutes • Cook time: 1 hour, 15 minutes • Serves 2

4 cups chicken stock

1 whole (2- to 3-lb.) chicken

2 TB. fresh lime juice

2 TB. fish sauce

2 kaffir lime leaves

2 green tomatoes, sliced

1 ($\frac{1}{2}$-inch) piece fresh ginger, peeled and sliced

1 tsp. sliced fresh garlic

2 green onions, trimmed and thinly sliced

4 sprigs Asian basil

5 bird's-eye chili peppers, sliced

5 small Thai chili peppers, seeded

Heat a wok over high heat, add chicken stock, and bring to a boil.

While stock is heating, cut chicken into pieces. Add chicken to stock with lime juice, fish sauce, lime leaves, tomatoes, ginger, and garlic. Bring to a boil. Immediately reduce heat and add green onion, basil, and *bird's-eye* and Thai chili peppers. Simmer for 20 minutes. When chicken is fork-tender and meat falls off bone, remove from heat. Serve hot.

Orient Expressions

Bird's-eye chilies, if you are lucky enough to find them, are tiny teardrop-shape chili peppers. They are also called piquino in Thailand or chili pequin in Mexican cuisine, so a substitute isn't too hard to find. A desperate grab for a fresh habanero would also be a wise move.

Chicken Braised with Kaffir Lime Leaf (Malaysia)

Prep time: 20 minutes • Cook time: 1 hour • Serves 2

2 TB. water	2 TB. canola oil
1 lemongrass stalk, trimmed and chopped	1 lb. chicken legs
1/2 cup white onion, diced	1/2 cup wet tamarind
3 small red chili peppers	5 kaffir lime leaves
1 tsp. sliced fresh garlic	1/2 tsp. salt
1 tsp. ground turmeric	8 oz. canned coconut milk

Pour water into a blender and add lemongrass, onion, red chilies, garlic, and turmeric. Process these spices on high speed for at least one minute or until you have a smooth paste.

Heat a wok until very hot and add oil. When oil begins to smoke, add spicy paste from the blender and stir-fry for three minutes, constantly moving paste around with a spatula. Be careful not to burn it.

Add chicken, coating it on all sides with paste; cook for three to five minutes. Chicken should be browned at this point. Toss in tamarind, lime leaves, and salt. When liquid starts to bubble, reduce heat, and simmer for 10 minutes. Pour in coconut milk and continue to simmer for 15 minutes or until chicken is fork-tender. Serve hot.

Lucky Treasures

Will the real tamaraind please stand up?! Wet tamarind and tamarind paste are completely different animals. You will probably have to go to a Thai market to get it, but wet tamarind is the real magilla, usually cleaned from the pods, with debris removed, and compressed into blocks or packaged in cans. It can be used in recipes as is, steeped in water for a refreshing drink, or frozen for ices. Chef Annie says that "tamarind paste" has additional ingredients that do not make it suitable for cooking.

Chili Crab (Singapore)

Prep time: 25 minutes • Cook time: 30 minutes • Serves 2

2 lb. whole Dungeness crab or blue crab

1 tsp. minced fresh garlic

1 tsp. minced fresh ginger

3 small Thai chili peppers, cut in half and seeded

$1/4$ cup peanut oil (divided use)

2 TB. sriracha sauce

$1/2$ cup chicken stock

1 TB. granulated sugar

3 TB. tomato ketchup

1 TB. tapioca starch

1 large egg

2 TB. fresh lime juice

1 tsp. fish sauce or nuoc mam

1 TB. soy sauce

$1/4$ cup sliced green onions

If crabs are alive, boil water in a wok with 1 teaspoon salt and add crab. Cook for two minutes or until crab turns bright orange or red. Remove from pot and cool.

If you are using frozen crab, rinse and resume the following instructions.

Remove and discard V-shape apron, or tail, on underside of crab. After you do this, you will see rows of gills; remove them also and discard. With a large sharp knife, cut claws and legs from body. Crack shells a bit for easier access when eating. Cut body down middle, and then cut into about four pieces each.

In a blender, purée garlic, ginger, red chilies, and 1 tablespoon peanut oil. Add sriracha sauce, chicken stock, sugar, and ketchup, blending for 30 seconds.

Toss crab in tapioca starch, then heat a wok to medium heat and put crab into it with remaining oil. Brown crab on all sides. Add sauce from the blender. Cover the wok and continue to cook for five more minutes.

Fortune Cookies

Live crab is best for this dish, but frozen will do if fresh is not available.

Remove the lid and crack egg into the wok, tossing until scrambled. Toss in lime juice, fish sauce, and soy sauce. Spoon chili crab onto a warm serving platter. Sprinkle with green onions and serve hot.

Spicy Beef in Dry Curry (Indonesia)

Prep time: 25 minutes • Cook time: 1 hour • Serves 2

1 lb. bottom round of beef

¹/₄ tsp. ground cumin

¹/₄ tsp. ground coriander

5 red chili peppers, cut in half and seeded

1 stalk lemongrass, trimmed and peeled to the soft core and chopped

1 shallot, peeled and quartered

¹/₂ tsp. ground ginger

¹/₄ tsp. salt

¹/₂ tsp. minced fresh garlic

2 TB. chicken stock

2 TB. canola oil

1 cinnamon stick

2 TB. dried unsweetened shredded coconut, toasted

2 kaffir lime leaves

1 tsp. granulated sugar

1 black cardamom pod

2 star anise pods

3 oz. wet tamarind

1 cup canned coconut milk

Steamed jasmine rice, for serving

Cut beef into one-inch cubes.

Place cumin in a blender with coriander, red chilies, lemongrass, shallot, ginger, salt, and garlic. Add chicken stock and purée to a paste-like consistency.

Heat a wok over medium-high heat. Add oil. When it starts to smoke, add spice purée. Cook purée for five minutes, stirring constantly. Add cinnamon stick, shredded coconut, lime leaves, sugar, cardamom pod, star anise pods, beef, and tamarind. Toss constantly with a spatula until beef is seared on all sides. Add coconut milk and bring to a boil. Reduce heat to low and simmer uncovered for 40 minutes or until beef is fork-tender. Liquid in the wok should be reduced until it is all but evaporated. Serve warm with steamed jasmine rice.

Recipes for Success _____

To toast unsweetened coconut, spread on a cookie sheet and bake in a 325°F oven for 5 to 7 minutes or until golden brown. Transfer immediately from the cookie sheet to another container or it will continue to toast.

Fish in Banana Leaf (Indonesia)

Prep time: 20 minutes • Cook time: 40 minutes • Serves 2

2 boneless filets Pacific red snapper (about 1 lb.), skin on

$1/4$ tsp. salt

1 white onion, roughly chopped

$1/4$ tsp. minced fresh garlic

$1/4$ cup ground macadamia nuts

4 small red chili peppers, cut in half and seeded

$1/4$ tsp. ground ginger

$1/4$ tsp. ground turmeric

1 TB. Asian basil, chopped

2 banana leaves, fresh or frozen

1 stalk lemongrass, trimmed and peeled to the soft core and finely chopped

2 roma tomatoes, sliced

$1/4$ cup green onions, sliced

Preheat the oven to 350°F. Rinse the fish clean and pat dry. Score fish four times with a knife on skin side and season both sides with salt.

In a food processor fitted with a metal blade, process onions, garlic, macadamia nuts, red chilies, ginger, turmeric, and basil to a paste.

Rub entire fish with paste. Place fish on the middle of each banana leaf. Arrange lemongrass, tomatoes, and green onions on top of fish. Wrap banana leaf around each fish filet and secure with toothpicks.

Place in the oven for 15 to 20 minutes; when fish feels firm, it is done. If you are nervous about judging when fish is done, poke a hole in the wrapping and take a peek to see whether fish flakes; if it does, it's ready.

Saffron Chicken (India)

Prep time: 25 minutes • Cook time: 1 hour, 20 minutes • Serves 2

2 medium white onions	1 tsp. garlic, minced
2 cups whole unsalted cashews	2 tsp. ginger, minced
1 TB. peanut oil	1/2 cup plain yogurt
1 whole (2- to 3-lb.) chicken	2 TB. fish sauce
3 TB. unsalted butter	1 pinch saffron threads
1 cinnamon stick	1/2 cup chicken stock
3 whole cloves	1/2 cup heavy cream
4 green cardamom pods	3 sprigs fresh cilantro

Peel white onions and boil them in water for 10 minutes. Drain and place onions, cashews, and peanut oil in a food processor fitted with a metal blade and purée until it turns to a paste. Remove from the food processor and set aside.

Cut chicken into 10 to 12 pieces. Heat a wok over medium heat, add butter, cinnamon stick, cloves, and cardamom pods. Sauté for two minutes and add onions, garlic, and ginger. While constantly tossing ingredients in the wok, add yogurt, fish sauce, and saffron and reduce heat to low. Cook for five more minutes. Add chicken pieces, chicken stock, heavy cream, and cashew paste. Turn heat up and bring to boil; reduce heat again and simmer for 30 minutes or until chicken is fork-tender. Garnish with cilantro and serve hot.

Lucky Treasures

Savor each bite of saffron—it is the most expensive and precious spice in the world! The dried stigmas of *Crocus Sativus* (there are only three per flower) have to be removed by hand. It takes more than 60,000 flowers to produce 1 pound of saffron! Luckily, a little goes a long way, so it's always used sparingly. Harvested all over the world, the saffron of Indian (specifically, Kashmiri) origin is considered some of the best.

Sizzling Sirloin (Malaysia)

Prep time: 15 minutes • Marination time: 4 hours • Cook time: 15 minutes • Serves 2

1 lb. sirloin steak, about 1-inch thick	1 TB. canola oil
1 tsp. ground ginger	$^1/_4$ cup chicken stock
1 tsp. garlic, minced	$^1/_4$ cup julienned carrot
1 TB. granulated sugar	$^1/_4$ cup green onions, sliced
1 tsp. freshly ground black pepper	1 tsp. sweet chili sauce
2 TB. wet tamarind	2 tsp. fresh lime juice
2 TB. sweet soy sauce	2 TB. sesame oil
1 TB. oyster sauce	1 TB. tomato ketchup

Cut steak into two pieces. With a meat mallet, pound beef as thinly as possible to tenderize it.

In a food processor fitted with a metal blade, blend ginger, garlic, sugar, black pepper, and tamarind. With the processor running, add soy sauce and oyster sauce. Spoon marinade over steaks and refrigerate for at least four hours.

Heat a cast-iron skillet over high heat and add oil. Scrape marinade off steaks into a 1-quart saucepan. Sear meat for three minutes on each side. Place steaks on two serving plates and keep warm.

Add chicken stock, carrots, green onions, chili sauce, lime juice, sesame oil, and ketchup to marinade in the small saucepan. Bring to a boil and immediately pour over warm steaks.

Beef with Madras Curry (Malaysia)

Prep time: 15 minutes • Cook time: 20 minutes • Serves 2

1 TB. canola oil

1 tsp. garlic, minced

$\frac{1}{2}$ cup white onion, diced

8 oz. lean ground beef

2 TB. Madras yellow curry powder

1 cup peeled and diced baking potatoes

1 cup chicken stock

2 TB. fish sauce

1 cup chopped fresh cilantro leaves

Steamed jasmine rice for serving

Heat a wok over high heat and add oil. When oil begins to smoke, add garlic and onion. Stir-fry for one minute. Add beef, curry powder, and potatoes. Continue to stir-fry for five minutes. Stir in chicken stock, fish sauce, and cilantro and bring to a boil. Lower heat and simmer until liquid has reduced in volume by two-thirds. Serve hot with steamed jasmine rice.

Braised Coriander Chicken (Singapore)

Prep time: 25 minutes • Marination time: 1 hour • Cook time: 1 hour, 10 minutes
• Serves 2

2 TB. ground coriander	1 TB. ginger, minced
2 TB. granulated sugar	2 cups chicken stock
1 tsp. freshly ground black pepper	1 bay leaf
2 TB. sweet soy sauce	2 TB. fish sauce
1 lb. chicken legs	$^1/_4$ cup fresh cilantro leaves
2 TB. canola oil	1 tsp. tapioca starch
1 whole white onion, sliced	2 TB. water
1 TB. garlic, minced	

Mix coriander, sugar, black pepper, and sweet soy sauce together and lather on chicken. Marinate for one hour, refrigerated.

When ready to cook, remove chicken from marinade and discard any excess marinade.

Heat a wok over high heat and add oil. Just as oil begins to smoke, add onion, garlic, and ginger. Stir-fry for two minutes, add marinated chicken legs, and sear legs on all sides.

Add chicken stock, bay leaf, fish sauce, and cilantro. Bring to a boil. Simmer 30 minutes. Mix tapioca with water and add to the wok. Bring to a boil and immediately turn off heat. Serve hot with Spicy Eggplant (see Chapter 11).

Grilled Lamb Kebabs (Singapore)

Prep time: 20 minutes • Marination time: 6 hours • Cook time: 20 minutes • Serves 2

1 tsp. garlic, minced

Juice of 1 whole lemon

1 TB. ginger, minced

1 tsp. freshly ground black pepper

1 TB. distilled white vinegar

1 tsp. chili powder

1 medium white onion, peeled and quartered

$^{1}/_{2}$ tsp. ground turmeric

1 tsp. salt

$^{1}/_{2}$ cup plain yogurt

1 lb. boneless leg of lamb, thinly sliced

In a blender, process garlic, lemon juice, ginger, black pepper, vinegar, chili powder, onion, turmeric, and salt; pulse until it turns into a paste. Pour paste into a nonreactive bowl big enough to hold lamb. Stir in yogurt. Add lamb and cover it well with marinade. Cover with plastic wrap and refrigerate for six hours.

When ready to cook, heat a grill until very hot and cook lamb for four minutes on each side. Serve hot.

Recipes for Success

Cutting meat at room temperature is like trying to slice a wet noodle, especially if you need to slice it thinly. Always chill the meat well or place it in the freezer for about 30 minutes before slicing. It will go much easier.

Recipes for Success

Use of the blender and food processor is not interchangeable. When you need to chop something or make a paste, use the food processor. When a very fine blend is required, such as for a sauce, use a blender and don't be afraid to let the thing run for a couple of minutes. Another word of warning: If you are puréeing something hot in the blender, *do not* use the lid. Cover the top with a towel or pressure will build up in the canister and blow the top and innards all over your walls.

Spicy Meatballs (India)

Prep time: 25 minutes • Cook time: 30 minutes • Serves 2

$^1/_4$ cup sliced green chilies

1 TB. chopped cilantro leaves

1 tsp. salt (divided use)

2 tsp. ginger, minced (divided use)

$^1/_4$ tsp. ground cloves

$^1/_4$ tsp. mace

1 pinch Garam Masala

1 lb. lamb stew meat, cubed

2 TB. unsalted butter (divided use)

$^1/_4$ cup unsalted cashews

$^1/_4$ cup whole toasted almonds

$^1/_2$ tsp. minced fresh garlic

$^1/_4$ tsp. ground turmeric

$^1/_2$ tsp. ground cayenne pepper

$^1/_2$ cup finely chopped yellow onion

3 roma tomatoes, finely chopped

$^1/_4$ cup plain yogurt

1 TB. chopped mint leaves

Put chilies, cilantro, half the salt and ginger, cloves, mace, and Garam Masala into a food processor fitted with a metal blade. Blend until finely ground. Add lamb and pulse only until meat is evenly ground and mixed in.

Scrape this mixture into a nonreactive bowl, cover with plastic wrap, and refrigerate for at least 15 minutes. When chilled, shape lamb mixture into one-inch balls. Heat a sauté pan over medium high heat and sauté lamb in 1 tablespoon butter until browned. Set aside and keep warm.

Place cashews and almonds in a small saucepan with water to cover plus about one inch. Bring to a boil over high heat; lower heat to medium and continue to cook for eight minutes.

Strain nuts and blend in the food processor fitted with a metal blade until you have a smooth paste. Heat a wok over medium heat and add the other 1 tablespoon butter, 1 teaspoon ginger, garlic, turmeric, and cayenne pepper. Stir-fry for two minutes. Add onion and tomatoes, cooking for 10 minutes. Stir in nut purée and yogurt and simmer for three more minutes.

Place meatballs back in the wok and toss with sauce. Simmer over medium heat for eight minutes. Ladle into a shallow soup bowl and sprinkle with chopped mint leaves.

Recipes for Success

Do not overprocess the lamb or it will have a grainy, dusty feel in the mouth.

Part  3

New Asian Primer

What's best about the two of us working together is the way we feed off each other. It's more East bounces off West than East meets West. Anyone dropping in on one of our "recipe development sessions" would probably find our conversations incomprehensible—"This would be great with that pork from the other day" or "What about adding some mango to that sauce we used to do with the pineapple?" We might start out with an idea for a beef curry, and wind up with Duck Cigars!

Our point is that new Asian cooking evolves from a willingness to experiment, to look at ingredients and combinations of food in a new way. Even though our kitchen is firmly planted in the East, the West is welcome to join us anytime. In this part, we'll mix and match flavors from India and China with Japan and Thailand, and concoct new Asian versions of some American classics.

Chapter 11

Appetizers and Sides

In This Chapter

◆ Awesome appetizers

◆ Brilliant veggies

◆ Add flair with succulent fare

◆ Some great recipes for satisfying appetizers and sides

In many Asian countries the idea of appetizers and sides is a completely foreign concept. In Thailand, for instance, all the components of a meal are brought out at the same time, even the soup. But many Asian dishes—especially finger foods and vegetarian dishes—can be adapted to the Western style of eating.

These intriguing new Asian style appetizers and side dishes are fantastic additions to an evening of Asian fare. Look to the Chicken Satay (see Chapter 24), Tuna Spring Rolls, and Ginger Mushrooms for a memorable cocktail hour. Even veggie haters will find it hard to resist these tempting recipes for Chinese Long Beans and Garlic Chinese Broccoli. Turn a simple dinner of grilled chicken into a savory feast with a side of Spicy Eggplant. Even the most diehard meat and potatoes fan will appreciate pumping up a meal with Wasabi or Red Curry Mashed Potatoes.

Or make a meal of appetizers and sides, eating much like the Chinese do at their dim sum restaurants. Dim sum comes from the centuries-old Cantonese custom of serving tasty tidbits at tea time. Modern dim sum restaurants are lively places with a stream of carts filled with an assortment of dumplings, spring rolls, and stuffed steamed buns and other treats rolling through the restaurant. As the carts stop at each table, guests choose what they want from that cart. Though the portions are small, by the time you've eaten 10 or 12 of them you'll be very satisfied. Just be sure to leave room for dessert!

Fortune Cookies

Threading skewers can be fraught with a couple issues. Either they burn to a crisp when you cook them, or the impaled food spins mercilessly on its axis, turning eating into a carnival game. There are two tricks to doing it successfully: (1) Submerge the bamboo skewers in water for at least 30 minutes. (2) Thread the meat or seafood with a slight side-to-side motion so the squid (for example) isn't impaled in a straight line. The slight tension will keep the food from spinning.

Orient Expressions

Dim sum translates as "touch your heart," and those luscious little dumplings and other tasty morsels that make up dim sum will do just that.

Roll 'Em, Roll 'Em, Roll 'Em

After you've made a couple of these babies, making fresh spring rolls is, well, a piece of cake. Rice papers are, simply put, the same dough for rice noodles, only schmoosed into a circle instead of being cut into "sticks."

Using one rice paper at a time, submerge each disk in simmering water for 45 seconds. After pulling it from water, hang it on a corner of the counter by its edge to dry for about 20 seconds. This will make it easy to roll.

Remove a softened rice paper from the counter's edge and place it on your workspace. Place the ingredients on the circle according to the recipe you are using. Pull bottom edge of rice paper up over filling using the thumb and forefinger of each hand while holding stuffing with the middle fingers. Keep rice paper tight as you roll, but not too tight or it will tear. Once you have covered filling, fold sides of rice paper in, and continue to roll until you have made a cylinder.

Forget the French onion dip, you're ready to prepare an array of Asian appetizers. The only problem is that now your guests will be reluctant to move on to dinner!

The Least You Need to Know

- ◆ Dim sum is making a meal of many small dishes.
- ◆ Perk up an ordinary meal with an Asian side.
- ◆ Asian-style appetizers are ideal for the cocktail hour.

Chinese Long Beans

Prep time: 6 minutes • Cook time: 8 minutes • Serves 2

1 TB. sesame oil

2 cups Chinese long beans

1 tsp. garlic, minced

1 tsp. sesame seeds

3 TB. chicken stock

3 TB. oyster sauce

$\frac{1}{2}$ tsp. freshly ground black pepper

Heat a wok over medium heat and add oil. When oil is hot, add long beans and garlic. Stir-fry for three minutes and add sesame seeds, chicken stock, oyster sauce, and black pepper. Stir-fry for two minutes longer and remove from heat. Serve hot.

Grilled Calamari

Prep time: 35 minutes • Marination time: 20 minutes • Cook time: 15 minutes • Serves 2

$\frac{3}{4}$ lb. squid

4 bamboo skewers, soaked in water for at least 30 minutes

$\frac{1}{2}$ cup soy sauce

1 tsp. granulated sugar

1 tsp. sesame seeds

1 TB. chopped fresh cilantro leaves

1 tsp. freshly ground black pepper

$\frac{1}{2}$ cup sweet chili sauce

$\frac{3}{4}$ cup shredded iceberg lettuce

$\frac{1}{4}$ cup shredded carrots

Cut body of squid into rings about $\frac{3}{4}$ inch wide. Thread each piece of squid onto skewer, ending with tentacles. You should have about four or five rings and tentacles on each skewer. Place squid into a nonreactive container.

Whisk together soy sauce, sugar, sesame seeds, cilantro, and black pepper in a small bowl. Pour over calamari. Marinate for 15 to 20 minutes, covered, in the refrigerator.

When ready to cook, remove calamari from marinade and discard marinade. Heat the grill to medium hot and cook calamari for three minutes on each side. Lay grilled calamari on a serving plate and pour chili sauce over it. Garnish with a little chopped lettuce and shredded carrots. Serve immediately.

Fresh Shrimp Rolls

Prep time: 25 minutes • Cook time: 10 minutes • Serves 2, makes 4 rolls

$1/2$ cup dry vermicelli noodles, soaked in cold water for 10 minutes

4 shrimp (16 to 20 count), peeled and deveined

1 cup shredded iceberg lettuce

$1/4$ cup bean sprouts

$1/4$ cup julienned carrot

1 TB. chopped Asian basil

4 spring roll wrappers

$1/4$ cup peanut sauce

1 TB. unsalted peanuts, crushed

Take soaked vermicelli noodles and blanch in boiling water for 15 seconds, remove, and drain. Cover and reserve in the refrigerator.

Place shrimp into boiling water for five minutes, remove, and pat dry. Cut shrimp in half lengthwise. Cover and reserve in the refrigerator.

Mix lettuce, bean sprouts, carrots, and basil together in a small bowl. Set up a sauté pan or 4-quart pot with simmering water.

Take noodles and shrimp out of the refrigerator. Create an assembly line by setting up your workspace next to the stove. Place shrimp, lettuce mixture, and noodles in a line just above your workspace. Using one wrapper at a time, submerge each disk in simmering water for 45 seconds. After pulling it from water, hang it on a corner of the counter by its edge to dry for about 20 seconds. This will make it easy to roll.

Remove a softened rice paper from the counter's edge and place it on your workspace. Place two shrimp halves end to end, centering them along the width on lower third of sheet. Place some lettuce mix on top of shrimp. Place a little vermicelli on top of lettuce mix. Pull bottom edge of rice paper up over filling using the thumb and forefinger of each hand while holding stuffing with the middle fingers. Keep rice paper tight as you roll, but not too tight, or it will tear. Once you have covered filling, fold sides of rice paper in, and continue to roll until you have made a cylinder.

Pour peanut sauce into a small dipping bowl and top with peanuts. Arrange rolls on a cold platter with peanut sauce. Serve at once or hold in the refrigerator for no longer than one hour covered with slightly damp paper towels. Serve whole or cut in half at an angle and serve the pieces placed vertically on the plate.

>─⊖─<

Khao Soi; Seafood Noodle Salad

Roasted Spare Ribs with Lemongrass and Chili; Wasabi Mashed Potatoes

Lobster Mango Roll;
Blue Champagne

Pepper in a Pepper; Garlic Chinese Broccoli

Grilled Lamb Kebabs; Thai Mango Beet Salad

Whole Fried Fish; Chinese Long Beans

Grilled Stuffed Lobster with Lemongrass Butter Sauce

Chicken and Pork Noodles

Grilled Lemongrass Beef

Steamed Snapper in Banana Leaf; Sprout and Scallion Stir-Fry

Grilled Swordfish and Asparagus; Mango Sticky Rice

Asian Beef Roulades with Teriyaki Garlic Sauce; Spicy Eggplant

Tofu Steaks with Ground Beef; Somen Noodles

Stuffed Prawns

Fuji Apple and Endive Salad with Ginger-Mint Dressing; Pork Panang

Coconut Cheesecake

Garlic Chinese Broccoli

Prep time: 15 minutes • Cook time: 8 minutes • Serves 2

2 TB. canola oil

2 tsp. minced fresh garlic

2 cups Chinese broccoli

$^{1}/_{4}$ cup chicken stock

$^{1}/_{4}$ cup oyster sauce

Heat a wok over high heat and add oil. When oil is smoking, add garlic and stir-fry for 30 seconds. Add broccoli and continue to stir-fry for two minutes. Then add chicken stock and oyster sauce. Bring to a boil and cook one minute longer. Remove from heat. Serve on a warm platter.

> **Fortune Cookies**
>
> Chinese broccoli comes in bunches that look like long, thin, stretched-out broccoli. Look for narrower leaves and firm bunches that should also have broccoli blossoms or buds. Trim off the large, thick stems from the broccoli. Leave the thinner stems intact, for they are tender and add a lot of flavor. If you can't find Chinese broccoli, a good substitute can be rapini or broccoli rabe.

Ginger Mushrooms

Prep time: 15 minutes • Cook time: 10 minutes • Serves 2

1 TB. oil for cooking

1 TB. pickled ginger, shredded

1 tsp. garlic, minced

$^{1}/_{2}$ cup shiitake mushrooms, quartered

$^{1}/_{2}$ cup button mushrooms, quartered

$^{1}/_{2}$ cup straw mushrooms

$^{1}/_{4}$ cup chicken stock

1 tsp. sugar

$^{1}/_{4}$ cup oyster sauce

Heat a wok over high heat and add oil, ginger, garlic, and shiitake, button, and straw mushrooms. Stir-fry for three minutes. Add chicken stock and sugar, and bring to a boil. Continue to cook for two minutes. Add oyster sauce. Bring to a boil again, then remove from heat. Serve hot.

Red Curry Mashed Potatoes

Prep time: 15 minutes • Cook time: 25 minutes • Serves 2

3 medium Idaho potatoes, peeled and quartered

2 tsp. salt (divided use)

1 TB. unsalted butter

2 tsp. red curry paste

2 TB. heavy cream

Recipes for Success

There's just no substitute for fluffy Idahoes when making mashed potatoes. New or waxy potatoes get too gummy for them to be mashers.

Place potatoes into a 3-quart pot filled with cold water and 1 teaspoon salt. Set the pot over high heat and bring to a boil. Boil potatoes until they are tender in the middle, about 15 to 20 minutes. Do not overcook potatoes or they will become mealy.

Drain potatoes and return to the pot. Turn heat on low and start to mash potatoes with a wire masher. The heat will dry potatoes some, giving them a finer texture. Add remaining salt, butter, curry paste, and cream. Mash until curry is fully infused throughout potatoes.

Wasabi Mashed Potatoes

Prep time: 15 minutes • Cook time: 25 minutes • Serves 2

3 medium Idaho potatoes

2 tsp. salt (divided use)

1 TB. wasabi paste

1 TB. unsalted butter

2 TB. heavy cream

Peel and quarter potatoes and place in a pot filled with cold water 1 teaspoon salt. Turn heat to high and lightly boil potatoes until they are tender in the center, about 15 to 20 minutes. Just poke them with a fork; if the fork goes in easily, potatoes are ready. Do not overcook potatoes or they will become mealy.

Drain potatoes and put them back in the pot. Turn heat on low and quickly begin to mash potatoes with a masher. The heat will dry out the potatoes to give them a finer texture. Add remaining salt, wasabi, butter, and cream and mash into potatoes. At this point, taste potatoes; flavor should be buttery with a slight piquancy. You might need to add more salt or wasabi if potatoes absorb too much liquid. Serve hot.

Sesame Ginger Crab Claws

Prep time: 20 minutes • Cook time: 15 minutes • Serves 2

$^1/_4$ cup chicken stock

2 TB. rice vinegar

1 tsp. sweet soy sauce

1 tsp. honey

1 tsp. minced fresh garlic

1 tsp. sesame seeds

1 TB. minced fresh ginger

$^1/_2$ tsp. red chili powder

1 TB. chopped fresh cilantro leaves

1 lb. pre-steamed blue crab claws

2 TB. chopped green onions

$^1/_2$ tsp. salt

1 TB. unsalted butter

Preheat the broiler.

Whisk together chicken stock, rice vinegar, sweet soy sauce, honey, garlic, sesame seeds, ginger, chili powder, and cilantro in a medium bowl.

Place crab claws in a large sauté pan. Pour sauce over crab, and top with green onions, salt, and butter. Place the pan under broiler and cook for five minutes.

Crab claws already come steamed at the market; placing in the broiler simply heats them up and gives them a nice color. Avoid using frozen or pasteurized crab.

Recipes for Success

Fresh blue crab claws are typically available from May through October; obviously, this is the best time to prepare this dish. Try to avoid using pasteurized crab. The freshness gives a clean, sweet flavor to the dish.

Fortune Cookies

The most important ingredient in your seafood recipe isn't on your shopping list. It's your fishmonger. Talk to him, become his best friend. Bring him a plate of cookies or better yet bring him a plate of Grilled Calamari. Find out when shipments come in. If fish comes in on Tuesday, don't buy it on Monday, for example. Now that we have the when-to-buy thing down, the next item to consider is finding the fishmonger himself. If you are landlocked, some of the best places to find a good fishmonger are at a natural foods market, large specialty grocery store, or a free-standing seafood shop where extra care is paid to seafood.

Spicy Eggplant

Prep time: 15 minutes • Cook time: 10 minutes • Serves 2

2 cups Chinese eggplant

2 TB. sesame oil

1 tsp. garlic, minced

1 tsp. red chili powder

1 tsp. granulated sugar

$^1\!/_4$ cup chicken stock

3 TB. oyster sauce

1 tsp. white vinegar

Trim ends from eggplant and cut into 1- × 3-inch chunks. Heat a wok over medium-high heat and add oil. When oil begins to smoke, add garlic and eggplant. Stir-fry for three minutes. Add chili powder, sugar, chicken stock, oyster sauce, and white vinegar. Continue to stir-fry for three more minutes, remove from heat, and spoon onto a warm serving platter. Serve hot.

Spicy Mixed Vegetables

Prep time: 20 minutes • Cook time: 10 minutes • Serves 2

2 TB. canola oil

2 tsp. garlic, minced

1 TB. black bean sauce

$^1\!/_4$ cup carrot, roughly chopped

$^1\!/_4$ cup zucchini, roughly chopped

$^1\!/_4$ cup broccoli florets

$^1\!/_4$ cup baby corn

$^1\!/_4$ cup red bell peppers, roughly chopped

2 jalapeño chilies, quartered

$^1\!/_4$ cup chicken stock

$^1\!/_4$ cup oyster sauce

1 tsp. granulated sugar

Heat a wok over high heat and add oil. When oil is smoking, add garlic and black bean sauce and stir-fry for one minute. Add carrots, zucchini, broccoli, corn, bell peppers, and chilies to the wok and continue to stir-fry for two minutes. Stir in chicken stock, oyster sauce, and sugar and bring to a boil. Immediately remove from heat. At this point, vegetables should be cooked tender-crisp. Spoon onto a warm serving platter and serve hot.

Sprout and Scallion Stir-Fry

Prep time: 5 minutes • Cook time: 8 minutes • Serves 2

1 TB. canola oil

1 cup bean sprouts

1 cup (3- to 4-inch) green onion pieces, loosely packed

$^{1}/_{4}$ cup oyster sauce

$^{1}/_{2}$ tsp. freshly ground black pepper

3 TB. chicken stock

Heat a wok over high heat and add oil. When oil begins to smoke, add bean sprouts and green onions. Stir-fry for two minutes and add oyster sauce, black pepper and chicken stock. Stir-fry for two minutes longer and remove from heat. Serve immediately.

Ginger Mushroom Stir-Fry

Prep time: 15 minutes • Cook time: 10 minutes • Serves 2

1 TB. canola oil

$^{1}/_{2}$ cup shiitake mushrooms, quartered

$^{1}/_{2}$ cup button mushrooms, quartered

$^{1}/_{2}$ cup straw mushrooms

1 TB. pickled ginger, shredded

1 tsp. garlic, minced

$^{1}/_{4}$ cup chicken stock

1 tsp. granulated sugar

$^{1}/_{4}$ cup oyster sauce

Heat a wok over high heat and add oil. When oil begins to smoke, add shiitake, button, and straw mushrooms; ginger; and garlic. Stir-fry for three minutes and add chicken stock. Bring to a boil, cook for two minutes, and add sugar and oyster sauce. Bring to a boil again and remove from heat. Spoon onto a warm platter and serve hot.

Tuna Spring Rolls

Prep time: 30 minutes • Cook time: 10 minutes • Serves 2

9 oz. ahi tuna

2 spring roll wrappers or rice skins

$^1/_2$ cup glass noodles, soaked in water for 20 minutes

$^1/_4$ cup fresh spinach

$^1/_4$ cup julienned carrot

1 TB. pickled ginger, optional

1 to 2 quarts canola oil

1 tsp. wasabi paste

$^1/_4$ cup soy sauce

Cut tuna into 1-inch strips.

Place spring roll wrappers in boiling water until soft. Hang on a work surface to dry. Take noodles from water and pat dry with a tea towel.

Place one spring roll wrapper in front of you on the counter. Place half the tuna on lower third of wrapper (but away from the edge). Place half the spinach, carrot, ginger, and noodles over tuna. Pull bottom edge of rice paper up over spinach and noodles using your thumb and forefinger of each hand while holding stuffing with the middle fingers. Keep rice paper tight as you roll, but not too tight, or it will tear. After you have covered filling, fold the sides of the rice paper in, and continue to roll until you have made a cylinder. Because the rice paper is damp, the seal should take care of itself.

Pour enough canola oil into the wok to reach with two inches in depth. Heat to 375°F. Place tuna rolls into oil and fry for three minutes or until golden brown. Gently press down on rolls with a spatula as they fry to keep them submerged; they tend to float to the top. Remove rolls from oil and drain on paper towels.

While rolls are cooking, mix wasabi with soy sauce and pour into a small bowl. Cut rolls in half and serve on small plates with sauce. Serve hot.

Chapter 12

Soups and Salads

In This Chapter

- ◆ Scintillating soups
- ◆ Sumptuous salads
- ◆ Some great soup and salad recipes

If the thought of soup and salad for dinner sounds about as exciting as a nice piece of dry toast, we want to take you for a delightful voyage through this chapter. Sky and sea, root and fruit brought together in graceful union elevate soup and salad to heavenly status in the following selection of new Asian soups and salads.

Soup's On!

Soups play more than a supporting role in Asian cuisine. Big, rich bowls of meat, vegetables, noodles, and spices are standard fare—in fact, often the main course—for breakfast, lunch, and dinner, while small, elegant sips of other soups are used as a beverage.

Asian soups can be divided into two basic groups—thin, brothy soups and thick, hearty soups. For thin soups like Japanese miso soups, the meats and vegetables are blanched or partly cooked and added to the broth at the last minute, then simmered for a very short time before serving. In contrast, for thick soups, like Chinese hot and sour soup, all the ingredients are cooked together for a longer period of time. Thick soups are often finished with a thickener such as cornstarch or tapioca.

Lucky Treasures
A cup of miso soup starts the day for many Japanese, from farmers and fisherman to policeman and politicians.

Thick soups are usually served as a main course, whereas thin ones are served between courses. Thin soups are often used as a palate cleanser between courses or as a stand-in for beverages throughout the meal.

Gorgeous Greens

Asian salads, whether new or traditional, are often the star of the show. Noodles, vegetables, fruits, seafood, and meat are artfully arranged, never tossed, with a piquant dressing. Toasted sesame oil, peanuts, lime, cilantro, ginger, miso, and soy sauce are frequently seen in the dressings.

Recipes for Success
Mama said "Don't play with your food!" We say when it comes to arranging a new Asian salad, it's all about playing. Let your creative juices flow as you play with the ingredients of your salad to create eye-candy on the plate.

Served as a main course, as a contrast to other dishes, or as a palate cleanser between courses, these salads will intrigue and please your taste buds. Once you're hooked on these new Asian salads, you may never eat another clump of iceberg with ranch dressing again.

Enjoy these soup and salad recipes as meals on their own or as partners to a main dish.

The Least You Need to Know

- There are two styles of Asian soup: thick, such as Chinese hot and sour, and thin, such as Japanese miso.
- Thick soups are often served as the main course of a meal, while thin soups are served as palate cleansers between courses or as substitutes for beverages.
- Asian salads often consist of a variety of ingredients, including noodles, vegetables, fruits, and seafood, and are dressed with toasted sesame oil, peanuts, lime, cilantro, ginger, miso, and soy sauce.
- Asian salads are not tossed—they are arranged.

Asian Pear Salad

Prep time: 20 minutes • Cook time: 5 minutes • Serves 2

1 tsp. Chinese five-spice powder

2 TB. chopped pecans

$\frac{1}{2}$ tsp. salt (divided use)

2 TB. firm goat cheese, chilled

$\frac{1}{2}$ cup cherry tomatoes

1 TB. minced fresh ginger

1 tsp. honey

1 tsp. minced fresh garlic

1 tsp. sweet soy sauce

$\frac{1}{4}$ cup rice vinegar

$\frac{1}{2}$ tsp. chili paste made with soybean oil

$\frac{1}{2}$ tsp. red chili powder

$\frac{1}{4}$ cup sesame oil

3 cups baby mixed greens

1 Asian pear

1 TB. sesame seeds

Preheat the oven to 350°F.

Mix Chinese five-spice powder with pecans and $\frac{1}{4}$ teaspoon salt. Mash pecan mixture into cheese and divide resulting mixture into two portions. Roll these into two balls. Chill.

Cut cherry tomatoes in half and set aside.

Whisk together ginger, honey, garlic, sweet soy sauce, rice vinegar, chili paste, and chili powder in a small bowl. Whisk in sesame oil and remaining salt. Chill for five minutes.

Toss greens and cherry tomatoes with dressing. Place goat cheese on a cookie sheet and bake for five minutes. While cheese is baking, peel and core pear and cut into thin julienne strips. Toss with dressed salad.

Divide salad between two chilled plates. Top each salad with warm goat cheese and sprinkle top with sesame seeds.

Coconut Cabbage Soup

Prep time: 15 minutes • Cook time: 15 minutes • Serves 2

6 cups chicken stock

1 cup chopped sweet potato, peeled and cut into 1-inch pieces

2 cups chopped napa cabbage, cut into 1-inch pieces

1 TB. ginger, sliced

3 kaffir lime leaves

1 TB. lemongrass, trimmed to the soft core and sliced into 1-inch pieces

2 tsp. chili paste made with soybean oil

$\frac{1}{2}$ tsp. red chili powder

3 TB. fresh lime juice

3 TB. fish sauce

2 cups canned coconut milk

2 TB. soy sauce

$\frac{1}{2}$ cup thinly sliced red onion

1 cup chantaboun rice sticks, soaked in water for 15 minutes

2 TB. chopped fresh cilantro leaves

Prepare a 1-quart saucepan of boiling water. Heat a wok over high heat. Add chicken stock, sweet potatoes, cabbage, ginger, lime leaves, lemongrass, chili paste, chili powder, lime juice, and fish sauce. Bring to a boil and lower the heat, simmering for five minutes. Add coconut milk, soy sauce, and red onion. Simmer for five minutes longer and turn off the heat.

Place presoaked rice sticks into boiling water and cook for two minutes. Remove from water, drain well, and place in the bottom of two warmed soup bowls. Ladle soup over noodles and garnish with the cilantro. Serve hot.

Fuji Apple and Endive Salad with Ginger-Mint Dressing

Prep time: 20 minutes • Serves 2

$^1/_4$ cup fresh orange juice

1 tsp. minced fresh ginger

$^1/_2$ tsp. Chinese mustard

1 tsp. granulated sugar

$^1/_2$ tsp. orange zest

1 Fuji apple

1 head Belgium endive

1 TB. fresh lime juice

$^1/_2$ cup julienne of carrot

$^1/_4$ cup raisins

Whisk together orange juice, ginger, Chinese mustard, sugar, and orange zest in a medium-size mixing bowl. Peel, core, and cut apple into a julienne. Remove any ragged outer leaves from endive and also cut into a julienne. Drizzle lime juice over apple and endive to prevent them from browning. Add apple, endive, carrots, and raisins to the bowl of dressing. Toss everything together. Spoon onto chilled plates and serve.

Seaweed Salad

Prep time: 20 minutes • Marination time: 15 minutes • Serves 2

$^1/_4$ cup rice vinegar

$^1/_4$ cup sesame oil

2 TB. toasted sesame seeds

2 TB. soy sauce

1 tsp. granulated sugar

$^1/_2$ tsp. freshly ground black pepper

2 cups kelp, shredded

$^1/_2$ cucumber, peeled, seeded, and sliced into rounds

Whisk vinegar, sesame oil, sesame seeds, soy sauce, sugar, and black pepper in a medium-size bowl. Toss in kelp and cucumbers. Marinate for 15 minutes in the refrigerator. Serve on chilled plates.

Fortune Cookies

Kelp, a type of seaweed, can be purchased at a health food store or at the local Asian market. It can also be found frozen. It's loaded with vitamins and iron, giving an energy rush—without the sugar.

Grilled Asparagus and Mushroom Salad

Prep time: 35 minutes • Marination time: 20 minutes • Cook time: 15 minutes • Serves 2

$^1/_2$ cup hoisin sauce

$^1/_4$ cup sesame oil

1 tsp. minced fresh garlic

$^1/_2$ cup black vinegar or balsamic vinegar

$^1/_2$ tsp. red chili powder

1 TB. honey

2 large portobello mushrooms caps

1 bunch (1 lb.) asparagus, trimmed

1 medium red onion, cut into $^1/_4$-inch slices

2 cups chopped romaine lettuce

4 roma tomatoes, quartered

Salt as needed

Whisk together hoisin sauce, sesame oil, garlic, vinegar, chili powder, and honey in a medium-size mixing bowl. Add mushrooms, asparagus, and red onion; cover and marinate for 20 minutes.

Heat the grill to medium heat. Remove vegetables from the marinade and place on the grill. Cook for three minutes and remove.

Place the romaine on two chilled plates and arrange tomatoes around lettuce. Place a grilled mushroom on top of each salad and lay asparagus over mushroom cap. Season with salt and pour marinade over lettuce. Serve at once.

Lucky Treasures

The warm vegetables against the cold lettuce is utterly refreshing, and the portobello mushroom lends a richness that makes this salad a meal in itself.

Japanese Beef Soup

Prep time: 30 minutes • Marination time: 10 minutes • Cook time: 20 minutes • Serves 2

8 oz. beef flank steak, trimmed of fat and cut into 2-inch pieces

1 tsp. granulated sugar

1 tsp. sesame seeds

1 TB. sesame oil

1 TB. oyster sauce

4 cups chicken stock

2 cups water

2 TB. fish sauce

$^1/_2$ cup julienne of shiitake mushroom caps

$^1/_2$ cup julienne of carrot

$^1/_2$ cup snow peas

2 TB. soybean sauce

$^1/_2$ tsp. freshly ground black pepper

2 tsp. beef-stock paste

1 cup fresh udon noodles

2 tsp. garlic, fried

2 TB. green onion, thinly sliced

2 TB. fresh cilantro leaves, chopped

Place flank steak pieces into a medium-size bowl. Add sugar, sesame seeds, sesame oil, and oyster sauce. Mix well and marinate in the refrigerator for 10 minutes.

Heat a grill to medium-high heat and grill beef until it is cooked medium, about two minutes on each side. Heat a wok over high heat. Add chicken stock, water, fish sauce, shiitake mushrooms, carrots, snow peas, soybean sauce, black pepper, and beef-stock paste. Bring to a boil.

Place noodles in a saucepan of boiling water and cook for six minutes. Drain noodles and divide between two bowls. Place cooked beef on top of noodles and ladle soup over noodles. Garnish with fried garlic, green onion, and cilantro.

Recipes for Success

To fry garlic, heat a small pan with $^1/_2$ tsp. canola oil over medium high heat and add the garlic. Stir-fry for about three minutes or until golden brown. Immediately remove from the heat and spoon into another container to cool.

Lobster Egg Drop Soup

Prep time: 20 minutes • Cook time: 15 minutes • Serves 2

1 quart canola oil	1 TB. tapioca starch
1/2 lb. lobster meat	2 TB. cold water
4 cups chicken stock	2 large eggs
2 cups water	1 cup fresh egg noodles
2 TB. fish sauce	2 TB. chopped fresh cilantro leaves
2 TB. soy sauce	1/4 cup sliced green onion
1 tsp. freshly ground black pepper	

Pour oil into fryer and heat to 375°F.

Cut lobster in large chunks, remove any shell that might still be left on, and set aside.

Heat a wok over high heat and add chicken stock, water, lobster, fish sauce, soy sauce, and black pepper. Bring to a boil. Reduce heat to low and simmer for six minutes. Whisk tapioca starch in cold water and slowly stir into soup. Bring soup to a boil and remove from heat. Whisk eggs together in a small bowl. Slowly pour eggs into the hot soup and stir.

Recipes for Success

Ahh, the drama of lobster … Don't sweat the expensive lobster in the shell. Because this is soup, frozen lobster will do; just don't go buying anything in a tin can.

Separate egg noodles into two batches. Fry each batch until golden brown, about 20 seconds, and drain on paper towels. Divide soup into two large, warm soup bowls. Insert a warm egg noodle nest into soup at the edge of each bowl. Sprinkle with cilantro and green onion. Serve hot.

Seafood Noodle Salad

Prep time: 25 minutes • Cook time: 15 minutes • Serves 2

1 cup sake

6 oz. black mussels

6 oz. squid, cut into 1-inch rings

1 tsp. chili paste made with soybean oil

1/2 tsp. red chili powder

2 tsp. sesame oil

1/4 cup fresh lime juice

1/4 cup fish sauce

1/4 cup julienne of carrot

1/4 cup red bell pepper, chopped

1/4 cup bean sprouts

1 bunch watercress

2 cups glass noodles, soaked in warm water for 15 minutes

2 TB. chopped fresh cilantro leaves

1 TB. fried garlic

Heat a wok over high heat. When the wok is hot, add sake and mussels. Cover and cook on high until mussels start to open, about three minutes. Just as mussels are opening, add squid. Continue to steam for two minutes and remove from heat. Spoon mussels and squid to a large heatproof bowl and keep warm. Discard any mussels that do not open. Reserve cooking liquid in the pot.

Add water to cooking liquid and bring to a boil. Whisk chili paste, chili powder, sesame oil, lime juice, and fish sauce together in a large bowl. Add carrot, red bell pepper, bean sprouts, and watercress, tossing to combine.

Bring a 1-quart saucepan of water to a boil. Remove noodles from presoak and place into boiling water for five seconds. Barely let noodles sit in boiling water. This is the key to cooking glass noodles; if left in water too long, noodles will become gummy. Drain noodles. Place in the bowl with sauce and vegetables, tossing well.

Divide noodles and vegetables between two large, warm soup bowls. Place mussels and squid around the rim of the bowl and sprinkle with cilantro and fried garlic, and serve.

Shredded Chicken Soba Salad

Prep time: 20 minutes • Cook time: 15 minutes • Serves 2

$^1/_2$ cup sake

1 cup water

1 lb. skinless, boneless chicken breasts

1 cup soba noodles, broken in half

$^1/_4$ cup sesame oil

2 TB. rice vinegar

1 TB. soy sauce

1 TB. sweet soy sauce

$^1/_4$ cup green onion, quartered

1 tsp. garlic, minced

1 tsp. ginger, minced

$^1/_4$ cup fresh cilantro leaves, chopped

$^1/_4$ cup julienne of shiitake mushroom caps

$^1/_4$ cup julienne of red bell pepper

$^1/_4$ cup shredded green cabbage

1 TB. fish sauce

1 TB. lime juice

$^1/_2$ tsp. red chili powder

1 TB. sesame seeds

Heat a sauté pan over medium-high heat, add sake and water, and bring to a simmer. Place chicken into the pan and poach for 10 minutes, flipping over halfway through. Remove from the pan, cool to room temperature, and shred breasts by tearing them with your hands or pulling with a fork. If the chicken is too cold, it's more difficult to shred.

Bring a 2-quart saucepan of water to a boil. Cook soba noodles for seven minutes, drain, and rinse with cold water until noodles are cool. Chill noodles in the refrigerator while putting salad together.

Toss together shredded chicken, sesame oil, vinegar, soy sauce, sweet soy sauce, green onion, garlic, ginger, and cilantro until thoroughly combined.

Place noodles in another bowl and add mushroom, red pepper, cabbage, fish sauce, lime juice, chili powder, and sesame seeds. Toss noodle mixture together with chicken and dressing. Divide between two chilled bowls and serve.

Spicy Chicken Bleu Cheese Salad

Prep time: 25 minutes • Cook time: 15 minutes • Serves 2

2 TB. soy sauce

2 egg whites

$\frac{1}{2}$ lb. skinless, boneless chicken breasts

$\frac{1}{4}$ cup tapioca starch

Canola oil, as needed

$\frac{1}{4}$ cup orange juice

1 tsp. sweet soy sauce

1 tsp. minced fresh garlic

1 tsp. minced fresh ginger

2 tsp. brown sugar

3 TB. sambal

1 cup curly endive (frisée)

$\frac{1}{2}$ head red leaf lettuce, washed and torn into bite-size pieces

$\frac{1}{4}$ cup red cabbage, shredded

$\frac{1}{4}$ cup julienne of green onion

$\frac{1}{4}$ cup julienne of red bell pepper

$\frac{1}{4}$ cup crumbled bleu cheese

1 TB. toasted sesame seeds

Mix soy sauce with egg whites. Pound chicken breast into a $\frac{1}{4}$-inch thin cutlet with a mallet. If you don't have a meat mallet, use the side of a soup can. Dip breasts into egg whites, and dredge in tapioca starch. Tap off any excess starch and set aside.

Pour enough canola oil into a frying pan to come up a depth of about $\frac{1}{4}$ inch or so. Heat the pan over high heat. When oil is hot, cook chicken on each side for three minutes. Cook chicken in a single layer, working in batches, if necessary.

Remove chicken from the pan and drain on paper towels. Whisk together orange juice, sweet soy sauce, garlic, ginger, brown sugar, and sambal. Cut chicken into long strips and combine with frisée, red lettuce, cabbage, green onion, and red bell pepper in a large bowl. Add dressing and toss well. Place on a large chilled serving platter or plates. Sprinkle bleu cheese and sesame seeds over salad and serve cold.

Spicy Duck Soup

Prep time: 15 minutes • Cook time: 25 minutes • Serves 2

10 oz. duck breast

3 tsp. red curry paste

3 cups chicken stock

1 cup water

2 cups canned coconut milk

2 TB. fish sauce or nuoc mam

½ cup pineapple chunks

½ cup cherry tomatoes

1 TB. granulated sugar

1 tsp. paprika

1 cup Chantaboun rice sticks, soaked in water for 15 minutes

2 TB. cilantro leaves, chopped

Heat a wok over medium heat. When hot, place duck breast into the wok, skin side down. Sear breast on both sides for three minutes and remove. Cool duck slightly (so it's easy to handle), and chop into bite-size pieces, leaving skin on.

Place cut duck back into the wok. Add curry paste and stir-fry until curry is worked well into duck. Add chicken stock and water; bring to a boil. Stir in coconut milk, fish sauce, pineapple, cherry tomatoes, sugar, and paprika. Return to a boil.

Bring a 2-quart saucepan of water to a boil. Cook rice sticks in boiling water for two minutes, drain, and place in two large, warm soup bowls. Ladle soup over noodles and sprinkle with cilantro. Serve hot.

Recipes for Success

One of the perfect balances in life is that of the duck breast. The yin of the skin, although fatty, is balanced by the yang of the leanness of the breast meat. So resist the urge to pull the skin off the duck. If you were to pull the skin off, the meat would become leathery and the dish would be missing an important flavor component.

Thai Mango Beet Salad

Prep time: 20 minutes • Serves 2

1 tsp. minced fresh garlic

1 TB. chopped cilantro leaves

1 TB. lemongrass

1 TB. fish sauce or nuoc mam

Juice of 2 limes

1 tsp. granulated sugar

1 tsp. yellow miso paste

$^{1}/_{4}$ cup rice vinegar

1 tsp. sesame oil

1 jalapeño, quartered

2 mangoes, firm and ripe

1 large beet

$^{1}/_{2}$ head green leaf lettuce, washed and torn into bite-size pieces

$^{1}/_{2}$ cup bean sprouts

$^{1}/_{2}$ cup julienne of carrot

2 tsp. pickled ginger

3 tsp. chopped fresh mint leaves

To make dressing, place garlic, cilantro, lemongrass, fish sauce, lime juice, sugar, miso paste, vinegar, sesame oil, and jalapeño in a food processor fitted with a metal blade; process on high until smooth. Pour dressing into a small bowl and chill.

Peel mango and make two cuts on either side of pit to remove flesh. Cut mango into two- or three-inch julienne. Peel raw beet, using gloves to keep red from getting on your hands. Cut the same as mango. Put lettuce, bean sprouts, carrot, pickled ginger, mint, mango, and beets into a large salad bowl. Pour dressing over salad and toss together. Serve cold on chilled plates.

Tomato Lemongrass Soup

Prep time: 15 minutes • Cook time: 25 minutes • Serves 2

$^1/_2$ cup sake

$^1/_4$ cup julienne of carrot

1 TB. thinly sliced fresh ginger

$^1/_2$ medium white onion, sliced

8 sprigs fresh cilantro

1 tsp. minced fresh garlic

2 tsp. red curry paste

2 stalks lemongrass, trimmed to the soft core and sliced into 1-inch pieces

3 kaffir lime leaves

4 cups chicken stock

2 cups water

3 TB. lime juice

2 cups canned plum tomatoes

1 tsp. chili paste made with soybean oil

2 cups fresh udon noodles

Salt to taste

$^1/_2$ avocado, cut into strips

4 green onions, trimmed and cut into thirds

$^1/_3$ cup frozen sweet corn, thawed to room temperature

Heat a wok over high heat. When the wok is hot, add sake, carrot, ginger, onion, cilantro, garlic, red curry paste, lemongrass, and lime leaves. Bring to a boil. Add chicken stock, water, lime juice, plum tomatoes, and chili paste. Bring soup to a boil again, reduce heat to low, and simmer for 15 minutes.

While soup is simmering, put udon noodles into a 2-quart saucepan of boiling water and cook for six minutes. Drain noodles and return to the pot, covered with a dishcloth to keep warm.

Purée soup in a blender in small batches, about two minutes per batch. Pass through a fine strainer into another saucepan over low heat. Season to taste with salt. Place noodles into warmed soup bowls and ladle in soup. Garnish soup with avocado, green onion, and corn. Serve hot.

Recipes for Success

People rarely think of physics when they cook. We guarantee it will come to mind if you purée the soup with the top snugly on the blender. Demonstrating the "every action has an equal and opposite reaction" theorem, the heat will build up in the canister and literally blow the top right off. When blending your batches, hold a thick towel snugly over the top instead of capping it and you won't have to clean the ceiling afterward.

Chapter 13

Land: Beef and Pork

In This Chapter

- ◆ Beefy dishes from the East
- ◆ Pork, more than the other white meat
- ◆ Western cuts meet Asian spices in new Asian meat dishes

New Asian meat dishes often differ from traditional Asian dishes in the amount of meat used. In traditional cooking, a big hunk of steak is rarely the focus of the meal. Rather, meat is used almost as a condiment, a flavor enhancer. These new Asian recipes call for more meat per serving than most traditional recipes. You won't be asking: "Where's the beef?"

Here's the Beef!

Convincing Texans there's any other way to eat beef than in big hunks of steak or between a bun is no easy task. On the other hand, introducing Chef Annie to Texas-style beef eating and Western cuts of beef has opened up new avenues for her. East truly met West when Annie showed up at the rodeo!

Fortune Cookies

In the mood to break the bank? Try a little real Kobe beef at about $150 a pound. True Kobe beef must be raised in Kobe, Japan where the Wagyu cattle are pampered like stud racehorses, fed on a diet of beer and grain to produce a sublimely marbled meat. Or you might be able to track down some domestically raised Wagyu beef at a more realistic price.

Our new Asian beef dishes incorporate western cuts like hanger steaks, Western foods like goat cheese, and such classic French preparations as roulades with Asian marinades and spices to create new Asian dishes that leave no doubt as to where the beef is.

Pork

Pork is popular throughout Asia, religious restrictions permitting, mostly because pigs are easy and cheap to raise. But our favorite cuts, chops and tenderloins, are not used as much. With all of Annie's training and years of experience, American-style pork chops were still somewhat of a mystery to her. So we went to Dallas's legendary fourth-generation Tex-Mex chef Matt Martinez, renowned for his mastery of beef, pork, and game, for Annie to learn everything she could about the art of the chop. And we are so glad we did! Annie's new Asian pork chops know no rival.

Lucky Treasures

Confucius said "The way you cut your meat reflects the way you live." Make sure your knife is sharp, clean, and well tended.

The Least You Need to Know

- ◆ In traditional Asian cooking, meat is used almost as a condiment, a flavor enhancer.
- ◆ New Asian meat dishes often have more meat in them than traditional dishes.
- ◆ Pork is popular throughout Asia, religious restrictions permitting.

Asian Basil Beef

Prep time: 15 minutes • Cook time: 18 minutes • Serves 2

2 TB. canola oil

2 (12-oz.) New York strip steaks

$^1/_4$ cup sake

1 TB. soy sauce

1 TB. thinly sliced garlic

2 TB. sliced shallot

1 tsp. thinly sliced spur chili pepper (if unavailable, substitute green Thai chili pepper)

1 cup sliced portobello mushroom

1 cup sliced red bell pepper

$^1/_2$ cup chicken stock

$^1/_2$ cup oyster sauce

1 TB. fish sauce

1 TB. granulated sugar

2 TB. chopped Asian basil

Heat a wok over high heat and add oil. When oil is smoking, sear steak for two minutes on each side. Add sake and soy sauce. Reduce heat to low. Simmer for four minutes. Remove steaks and any remaining sauce from the wok and reserve.

Add garlic, shallot, spur chili, mushroom, and red bell pepper to the wok and stir-fry for three minutes. Add chicken stock, oyster sauce, fish sauce, and sugar. Bring to a boil. Stir in basil and immediately remove from heat.

Place each steak on a warm serving plate. Ladle sauce and vegetables on top of steaks, and serve hot.

Asian Beef Roulades with Teriyaki Garlic Sauce

Prep time: 35 minutes • Cook time: 20 minutes • Serves 2

1 cup soy sauce

$^1/_2$ cup mirin

$^1/_4$ cup chicken stock

$^1/_4$ cup orange juice

2 TB. fish sauce or nuoc mam

1 tsp. minced fresh garlic

1 TB. minced fresh ginger

1 TB. brown sugar

1 lb. beef skirt steak

2 TB. canola oil

$^1/_4$ tsp. salt

1 tsp. freshly ground black pepper

6 medium green onions, cut in half lengthwise

$^1/_2$ cup fontina cheese, shredded

$^1/_2$ cup pine nuts

Asian basil sprigs for garnish

6-inch bamboo skewers, as needed, soaked in water for 30 minutes

Heat a 1-quart saucepan over high heat. Add soy sauce, mirin, chicken stock, orange juice, fish sauce, garlic, ginger, and brown sugar. Cook until liquid is reduced in volume by half, about 15 minutes. Remove from heat and set marinade aside.

Place skirt steak on a cutting board and rub both sides with oil, salt, and black pepper. Place green onions in a row on center of meat, about $^1/_2$-inch from the end. Spread cheese, pine nuts, and Asian basil alongside green onions. Roll beef tightly until both ends meet and overlap slightly. Cut beef into 3-inch long rolls and thread the skewers along seam of each roll, sealing it closed.

Heat the grill to medium heat, brush beef with sauce, and place on the grill. Cook for three minutes on each side, basting every minute with teriyaki garlic sauce. When rolls are cooked, arrange on a warm plate and serve with extra sauce on the side in a small bowl for dipping.

✂ ☺ ✂

Beef Musman

Prep time: 15 minutes • Cook time: 20 minutes • Serves 2

1 cup chopped raw potato

2 TB. canola oil

1 lb. beef flank steak, cut into 2-inch pieces

2 TB. musman curry paste

1 cup canned coconut milk

2 TB. fish sauce or nuoc mam

2 TB. wet tamarind

1 TB. granulated sugar

2 bay leaves

1/2 cup pineapple chunks

1/2 cup crushed unsalted peanuts

Put potatoes in a 1-quart pot filled with water. Bring to a boil, cook for five minutes, remove from heat, and cool. The center of the potato should still be firm to the bite.

Heat a wok over high heat and add oil. When oil is smoking, add beef and curry paste. Stir-fry for two minutes; add coconut milk, fish sauce, tamarind, sugar, and bay leaves. Bring to a boil. Add pineapple, potatoes, and peanuts. Return to a boil. Remove from heat and ladle mixture into two warmed serving bowls. Serve hot.

Beef with Chinese Broccoli Stir-Fry

Prep time: 35 minutes • Marination time: 10 minutes • Cook time: 15 minutes • Serves 2

1 lb. beef flank steak, cut into 1-inch strips, across the grain

1 TB. tapioca starch

1/4 cup oyster sauce

2 TB. soy sauce

1 TB. sugar

1 tsp. freshly ground black pepper

1 bunch Chinese broccoli

1 TB. canola oil

1/2 cup shiitake mushroom caps

1/4 cup chicken stock

Mix beef, tapioca starch, oyster sauce, soy sauce, sugar, and black pepper together in a medium-size bowl, coating the beef well. Refrigerate for 10 minutes.

Bring a 3-quart saucepan of lightly salted water to a boil, add Chinese broccoli, and cook for three minutes. Remove from heat, drain, and divide between two serving plates.

Heat a wok over high heat and add oil. When oil is smoking, add mushrooms and beef and stir-fry for three minutes. Add chicken stock and bring to a boil. Turn off heat and ladle beef mixture over Chinese broccoli. Serve hot.

Ginger Flank Steak

Prep time: 20 minutes • Cook time: 12 minutes • Serves 2

2 TB. canola oil

1 tsp. minced fresh garlic

2 TB. shredded fresh ginger

1 lb. beef flank steak, sliced into 2-inch strips

$\frac{1}{2}$ cup sliced green bell pepper

$\frac{1}{2}$ cup sliced white onion

$\frac{1}{2}$ cup sliced white mushroom

$\frac{1}{2}$ cup broccoli florets

2 TB. sliced green onion

$\frac{1}{4}$ cup chicken stock

$\frac{1}{2}$ cup oyster sauce

2 TB. distilled white vinegar

2 tsp. granulated sugar

1 tsp. freshly ground black pepper

Heat a wok over high heat and add oil. When oil is smoking, add garlic, ginger, and beef. Stir-fry for two minutes and add green bell pepper, white onion, mushrooms, broccoli, and green onion. Stir-fry for two minutes and add chicken stock, oyster sauce, vinegar, sugar, and black pepper. Bring to a boil, reduce the heat to low, and simmer for one minute. Remove from heat and divide between two warm plates.

Red Thai Curry Pork

Prep time: 25 minutes • Cook time: 15 minutes • Serves 2

2 TB. canola oil

2 tsp. minced fresh garlic

1 tsp. kaffir lime leaf, thinly sliced

1 tsp. thinly sliced lemongrass

2 TB. red curry paste

2 (8-oz.) pork cutlets, 1-inch thick

$\frac{1}{4}$ cup chicken stock

$\frac{1}{2}$ cup thinly sliced white onion

$\frac{1}{2}$ cup pineapple chunks

$\frac{1}{2}$ cup julienne of red bell pepper

$\frac{1}{2}$ cup julienne of green bell pepper

1 cup canned coconut milk

2 TB. fish sauce or nuoc mam

1 TB. granulated sugar

3 medium green onions, cut in thirds

2 TB. thinly sliced Asian basil leaves

Heat a wok over high heat and add oil. When oil is smoking, add garlic, lime leaf, lemongrass, and red curry paste. Stir-fry for one minute. Add cutlets to the wok and sear on both sides for one minute. Add chicken stock, white onions, pineapple, and red and green bell peppers. Stir-fry for one minute. Add coconut milk. Turn heat to high and bring to a boil. Add fish sauce, sugar, green onion, and basil. Return to a boil and remove from heat.

Remove pork, place on two warm serving plates, and ladle curried vegetables over pork. Serve hot.

Pork Chopper

Prep time: 40 minutes • Cook time: 35 minutes • Serves 2

1 cup tempura flour

$^1/_2$ cup very cold water

1 cup sake

Juice of 2 lemons

1 Asian pear, peeled and diced

2 tsp. brown sugar

1 tsp. red chili powder

1 cinnamon stick

2 (8-oz.) center cut pork chops

1 tsp. Chinese five-spice powder

$^1/_2$ cup chopped pecans

$^1/_2$ cup shredded Gruyere cheese

1 cup panko (Japanese breadcrumbs)

1 cup canola oil

Preheat the oven to 350°F.

Mix tempura flour with water and chill for at least 15 minutes.

In a 2-quart saucepan, add sake, lemon juice, pears, brown sugar, chili powder, and cinnamon stick. Bring to a boil and reduce heat, simmering for five minutes. Remove from heat and cool to room temperature.

Cut a pocket in side of pork chop and set aside.

Mix five-spice powder with pecans. Stuff pork chop with pecans and Gruyere, firmly pressing opening closed. Remove tempura batter from refrigerator and dip pork chops into batter. Dredge chops in *panko* breadcrumbs, covering completely.

Heat oil in a frying pan to 350°F and fry chops for three minutes on each side. Immediately place chops on a baking sheet and bake for 15 minutes. Pork should have a golden-brown crust and cheese should be melted in center. Place pork chops on a plate and ladle the Asian pears over chops. Serve hot.

Orient Expressions

Japanese breadcrumbs are called **panko.** Why use it instead of the American version? The crumbs are unseasoned and flaked instead of ground, so they have a clean flavor and extra crispness when cooked.

Steak Udon

Prep time: 15 minutes • Marination time: 20 minutes • Cook time: 20 minutes • Serves 2

2 (8-oz.) sirloin steaks

$^1/_2$ cup soy sauce

3 TB. canola oil (divided use)

2 cups dry udon noodles

$^1/_2$ bunch asparagus, trimmed

1 tsp. minced fresh garlic

$^1/_2$ cup sliced fresh button mushrooms

1 small white onion, sliced lengthwise

$^1/_2$ cup julienne of carrot

$^1/_2$ cup green onion, cut into thirds

$^3/_4$ cup hoisin sauce

$^1/_2$ cup chicken stock

2 TB. fish sauce

1 TB. granulated sugar

2 TB. Asian basil, sliced

1 tsp. chili powder

Place steaks into a medium-size, nonreactive bowl and pour soy sauce over them, turning to coat. Refrigerate for 20 minutes.

Heat a sauté pan over medium heat and add 1$^1/_2$ tablespoons oil. When oil is hot, remove steaks from marinade and discard marinade. Sear steaks for five minutes on each side. Remove from the pan and let steaks rest in a warm spot.

Bring a 2-quart saucepan of water to a boil, add noodles, and cook for six minutes. Remove noodles with tongs or a large slotted spatula and drain in a colander. Reserve cooking liquid in the pot.

Cook asparagus in the same water for four minutes. Remove asparagus and place in an ice water bath to stop the cooking. Chill for at least one minute or until chilled, drain and cut each stalk into three pieces.

Heat a wok over high heat and add remaining oil. When oil is hot, add garlic, mushrooms, and white onion; stir-fry for two minutes. Add carrot, asparagus, and green onion and stir-fry for one minute longer. Add hoisin sauce, chicken stock, fish sauce, sugar, and noodles. Stir-fry for one minute. Add basil and chili powder, and remove from heat. Ladle noodles into a bowl. Slice steak $^1/_4$- to $^1/_2$-inch thick and add to soup.

Recipes for Success

Dropping the asparagus into an ice water bath will stop the cooking and set the color. Just drop them directly into the water, let sit until at least room temperature, and remove and drain.

Sweet Pineapple Beef

Prep time: 20 minutes • Cook time: 12 minutes • Serves 2

2 TB. canola oil	$^1/_2$ cup julienne of red bell pepper
1 tsp. minced fresh garlic	$^1/_4$ cup chicken stock
1 TB. chili paste made with soybean oil	3 TB. fish sauce or nuoc mam
12 oz. beef flank steak, sliced into 2-inch strips	2 TB. sweet soy sauce
1 cup pineapple chunks	3 cups chow fun noodles
1 jalapeño chili pepper, quartered	2 tsp. tapioca starch
$^1/_2$ cup quartered shiitake mushrooms caps	3 TB. water
$^1/_2$ cup snow peas	2 TB. chopped cilantro leaves
$^1/_2$ cup sliced white onion	

Heat a wok over high heat and add oil. When oil is smoking, add garlic, chili paste, and beef. Stir-fry for two minutes and add pineapple, jalapeño, mushrooms, snow peas, white onion, and red pepper. Stir-fry for two minutes longer. Add chicken stock, fish sauce, sweet soy sauce, and chow fun noodles. Cook, stirring for two minutes. Mix tapioca with water and stir into the wok. Bring to a boil and remove from heat. Stir in cilantro and ladle onto two warm plates. Serve hot.

Thai Beef Kebab

Prep time: 20 minutes • Marination time: 1 hour • Cook time: 20 minutes • Serves 2

1 lb. beef rib-eye, cut into 2-inch cubes

$\frac{1}{2}$ cup olive oil (divided use)

1 TB. garlic, minced

1 tsp. salt

1 tsp. freshly ground black pepper

$\frac{1}{4}$ cup fresh cilantro leaves, chopped

$\frac{1}{2}$ cup green bell pepper, cut into 2-inch square pieces

$\frac{1}{2}$ cup white onion, cut into 2-inch square pieces

1 beefsteak tomato, cut into 2-inch square pieces

2 jalapeño peppers, quartered

Metal skewers or bamboo skewers soaked in water

Place cubed beef into a medium-size bowl with all but 1 teaspoon oil, garlic, salt, black pepper, cilantro, green bell pepper, white onion, tomato, and jalapeño. Cover and marinate in the refrigerator for one hour.

When you are ready to cook, remove beef from marinade. Thread a piece of beef on a skewer. Push toward the top of the skewer, leaving about two inches for a handle. Thread on each vegetable chunk and another piece of beef at the end. Alternate in this way until all the skewers are made.

Brush remaining olive oil from marinade on the grill and heat the grill to high heat. Sear skewered beef on the hottest area of the grill, about two minutes each side. This length of time will grill meat to slightly rarer than medium and give vegetables a slightly charred glow.

Wasabi Goat Cheese Filet Mignon

Prep time: 25 minutes • Cook time: 25 minutes • Serves 2

1 tsp. canola oil

$\frac{1}{4}$ cup chopped shallot

2 (8-oz.) beef tenderloins

2 TB. sesame oil (divided use)

$\frac{1}{4}$ tsp. salt

$\frac{1}{2}$ tsp. freshly cracked ground black pepper

3 TB. soft goat cheese

1 tsp. wasabi paste

1 tsp. minced fresh garlic

1 TB. black bean sauce

$\frac{1}{4}$ cup sweet soy sauce

$\frac{1}{4}$ cup chicken stock

Preheat the oven to 350°F.

Heat canola oil in a small sauté pan; when oil is hot, add shallots and sauté until golden brown. Scrape fried shallots onto a paper towel to drain. When cool, shake the towel off into a small bowl to catch the fried shallots. Reserve.

Rub tenderloins with 1 tablespoon sesame oil and season with salt and pepper. Heat a grill to medium-hot heat and grill tenderloins for three minutes on each side. Remove from the grill and reserve.

Mash goat cheese and wasabi paste in a small bowl using a fork. Top each tenderloin with wasabi goat cheese, place on a baking sheet or small roasting pan, and bake for seven minutes.

Heat a wok over high heat and add remaining sesame oil. When oil is smoking, add garlic, black bean sauce, sweet soy sauce, and chicken stock. Bring to a boil. Reduce heat and simmer for three minutes.

Remove from heat. Ladle sauce on the bottom of a plate and place filet on top. Sprinkle fried shallots over top and serve at once.

Chapter 14

Air: Chicken and Duck

In This Chapter

- Fun with fowl
- New Asian comfy food
- Some great chicken and duck recipes

From everyday chicken to lofty duck, Asian cuisine focuses on these ingredients in new ways. In this chapter, we'll show you how to push the envelope with chicken and prepare duck with confidence.

Dandy Duck Dishes

"What? Are we crazy?" seem to be questions we ask ourselves every day, especially when we find ourselves coming up with something as daffy sounding as Duck Cigars! No, they are not soaked in tobacco juice or wrapped in tobacco leaves. They are lovely, elongated spring rolls stuffed with duck and vegetables with a "cigar wrapper" of rice paper and are just the kind of indulgence that keeps us excited about new Asian food.

We love cooking with duck for its robust flavor, but it does require more care in cooking than chicken. Whether you buy your duck fresh or frozen, whole or in parts, with the bones in or not, here are some tips on getting the most quack for your cash.

First, you'll need a bigger duck than you would think. Its huge chest cavity makes a 5-pound duck look like a 10-pound chicken. And that 5-pound duck will really only feed a couple hungry people.

Thoroughly wash the cavity, making sure you remove any excess fat that might be floating around in there.

Because of its high fat content, Mother Nature has provided us with a self-basting bird. Resist the urge to start with oil in the pan. When roasting the whole bird, prick the skin on the thighs and the bottom of the breast to allow some of the fat to drain off while cooking; discard the fat before serving. When pan-frying the breast, be sure to score the skin.

Lucky Treasures
Domesticated ducks have been a part of the Chinese diet for more than 2,500 years, which explains why Chinese cooks have such an enormous repertoire of duck dishes.

Armed with this knowledge, feel free to substitute duck for chicken in most recipes.

Feel free to dispense with the carving knife and use poultry shears or heavy scissors to carve a duck.

Recipes for Success
Do not use ultra hot temperatures with duck or you will wind up with one tough superball of a bird. Remember movies where the dinner guests take a tiny bite and are chewing, and chewing, and chewing? Well, this is a big movie secret, but all they do is make a duck this way and feed it to the actors. Shh, don't tell anyone …

Chicken

Chicken. It's easy to cook, economical, and virtually available all day, every day, so much so that sometimes you just want to scream at the thought of yet another chicken dish. And yet for all those reasons, we love to use it.

Novices to new Asian food find a comfort level knowing that the main ingredient in a dish is something they eat every day.

For those who have ended up at our new Asian restaurant only because everyone else was going, we created Pan-Fried Chicken. Even the biggest Bubba in Texas loves this new Asian version of a Southern staple. Going one step further, Annie came up with the idea of using a pumped-up, chili-enhanced, sweet and sour sauce instead of cream gravy.

Our Musman Chicken is one of those dishes that started out as one thing and ended up as another. Annie's teacher from Taiwan was in town and we were having one of our culinary meetings with a group of chefs and friends. Annie and her teacher got in the kitchen and started sending out stuff. The first version of this dish came out as sort of a stew with pork and potatoes, and we all loved the flavor, but we kept tweaking it until it morphed into a new Asian chicken dish over rice.

So now you know the big secret of new Asian cooking (or any cooking for that matter): keep tweaking 'til you get it where you want it.

Flying or not, fowl dishes Asian style are never foul. These recipes will get you to spread your wings in the kitchen and we promise no one will ever say "What? Chicken again?"

The Least You Need to Know

- ◆ Be sure to score or prick the duck skin before cooking.
- ◆ New Asian chicken is not your mother's chicken.
- ◆ If you prefer, you can substitute chicken for duck in any of these recipes.

Chicken Panang with Rice Vermicelli

Prep time: 25 minutes • Cook time: 15 minutes • Serves 2

2 TB. canola oil

1 TB. Panang curry paste

3 kaffir lime leaves

1 lb. skinless, boneless chicken breast, cut diagonally against the grain

1/2 cup julienne of red bell pepper

1/2 cup julienne of green bell pepper

1 TB. granulated sugar

1/4 cup chicken stock

1 cup canned coconut milk

2 tsp. lime juice

2 TB. fish sauce

2 cups rice vermicelli noodles, soaked in water 15 minutes

2 TB. chopped Asian basil

2 TB. chopped fresh cilantro leaves

Heat a wok over high heat and add oil. When oil is hot, add curry paste, lime leaves, and chicken. Stir-fry for three minutes. Add red and green peppers, sugar, and chicken stock. Bring to a boil, and cook for two minutes. Add coconut milk, lime juice, and fish sauce. Simmer for five minutes. Remove from heat and keep warm.

Bring a 2-quart saucepan of water to a boil. Put noodles into boiling water for 40 seconds. Try not to overcook noodles because they will get soft and gummy. Divide noodles between two large, warm soup bowls and ladle chicken curry over noodles. Sprinkle with fresh basil and cilantro. Serve hot.

Chow Fun Duck

Prep time: 20 minutes • Cook time: 15 minutes • Serves 2

1 (8-oz.) duck breast, skin on	$^1/_2$ cup pineapple chunks
2 tsp. red curry paste	3 cups chow fun noodles
$^1/_4$ cup sliced white onion	$^1/_2$ cup canned coconut milk
4 green onions, cut into 2- to 3-inch pieces	2 TB. chopped Asian basil
$^1/_4$ cup chicken stock	2 TB. granulated sugar
2 TB. fish sauce	1 TB. paprika
$^1/_4$ cup cherry tomatoes, halved	

Heat a wok over medium heat. When the wok is hot, place duck breast in it skin side down and sear for three minutes on each side. Remove duck from the wok and cool for a minute until it's easy to handle. Slice duck into bite-size pieces and reserve.

There should be some fat from duck in the wok. Pour out all but 1 teaspoon and heat over medium heat. Stir-fry curry paste in duck fat for 30 seconds. Add white onion, green onion, and duck breast pieces to the wok and stir-fry for one minute. Add chicken stock, fish sauce, cherry tomatoes, and pineapple; bring to a boil. Reduce heat to a simmer and add chow fun noodles, coconut milk, basil, sugar, and paprika, tossing frequently for two minutes. Remove from heat and ladle soup into two large, warm soup bowls. Serve hot.

Duck Cigars

Prep time: 30 minutes • Cook time: 1 hour, 20 minutes • Serves 2

6 cups water

1 cup soy sauce

2 TB. minced fresh garlic

$^{1}/_{2}$ cup granulated sugar

2 TB. salt

1 TB. freshly cracked black pepper

$^{1}/_{2}$ whole duck

8 rice paper wrappers

$^{3}/_{4}$ cup finely julienned carrot (divided use; reserve $^{1}/_{4}$ cup for dipping sauce)

$^{1}/_{2}$ cup shredded iceberg lettuce

$^{1}/_{4}$ cup julienne of seeded cucumber

4 green onions, trimmed to within 1 inch of the white part, halved lengthwise

$^{1}/_{2}$ cup bean sprouts

$^{1}/_{4}$ cup lightly packed fresh cilantro sprigs

$^{1}/_{4}$ cup distilled white vinegar

$^{1}/_{2}$ cup sriracha sauce

1 TB. granulated sugar

2 TB. crushed unsalted peanuts

In a large stockpot, bring water, soy sauce, garlic, sugar, salt, and black pepper to a boil. Add duck and reduce heat; simmer for one hour. Remove duck; when it's cool enough to handle, discard skin, pull meat from bone, and shred it with a fork into thin pieces.

Using one rice paper at a time, submerge each disk in simmering water for 45 seconds. After pulling it from water, hang on a corner of a counter by its edge to dry for about 20 seconds. This will make it easy to roll.

Remove the softened rice paper from the counter's edge and place it on a work surface. Place $^{1}/_{2}$ cup duck on the lower third of the sheet. Place a little bit each of carrot, lettuce, cucumber, green onion, and bean sprouts, and top with a couple cilantro sprigs. Pull bottom edge of rice paper up over salad and noodles using your thumb and forefinger of each hand while holding stuffing with your middle fingers. Keep rice paper tight as you roll, but not too tight, or it will tear. Once you have covered filling, fold sides of rice paper in and continue to roll until you have made a thin cigar shape. Repeat with remaining wrappers.

Recipes for Success
Make one roll at a time. If too much water evaporates from the wrapper it will become sticky and tear easily.

Dipping sauce: Whisk together vinegar, sriracha sauce, sugar, peanuts, and $^{1}/_{4}$ cup of carrot. Pour into two dipping bowls and serve with the duck cigars.

Duck and Ginger Stir-Fry

Prep time: 25 minutes • Cook time: 1 hour, 20 minutes • Serves 2

8 cups water

1 cup soy sauce

3 TB. fish sauce

$^{1}/_{2}$ cup granulated sugar

2 TB. salt

1 tsp. freshly cracked black pepper

1 whole Muscovy duck

2 TB. canola oil

1 tsp. minced fresh garlic

$^{1}/_{4}$ cup pickled ginger

$^{1}/_{2}$ cup straw mushrooms

$^{1}/_{2}$ cup snow peas

$^{1}/_{2}$ cup sliced green onion

$^{1}/_{2}$ cup chicken stock

$^{1}/_{2}$ cup oyster sauce

Bring water to a boil in a 2-gallon stockpot and add soy sauce, fish sauce, sugar, salt, and black pepper. Add duck and return to a boil. Lower the heat and simmer duck for one hour. Remove duck from the pot and set aside until it's cool enough to handle. Remove skin and discard. Pull meat off bone and cut into large bite-size pieces.

Heat a wok over high heat and add oil. When oil is smoking, add garlic, ginger, and duck. Stir-fry for three minutes and add mushrooms, snow peas, and green onion. Stir-fry for three minutes and add chicken stock and oyster sauce; return to a boil and immediately remove from heat. Divide between two warm serving plates and serve with steamed rice.

Fried Pandan Leaf Chicken

Prep time: 20 minutes • Marination time: 30 minutes • Cook time: 15 minutes • Serves 2

1 lb. boneless, skinless chicken breast, cut into large chunks

1/2 cup canned coconut milk

2 TB. fish sauce

1 tsp. minced fresh garlic

2 TB. chopped cilantro leaves

1/2 tsp. freshly ground black pepper

2 pieces Pandan or banana leaf, cut into an approximately 8 × 10-inch sheet

2 cups canola oil

1/2 cup sweet chili sauce

Mix chicken, coconut milk, fish sauce, garlic, cilantro, and black pepper together, tossing well. Cover, and marinate in the refrigerator for 30 minutes.

Place pandan leaf or banana leaf on a work surface. Remove chicken from marinade, place a chunk of chicken in center of leaf, and roll tightly. Secure with a toothpick and repeat the process until all chicken is wrapped. Steam bundles in a steamer for eight minutes. Remove from the steamer and pat them dry with paper towels.

Heat a wok over medium-high heat and add oil. Heat oil to 350°F. Drop chicken wraps in oil and cook for three minutes. Drain chicken wraps briefly on paper towels. Pour chili sauce into a dipping bowl and place the bowl on a warm platter next to wraps. To eat, unwrap chicken before eating and dip, dip, dip!

Fortune Cookies _____

More fun and less fattening than making fudge, this is the ultimate in group cooking. These chicken wraps are tasty and so easy that everyone will be interested in cooking.

Orient Expressions _____

Sweet chili sauce is a purée of fresh chili peppers with vinegar and sugar added. It makes a great marinade for duck, chicken, and shrimp.

Garlic Duck

Prep time: 1 hour • Marination time: 30 minutes • Cook time: 1 hour, 20 minutes • Serves 2

6 cups water

1 cup soy sauce

$^{1}/_{2}$ cup granulated sugar

1 cup sliced celery

3 TB. salt

2 TB. freshly ground black pepper (divided use)

$^{1}/_{4}$ cup minced fresh garlic (divided use)

1 whole Muscovy duck (or Peking duck can be substituted)

1 bunch fresh cilantro

$^{1}/_{4}$ cup fish sauce

2 TB. canola oil

$^{1}/_{4}$ cup pickled ginger

Heat water, soy sauce, sugar, celery, salt, 1 tablespoon black pepper, $^{1}/_{8}$ cup garlic in a 4-quart stockpot. Place duck in the pot and return to a boil. Lower heat and simmer for one hour. Remove duck from the pot and set aside to cool.

Place cilantro, fish sauce, and remaining black pepper and garlic in a food processor fitted with a metal blade. Process to a paste and set aside.

Skin duck and discard the skin. Remove meat from the bone in large pieces and marinate in paste, refrigerated, for 30 minutes.

Heat a wok over high heat and add oil. When oil is smoking, stir-fry duck meat until golden-brown. Arrange duck meat on a platter with pickled ginger on the side. Serve warm.

Island Chicken

Prep time: 40 minutes • Cook time: 20 minutes • Serves 2

1 cup tempura flour

$^1/_2$ cup water, iced and strained

2 to 3 quarts + 1 TB. canola oil (divided use)

1 lb. skinless, boneless chicken breasts, diced

$^1/_2$ cup diced white onion

$^1/_2$ cup diced pineapple

$^1/_2$ cup diced red bell pepper

$^1/_2$ cup diced seeded cucumber

1 cup tomato ketchup

3 TB. fresh lime juice

3 TB. granulated sugar

$^1/_2$ tsp. salt

1 TB. tapioca starch

2 TB. water

Mix together tempura flour and ice water with a fork.

Fill a wok with canola oil until it's about half full. Heat oil to 350°F. Dip chicken into tempura batter, carefully place it into oil, and fry until golden brown, about 4 to 6 minutes. Remove from the wok and place on paper towels to drain. Pour off oil and wipe out the wok.

Heat the wok over high heat and add 1 tablespoon canola oil. When oil is smoking, add onion, pineapple, red peppers, and cucumber, and stir-fry for three minutes. Add ketchup and lower the heat. Stir in lime juice, sugar, and salt. Mix tapioca starch with water and add to wok. Bring to a boil and toss in chicken. Remove from heat and spoon onto warm serving plates. Serve immediately.

≻⊖≺

Musman Chicken

Prep time: 25 minutes • Cook time: 12 minutes • Serves 2

1 cup green beans

$^1/_4$ cup diced potatoes

8 oz. skinless, boneless chicken breast, sliced thinly across the grain

2 TB. canola oil

2 tsp. musman curry paste

1 tsp. minced fresh garlic

$^1/_2$ cup thinly sliced Chinese sausage

$^1/_4$ cup chicken stock

2 TB. fish sauce

$^1/_4$ cup sliced white onion

2 TB. chopped green onion

$^1/_2$ cup canned coconut milk

1 tsp. Chinese five-spice powder

1 tsp. paprika

$^1/_4$ cup crushed unsalted peanuts

1 TB. granulated sugar

Bring a 2-quart saucepan of lightly salted water to a boil and add green beans. Lower to a medium boil and cook for three to four minutes. Remove beans with a slotted spoon and reserve.

Keep water on the stove and return it to a boil, add potatoes, and cook for five minutes. Remove potatoes with the slotted spoon and set atop green beans.

Bring water back to a boil one last time, add chicken, and cook for four minutes. Drain chicken.

Heat a wok over high heat and add oil. When oil is smoking, add curry paste, garlic, Chinese sausage, and chicken. Stir-fry for two minutes and add chicken stock and fish sauce. Bring to a boil and add potatoes, green beans, white onion, and green onion, tossing for two minutes. Add coconut milk, Chinese five-spice powder, paprika, peanuts, and sugar, and cook for two minutes longer. Remove from the heat. Ladle onto two warm serving plates.

Oven-Roasted Spicy Chicken with Noodles

Prep time: 20 minutes • Cook time: 1$\frac{1}{2}$ hours • Serves 2

1 whole (about 2- to 3-lb.) chicken	$\frac{1}{2}$ cup broccoli florets
2 TB. chopped fresh cilantro leaves	1 TB. shredded fresh ginger
2 TB. chopped Asian basil	$\frac{1}{2}$ cup sliced button mushrooms
1 TB. yellow curry powder	$\frac{1}{2}$ cup diced red bell pepper
1 tsp. salt	$\frac{1}{2}$ cup diced green bell pepper
$\frac{1}{4}$ cup canola oil	$\frac{1}{2}$ cup chicken stock
8 oz. dry udon noodles	$\frac{1}{2}$ cup oyster sauce
2 tsp. minced fresh garlic	2 TB. sweet soy sauce

Heat oven to 400°F.

Rinse chicken and dry with a paper towel.

Mix cilantro, basil, curry powder, and salt together in a large mixing bowl. Place chicken in the bowl, rub in 2 tablespoons oil, and rub curry mixture all over it, coating chicken well. Put chicken on a roasting pan and bake for 45 minutes or until golden brown. Remove from the oven and when cool enough to handle (about 20 minutes), pull meat off bone, leaving as much of the skin on as possible.

Bring a 2-quart saucepan of water to a boil and cook udon noodles for 6 minutes; drain and reserve.

Heat a wok over high heat and add remaining oil. When oil is smoking, add garlic, chicken, noodles, broccoli, ginger, mushrooms, and red and green peppers. Stir-fry for four minutes and add chicken stock, oyster sauce, and sweet soy sauce. Give everything one last toss and remove from the heat. Divide between two large, warm soup bowls.

Fortune Cookies

This recipe is perfect to start a day or two before. Prepare the recipe through the roasting or boning step and refrigerate. When you are ready to finish the dish, bring the meat to room temperature before carrying on.

Pan-Fried Chicken

Prep time: 25 minutes • Cook time: 15 minutes • Serves 2

1 cup tempura flour	1 cup panko (Japanese bread crumbs)
$1/2$ cup ice cold water	$1/2$ cup sweet chili sauce
2 to 3 quarts canola oil	1 cup sliced cucumber, cut into 1-inch slices
2 (8-oz.) boneless, skinless chicken breasts	1 cup sliced roma tomatoes, cut into 1-inch slices

Whisk tempura flour with ice water until smooth. Cover and let rest for at least 20 minutes.

Fill a heavy-duty frying pan with canola oil until it comes halfway up the side. Heat oil to 350°F. When oil is hot, dip chicken into batter and then into panko. Dredge all sides of chicken well. Quickly place chicken into the frying pan and cook for four minutes on each side. Remove from the pan and set on paper towels to drain.

Divide chili sauce between two small bowls and put them on two warm serving plates. Place breast, cucumbers, and roma tomatoes on each plate. Serve chicken hot.

Pot See You

Prep time: 15 minutes • Cook time: 15 minutes • Serves 2

1 (8-oz.) boneless, skinless chicken breast, cut into chunks

2 TB. canola oil

1 tsp. minced fresh garlic

2 eggs, beaten

2 cups Chinese broccoli

$^1/_4$ cup chicken stock

3 cups fresh chow fun noodles

2 TB. fresh lime juice

$^1/_2$ cup oyster sauce

2 roma tomatoes, quartered

2 tsp. granulated sugar

2 TB. soy sauce (Golden Mountain brand)

2 TB. sweet soy sauce

Bring a 2-quart pot of water to a boil. Place chicken in boiling water for three minutes and remove.

Heat a wok over high heat and add oil. When oil is smoking, add garlic, eggs, and chicken. Stir-fry for two minutes and add broccoli and chicken stock. Stir-fry for two minutes. Add chow fun noodles, lime juice, oyster sauce, tomatoes, sugar, soy sauce, and sweet soy sauce. Stir-fry ingredients together for two minutes longer and remove from heat. Divide between two warm serving plates. Serve hot.

Recipes for Success

Our preferred brand of soy sauce is called Golden Mountain. We have found major differences in soy sauces across the board, especially regarding the right balance of saltiness to sweetness. If you cannot find this brand, another one to try is Kikkoman Lite; not the same, but still a good choice.

Yum Yum Chicken

Prep time: 25 minutes • Cook time: 15 minutes • Serves 2

$^1/_2$ cup diced raw Idaho potatoes

1 TB. canola oil

1 lb. boneless, skinless chicken breast, sliced across the grain

2 TB. yellow curry paste

2 cups chicken stock

1 tsp. yellow curry powder

$^1/_2$ cup diced white onion

$^1/_2$ cup diced red bell pepper

$^1/_2$ cup diced green bell pepper

$^1/_2$ cup snow peas, rinsed and trimmed if necessary

$^1/_2$ cup diced carrot

2 cups canned coconut milk

2 TB. fish sauce

2 tsp. granulated sugar

2 TB. tapioca starch

$^1/_2$ cup water

2 cups chantaboun rice sticks, soaked in water for 15 minutes

Bring a 1-quart saucepan of water to a boil; cook potatoes for 5 minutes, drain. Potatoes should not be cooked through fully, but firm to the bite.

Heat a wok over high heat and add oil. When oil is smoking, add chicken slices and curry paste. Stir-fry for one minute and add chicken stock and curry powder; bring to a boil. Add potatoes, onion, red and green peppers, snow peas, and carrot. Bring to a boil again and add coconut milk, fish sauce, and sugar. Return to a boil. Mix tapioca starch with water and stir in. Bring to a boil one last time and remove from heat.

Place noodles in a 2-quart saucepan of boiling water and cook for 1 minute; drain well. Divide noodles between two large, warm soup bowls and ladle curried chicken over noodles. Serve hot.

Chapter 15

Seafood, Eat It

In This Chapter

- Identifying shellfish
- How to pick out a good piece of fish
- Methods for preparing new Asian seafood dishes
- Recipes for preparing new Asian seafood dishes

"Ruling a large kingdom is like cooking a small fish."
(Handle gently and never overdo it.)

—Lao-tse, Chinese philosopher (sixth century B.C.E.)

What is it about seafood that makes us salivate so? Is it the fantasy of seafaring adventures from long ago? Is it the lure of exotic flavors from faraway lands? I think it is simply because seafood offers some of life's most exquisite tastes. In almost every cuisine, bounty from the sea provides some of the most delicious and exciting dishes. New Asian cooking is no different.

In this chapter, we are going to dive into the real depths of new Asian cooking with methods and recipes for preparing seafood. With each dish, we will blend tastes and techniques from several Asian countries. So prepare for a crowd, because when the wok starts rockin', your friends will come a knockin'.

Shell Game

In today's casual vocabulary, when we talk about shellfish, we could be discussing mollusks like clams, scallops, and mussels or we could be talking about crustaceans like lobsters, shrimp, and crabs.

> **Recipes for Success**
>
> Look before you cook: Some people have lethal allergies to shellfish. If you are unsure whether you are one of them, consult your doctor. And consult your dinner guests about their allergies before planning a shellfish feast that could turn into a voyage to the emergency room. This is particularly important if you are planning a stew or soup in which the shellfish might not be immediately apparent.

Home Is Where the Shell Is

Mollusks are the ocean's equivalents of mobile homes. These animals live in their shells and take their homes with them. Like in a trailer park, there are some smaller homes and some double-wides. While these shells are prized souvenirs from summer vacations in Florida, it is what is inside these shells that becomes the prize of restaurants and kitchens around the world.

Here are some of the most popular shellfish used in recipes throughout Asia:

- **Abalone.** Spiral, ear-shaped shell with pearly interior; highest-class sushi topping.
- **Ark shell.** Rare unless you're there, a spiky shelled creature with bright red flesh; loses freshness quickly.
- **Clam.** Because of their variety and ease of preparation, clams are one of the most popular shellfish. There are more than 2,000 varieties. They come in hard-shell and soft-shell varieties and can be steamed, grilled, fried, or served raw.
- **Conch.** Delicious creature, resides in the big shells that can be used as blow horns.
- **Mussels.** One of the tastier shellfish, mussels are ovular and darker in color.
- **Ormer.** Smaller, tougher version of abalone.
- **Oyster.** Rumored to be an aphrodisiac, oysters have irregular shaped shells.
- **Scallops.** The versatile scallops comes in a highly sought-after fan-shaped shell.

> **Lucky Treasures**
>
> World-famous explorer Jacques Cousteau wanted the ocean to become a gigantic farm instead of a watery hunting ground. Rather than chase down food, he thought that the world would benefit more if we learned to cultivate seafood. Today, shrimp is harvested from Texas' Gulf Coast to Vietnam's South China Sea.

Wonderful World of Crustaceans

Crustacean is such an unappetizing name for some of the most delicious offerings from the sea. They are considered shellfish because of the chemical similarity of the meat and also because their bodies are shell-like. Lobster, shrimp, and crab are the big three in the crustacean world. From tacos to spring rolls, they appear in dishes all over the world. Crayfish, also known as crawfish or crawdads, are in the same family. They are basically miniature freshwater lobsters. Squilla are popular in sushi and are best around spawning season, which is June and July.

Perfect Ten-tacles: Squid and Octopods

Basically, squid and octopods are mollusks without shells. We separated them from the other shelled mollusks, because of their unique, if not unusual, physical characteristics.

Call to Arms: Differences Between the Squid and the Octopus

If you believe the old cartoon image, an octopus and a squid are the same creature. Most people only know about these creatures from cartoons or sea legends depicting 200-foot-long monsters that swallow boats whole.

There are two main differences between the squid and octopus that, once learned, will easily enable you to tell them apart. The main difference is the number of tentacles, or arms. As the name implies, the octopus has eight arms. The squid has 10. The other difference is the shape of their body. The octopus is rounded and the squid is a sleek, oblong shape and pointed with two fins at the end.

 **Lucky Treasures**
Octopus and squid have similar tastes and texture. Squid is a little more tender. Next time you are grilling, throw some octopus or squid on the barbie and enjoy.

Gone Fishin'

Fish can be among the easiest and most rewarding dishes to prepare. If you can flip a steak or bake lasagna, you can cook fish. Some of the techniques might be a little different, but they are easy to master.

A Trip to the Fishmonger: Picking Out Fish

I know some people are scared of buying fresh fish. They'll skip the fresh fish section of the grocery store and head straight to the freezers to grab some frozen salmon. We tend to fear that which we don't understand. Follow these simple guidelines and go fishin'.

For whole fish, one that hasn't been filleted yet, look at the eyes. I admit, it might seem a bit weird to stare down a mackerel, but the eyes are the windows to the freshness of the fish. If the eyes are cloudy, keep looking for another fish. At this point, you may find a fish with bloodshot eyes; if the eyes are clear it's still a good choice, it just means the fish was held in the wrong position or someone had bad aim with the club. So now that you've found one with eyes that aren't cloudy, press the skin right there on the scales. If the indentation left from your touch springs back into form, then congratulations, you're almost there. If the indentation sags and becomes permanent, then you need to find another fish.

> **Fortune Cookies**
>
> If you are in the mood for some fresh fish on a Sunday, it is going to be difficult to find at your favorite market. Grocers usually don't get fish deliveries on Sundays. Sunday is a good day for chicken, beef, or tofu.

The last test is the smell. It sounds ironic, but a fish that smells like fish is a bad fish. Fresh fish should not have that stinky fish smell. There will be a natural fish odor (you'll know it when you smell it), but if it is highly noticeable, buyer beware.

> **Fortune Cookies**
>
> If you buy a whole fish, you will save time and sanity by letting the butcher or fishmonger clean it for you.

When buying filleted fish, again keep the smell test in mind. When buying tuna, it should be a deep red color. Watch out for fillets with a heavy concentration of brown spots. Salmon should be an orange-pink color and firm. Swim away from salmon that has a high gloss on the meat.

Supporting Cast: Substituting Hard to Find Fish

I've tried to use recipes in this book with ingredients that are easy to obtain. Sometimes, even the best-stocked meat purveyors, grocery stores, and Asian markets will run out of a certain fish.

Let's take a dip in the ocean now with these delicious recipes.

Recipes for Success _____

Do not cross-contaminate seafood, meat, chicken, or vegetables. That means washing your hands between handling seafood, meat, and chicken for the same recipe. If you do a lot of cooking it's a good idea to keep a separate cutting board for each type—that's at least four and sanitize them after each use. To sanitize, add 2 teaspoons bleach to 1 gallon hot water, soak for 10 minutes and rinse clean. While you're at it, toss in your knives for five minutes, but no longer as long exposure to water can pit the blade.

The Least You Need to Know

◆ Unless you like the texture of leather, do not overcook shellfish and fish.

◆ When buying fish, use the eye, press, and smell tests to determine freshness.

◆ An octopus has 8 arms and a squid has 10.

◆ The bottom line for freshness: When in doubt, throw it out.

Green Chow Fun

Prep time: 15 minutes • Cooking time: 15 minutes • Serves 2

2 TB. canola oil

2 tsp. green curry paste

6 shrimp (16 to 20 count), peeled and deveined

6 sea scallops (20 to 30 count)

6 New Zealand green-lipped mussels

2 large crab claws

¼ cup chopped red bell pepper

¼ cup chopped green bell pepper

¼ cup chopped carrot

¼ cup broccoli florets

¼ cup chopped roma tomato

½ cup chicken broth

2 tsp. fish sauce

2 tsp. granulated sugar

1 cup canned coconut milk

2 tsp. cornstarch

1 TB. cold water

2 cups fresh chow fun noodles

Fortune Cookies

A good way to tell when you have reached a sauce consistency is when the liquid coats the back of a wooden spoon. Dip the spoon into the sauce and run your finger along the back of the spoon. If your finger leaves a path, it's good to go.

Heat a wok over medium heat and add oil and green curry paste and stir. As curry starts to release its flavors, add shrimp, scallops, mussels, and crab claws and toss to coat well with curry.

Next, add red and green bell peppers, carrot, broccoli, and tomatoes and stir-fry for a few seconds. Pour in chicken broth, fish sauce, sugar, and coconut milk and reduce by half. Dissolve cornstarch in cold water. Slowly add to the wok. Bring to boil, stirring constantly; remove from heat. Cut chow fun noodles into two-inch strips, making sure noodles are soft. (A good way to soften noodles is to warm them up in the microwave on defrost.) Put noodles into a bowl. Ladle hot curry over noodles and serve.

Orient Expressions

Shrimp and scallops are classified by weight. Shrimp classified as "12 to 16 count" means that 12 to 16 shrimp come in a pound. The larger the classification numbers, the smaller the shrimp.

Red Sea

Prep time: 20 minutes • Cooking time: 12 minutes • Serves 2

2 quarts canola oil

³/₄ cup fresh egg noodles, fried

2 TB. canola oil

2 TB. red curry paste

10 shrimp (16 to 20 count), peeled and deveined

¹/₂ cup sea scallops (20 to 30 count)

4 crab claws

1 lb. New Zealand green lipped mussels

¹/₄ cup sliced red bell pepper

¹/₄ cup sliced green bell pepper

4 cups chicken broth

2 TB. fish sauce

2 TB. paprika

3 cups canned coconut milk

2 tsp. cornstarch

1 TB. cold water

10 sprigs Asian basil

¹/₂ cup chantaboun noodles or rice sticks, soaked in water until soft

Heat 2 quarts canola oil in a heavy stock pot or fryer to 350°F. Divide the egg noodles in half. Drop each batch of egg noodles into oil one at a time. In about 15 seconds they will poof up into clouds of crispy egg noodle. Remove from oil and reserve for garnish.

Heat a wok over medium heat. Add 2 tablespoons oil and curry paste, stirring to release flavors. Add shrimp, scallops, crab claws, and mussels and coat well with curry. Add red and green peppers, chicken broth, fish sauce, paprika, and coconut milk.

When seafood is almost cooked, the dish should have a nice vibrant red color. If not, add more paprika.

Dissolve cornstarch in water. Slowly stir it into mixture in the wok. Bring to a boil and cook until liquid coats the back of a spoon. Remove from heat and stir in basil.

Add presoaked noodles to a pot of boiling water for 30 seconds to cook through. Place noodles into two warm serving bowls, and ladle ingredients over rice noodles. Garnish each bowl with half of fried egg noodles.

Recipes for Success

To monitor the temperature of your pot of oil, use a candy thermometer.

Shrimp and Scallops over Curried Fried Rice

Prep time: 5 minutes • Cooking time: 20 minutes • Serves 2

2 TB. canola oil

2 medium eggs

4 cups steamed jasmine rice

2 tsp. yellow curry powder

1 TB. fish sauce

2 tsp. soy sauce (Golden Mountain brand)

10 small scallops (20 to 30 count)

8 medium shrimp (16 to 20 count)

2 tsp. garlic

Freshly ground black pepper to taste

¾ cup Chinese broccoli

½ cup oyster sauce

½ cup chicken broth

Heat a wok over medium heat, and add oil and eggs. Scramble eggs, using a quick stirring motion with a wok spatula. Toss in rice, curry powder, fish sauce, and soy sauce. Toss well in wok, and remove from heat. Place in two warm soup bowls.

Heat a wok over medium heat and sear scallops and shrimp for three minutes. Add garlic, black pepper, and Chinese broccoli. As broccoli starts to wilt, add oyster sauce and chicken broth. Bring to a boil, then remove from heat. Ladle wok ingredients on top of rice. Serve immediately.

Spicy Shrimp Chow Fun

Prep time: 15 minutes • Cooking time: 8 minutes • Serves 2

¼ cup canola oil

14 medium shrimp (16 to 20 count), peeled and deveined

2 tsp. garlic, chopped

1 jalapeño, quartered

½ cup chopped red bell pepper

½ cup chopped green bell pepper

1 roma tomato, quartered

2 TB. diced green onion

3 cups chow fun noodles, cut in 1-inch strips

¼ cup chicken broth

2 TB. sweet soy sauce

⅓ cup oyster sauce

2 TB. sugar

10 sprigs Asian basil

Heat a wok to medium heat and add oil and shrimp. Sear for three minutes. Add garlic and sauté for 10 seconds. Add jalapeño, red and green bell peppers, tomato, and onion and sauté for another minute. Add chow fun noodles and toss with other ingredients, stir-frying constantly. Add chicken broth, sweet soy sauce, oyster sauce, and sugar, and cook for four minutes. Ladle into serving bowl and garnish with basil. Serve hot.

Grilled Stuffed Lobster with Lemongrass Butter Sauce

Prep time: 15 minutes • Cook time: 25 minutes • Serves 2

2 (1- to 1^{1}/$_{2}$-lb.) live lobsters

^{1}/$_{4}$ cup Chinese sausage

^{3}/$_{4}$ cup lump crabmeat

1 minced jalapeño pepper

4 green onions

6 sprigs fresh cilantro

4 TB. lemon juice (divided use)

2 TB. mayonnaise

^{3}/$_{4}$ cup white wine

2 TB. chopped lemongrass

^{3}/$_{4}$ cup heavy cream

^{1}/$_{2}$ cup unsalted butter, room temperature, cut into 1-inch pieces

Salt to taste

4 TB. bread crumbs

Bring a three-gallon stock pot of water to a boil. Add lobsters. Cook for four minutes. Remove and keep cool. Insert a sharp knife in the center, just above the head, and cut shell, moving the knife downward to the bottom, splitting lobster in half. Discard contents of head cavity and the green tomalley (unless you love that stuff). Set lobster aside.

Grill Chinese sausage over medium high heat, dice, and place in mixing bowl. Add crabmeat, jalapeño, green onion, cilantro, 2 tablespoons lemon juice, and mayonnaise. Toss together and set stuffing aside.

In a small saucepan over medium-high heat, add wine and lemongrass and reduce the liquid in the pan by half. Add heavy cream and reduce by half. Turn the heat to medium low and slowly whisk in butter piece by piece. Season sauce with salt and lemon juice to taste. Keep the sauce warm.

Preheat a broiler. Grill lobster for four minutes over medium heat. Fill head cavity with stuffing and top with bread crumbs. Broil for four minutes. Place on a plate and ladle sauce over lobster.

Recipes for Success

When you remove the lobster from the pot, weight it down with a large plate to keep it flat. This will keep the tail from curling as it cools.

Five-Spice Pecan Trout

Prep time: 15 minutes • Cook time: 15 minutes • Serves 2

1 lb. whole boneless dressed trout, skin on
$1\frac{1}{2}$ cup chow mein noodles
$\frac{1}{4}$ cup pecan pieces
2 tsp. Chinese five-spice powder
1 tsp. salt
$\frac{1}{2}$ cup canola oil
1 tsp. garlic, minced
1 tsp. chili paste made with soybean oil
1 roma tomato, quartered
$\frac{1}{4}$ cup green onions
$\frac{1}{4}$ cup carrots, sliced matchstick-size
10 sprigs cilantro
1 tsp. red curry paste
$\frac{3}{4}$ cup canned coconut milk
$\frac{1}{4}$ cup lime juice

Rinse trout under cold water, and dry with a paper towel. Set aside.

Boil the chow mein noodles in a 2-quart pot of water for 5 minutes. Drain and set aside.

In a food processor fitted with a metal blade, blend pecans, Chinese five-spice powder, and salt until fine. Put pecan mixture on a plate and dredge the meat side only of the fish through the mixture.

Heat a sauté pan over medium heat. Add half the oil. Place the trout skin side up in the sauté pan and cook three minutes. Turn over and cook two more minutes. Carefully remove from pan and flip fillets over onto a plate and set aside.

Heat the wok over medium heat and add remaining oil, garlic, and chili paste. As the wok releases a fragrant smell, add tomatoes, green onions, carrots, and chow mein noodles. Toss together until heated through. Add cilantro and ladle onto two warm serving plates.

Clean the wok, reheat over medium heat, and add a small amount of oil and red curry paste, cooking until the fragrance is released. Add coconut milk and lime juice. Bring to a boil and remove from heat.

Place trout over noodles on the serving plates, spoon sauce over trout, and serve.

Red Curry Cashew Halibut

Prep time: 1 hour • Cooking time: 15 minutes • Serves 2

1 1/2 cups soba noodles

4 oz. (1/4-lb.) piece Chinese sausage

1/4 cup cherry tomatoes, halved

1/4 cup bean sprouts

1 bunch watercress

2 tsp. rice vinegar

1 tsp. salt

1 tsp. honey

4 TB. sesame oil (divided use)

2 tsp. sweet soy sauce

1/2 tsp. chili paste made with soybean oil

Pinch Thai chili powder

1/4 cup cashews, chopped

1 tsp. red curry paste

1 lb. skinless, boneless halibut

1 1/2 cups canned coconut milk

1/4 cup pineapple purée with juice

1/2 tsp. cornstarch

2 tsp. water

2 tsp. granulated sugar

Boil 2 quarts water in a large saucepan, add noodles, and cook for 6 minutes. Remove from heat, drain, and place in a bowl covered with plastic wrap. Set aside in the refrigerator.

Grill Chinese sausage and cut into 1/4-inch slices. Toss tomatoes in the mixing bowl with sausage, noodles, bean sprouts, and watercress. Add vinegar, salt, honey, 2 tablespoons sesame oil, sweet soy sauce, chili paste, and chili powder. Toss well, taste, adjust seasoning if necessary, and set aside.

Place cashews and red curry in a food processor fitted with a metal blade and pulse for five seconds until mixture is fine. Heat a sauté pan over medium heat, and add in 2 tablespoons oil. Dredge halibut in cashew mixture, and place in the pan. Cook on each side for five minutes.

While halibut is cooking, take a separate pan and combine coconut milk and pineapple purée. Reduce to half. Combine cornstarch with water and add it to the pan with sugar, and bring to boil. Immediately remove from heat. Place noodle salad on two large serving plates and lay fish on top. Ladle sauce around the plate and serve.

Grilled Salmon

Prep time: 20 minutes • Marination time: 30 minutes • Cook time: 15 minutes • Serves 1

$^1/_2$ tsp. garlic, minced

$1^1/_2$ TB. granulated sugar

$^1/_2$ tsp. Madras curry powder

2 TB. canola oil

$^1/_4$ tsp. freshly ground black pepper

8 oz. boneless salmon fillet

8 stems Chinese broccoli, trimmed

1 cup steamed rice

$^1/_4$ cup Korean sauce (see recipe in the following Recipes for Success sidebar)

1 tsp. sesame seeds

Mix garlic, sugar, curry powder, oil, and black pepper together in a bowl. Rub this mixture on salmon. Cover with plastic wrap and refrigerate for 30 minutes.

Heat a grill to medium, and grill the fish for three minutes on each side so it picks up the grill markings. Lower the heat or move over to a lower flame on the grill and finish cooking for about two minutes or until salmon is firm to the touch. Remove fish from the grill and set aside.

Steam Chinese broccoli for two minutes; remove from heat and drain excess water. Divide the steamed rice onto two large serving plates, and place fish on top of rice. Place broccoli on the side and ladle Korean sauce over fish. Sprinkle with sesame seeds and serve hot.

Recipes for Success

To make Korean sauce, in a saucepan over high heat combine $^1/_2$ teaspoon minced ginger, $^1/_4$ teaspoon minced fresh garlic, 1 tablespoon finely chopped white onion, $^1/_4$ cup soy sauce, $^1/_4$ cup soy bean sauce, and 1 tablespoon sweet soy sauce. Bring to a boil. Combine $^1/_2$ teaspoon tapioca starch and 1 tablespoon water and add the mixture to the saucepan. Bring to a boil and remove from heat.

Royal Typhoon

Prep time: 15 minutes • Cook time: 8 minutes • Serves 1

2 TB. canola oil

$^1/_4$ cup squid bodies, sliced

1 tsp. minced fresh garlic

2 TB. chopped carrot

2 TB. chopped yellow squash

2 TB. chopped zucchini

2 TB. chopped red bell pepper

2 TB. chopped green bell pepper

2 TB. sliced fresh mushrooms

2 TB. chopped white onion

4 medium green onions, cut into 2- to 3-inch pieces

6 oz. rice noodles (soak in cold water)

1 tsp. soy sauce (Golden Mountain brand)

$^1/_4$ cup oyster sauce

$^1/_2$ tsp. granulated sugar

1 tsp. chili paste made with soybean oil

$^1/_4$ cup chicken broth

5 sprigs Thai basil

Heat a wok over medium heat. Add the oil, and when the oil begins to smoke, add the squid and sear for three minutes. Add garlic, carrot, yellow squash, zucchini, red and green bell peppers, mushrooms, white onion, and green onion and stir-fry for one more minute.

Place softened rice noodles into a pot of boiling water. The trick for noodles is to shake them while they're in water so they can roll up. This should take about a minute. After noodles roll up, drain them and add them to the wok. Toss with soy sauce, oyster sauce, sugar, chili paste, and chicken broth. Garnish with basil, ladle noodles into bowl, and serve hot.

Orient Expressions _____

Squeamish on squid? So are a lot of folks, which might explain why we in the United States have adopted the far more edible sounding Italian word _calamari_ as our preferred name for squid. Calamari served up with leeks, warm soba noodles, and a nice glass of Riesling sound far more inviting than squid with noodles.

Octopus Skewers

Prep time: 15 minutes • Cook time: 14 minutes • Serves 1

1/4 cup soy sauce

1/2 tsp. minced fresh garlic

1/2 tsp. sugar

1/2 bunch fresh cilantro, chopped

1/2 tsp. freshly ground black pepper

1 medium-size (8 oz.) octopus

1/4 cup shiitake mushroom caps

2 TB. sliced green onions

Generous 1/4 cup cherry tomatoes, halved

2 TB. chopped yellow bell peppers

6 to 8 bamboo skewers, soaked in water for at least 30 minutes

1 cup steamed jasmine rice

1/4 cup sweet chili sauce

1 tsp. sesame seeds

Mix soy sauce, garlic, sugar, cilantro, and black pepper in a bowl. Alternate octopus, mushrooms, onions, tomatoes, and peppers on the skewers.

Pour marinade over the skewers and refrigerate for 15 minutes. Heat a grill to medium and grill the skewers for four minutes on each side. Once the skewers are fully cooked through, put on two serving plates with a side of steamed rice. Ladle sweet chili sauce over the skewers, top with sesame seeds, and serve.

Calamari and Rice Stir-Fry

Prep time: 15 minutes • Cook time: 10 minutes • Serves 1

2 TB. canola oil

1 medium egg

2 cups steamed jasmine rice

1 tsp. yellow curry powder

1 TB. fish sauce

1 tsp. soy sauce (Golden Mountain brand)

1 tsp. granulated sugar

8 oz. calamari bodies or tubes, sliced into thin rings

$^1\!/_2$ tsp. garlic, minced

$^1\!/_4$ cup sliced white button mushrooms

2 TB. sliced white onion

2 TB. snow peas, cut lengthwise

2 TB. chicken broth

1 lime, cut into 4 wedges

Heat a wok over medium heat. Add 1 tablespoon oil and egg. Quickly scramble egg and add rice, yellow curry powder, fish sauce, soy sauce, and sugar. Mix well until rice has a nice yellow color to it. Transfer to a bowl. Add remaining tablespoon oil to wok. When the oil is smoking, add the squid, and sear for three minutes; add garlic. Stir-fry for one minute. Add mushrooms, onion, and snow peas and cook for another minute. Add chicken broth and toss well. Spoon into two serving bowls and garnish with lime wedges.

Chapter 16

Desserts

In This Chapter

- ◆ Exotic sweet treats
- ◆ A New Asian kink to Old World classics
- ◆ Fun with fruit

Belgian chocolate. American apple pie. French pastry. Italian gelato. There are all sorts of places in the world where desserts and sweet treats are inextricably linked with the dining experience. Even though legend has it that ice cream was invented in China, Asian countries are rarely what pop into most people's minds when they're looking for desserts.

This isn't because of any particular boneheadedness on our part. Rather it's because dessert in Asia is more likely to be a piece of fruit than a show-stopping, over-the-top, spun-sugar extravaganza of some deranged pastry chef let loose in the kitchen.

Though they've never really caught on in the West, there are plenty of Asian desserts. Many are rice- or nut-based, generally not as sweet as what we are used to, and often have a consistency that is considered too gelatinous by many Westerners.

Fortune Cookies

According to Chinese tradition, the Kitchen God comes to check out your house the week before the start of the Chinese New Year festival. To make sure the Kitchen God has a favorable opinion of your home, Neen Gao, a steamed Chinese fruit cake, is prepared as an offering.

Orient Expressions

Even today, ovens aren't standard issue in Chinese kitchens. Traditional Chinese cakes are steamed, not baked, which gives them a spongy texture very different from our cakes. But they can still support a birthday candle.

Though few of us would have any objection to the French-influenced custards of Thailand or the fried fruits of many Southeast Asian countries, they don't show up nearly as often as they ought to on the menus of Asian restaurants in the West.

Whether it's a little something picked up on the street for a quick breakfast or mid-afternoon snack, eaten for good luck, served after a meal, or as a part of a traditional celebration, sweets are an integral part of dining in Asia. Sweet red bean paste, made from a mix of sugar and puréed red beans, taro root, jujubes, lotus seeds, and even turnips find their way stuffed into dumplings and put on Asian dessert and dim sum menus.

When we came up with these desserts, we looked to update some traditional Asian desserts and add an Asian twist to some Western favorites. And some, like the Wapples, are off the cuff. Annie just started doing these one day, wrapping bits of fruit in wonton wrappers and rewarding us with these delicious little treats. Once you've tried one, we'll bet you can't eat just one.

The Least You Need to Know

- Fruit is most often the dessert of choice after a meal in Asia.
- Many Asian desserts are rice- or nut-based and are generally not as sweet as what Westerners are used to.
- Many New Asian desserts have their roots firmly planted in the West.

Asian Pear Tart

Prep time: 45 minutes • Chill time: 20 minutes • Cook time: 1 hour • Serves 8

1 cup all-purpose flour	1 tsp. vanilla extract
$^1\!/_2$ tsp. salt	1 tsp. ground cinnamon
$^1\!/_2$ cup solid vegetable shortening	Juice of 1 lemon
3 TB. ice water	2 cups heavy cream
3 large eggs	Nonstick vegetable oil spray
2 TB. brown sugar	4 Asian pears, washed, peeled, and cored
1 tsp. ground nutmeg	

Preheat the oven to 325°F.

Sift flour into a large mixing bowl. Add salt and cut shortening in with a pastry cutter or use your hands. When the mixture looks like lumpy cornmeal, slowly add water, mixing lightly with your hands just until dough holds together. Press dough together, cover the surface with plastic wrap, and rest in the refrigerator for 20 minutes.

While dough is setting, whisk eggs, brown sugar, nutmeg, vanilla extract, and cinnamon together in a medium bowl. Squeeze lemon juice into batter. Whisk ingredients until eggs are completely combined and then whisk in heavy cream.

Dust a cutting board and rolling pin with flour. Remove dough from the refrigerator. Push down on dough with your hands until flattened like a thick pancake. Place the rolling pin in center of dough and roll outward. Turn dough a quarter turn every couple rolls until dough is $^1\!/_8$-inch thick.

Take a fluted tart pan and spray with vegetable spray on the bottom to prevent sticking. Lay dough inside the pan and gently press sides into fluted sides, making sure there are no air pockets. Scrape off any remaining dough that might hang off the edges.

Slice pears as thinly as possible. Arrange sliced pears on the bottom of tart, overlapping slightly to form overlapping circles. When you have covered the entire surface, pour some of the batter over pears. Repeat if necessary, until all pears and liquid are used.

Bake for 45 minutes. Let tart cool to room temperature for 30 minutes before cutting. Serve at room temperature or chilled.

Chocolate Tempura Bananas

Prep time: 20 minutes • Cook time: 15 minutes • Serves 2

½ cup chocolate chips

1 tsp. granulated sugar

¼ cup heavy cream

½ tsp. unsalted butter

4 bananas

1 cup tempura flour

½ cup ice water

1 to 2 quarts canola oil

1 tsp. powdered sugar

Heat chocolate chips, sugar, heavy cream, and butter in a 1-quart saucepan set over low heat. Stir constantly with a wooden spoon so it doesn't burn. When chocolate has melted and sauce is smooth, turn off heat and let sit on stove.

 Recipes for Success
Make sure the bananas are not fully ripened. If they are too soft, they will not cook properly.

Peel bananas. Mix tempura flour with water. Fill a wok a quarter full with oil and heat to 350°F. Dip bananas into the tempura batter, gently drop in oil, and cook for three minutes. Remove from oil with a slotted spoon and drain on a paper towel.

Place two bananas on each serving plate, sprinkle with powdered sugar, and drizzle with chocolate sauce. Serve hot.

Ginger Crème Brulée

Prep time: 4 hours • Cook time: 25 minutes • Serves 4

1 cup heavy cream

½ vanilla bean

2 TB. + ¼ cup granulated sugar (divided use)

1 egg yolk

2 tsp. candied ginger, a.k.a. crystallized ginger

Preheat the oven to 325°F.

In a 2-quart saucepan, stir heavy cream, vanilla bean, and 1 tablespoon sugar over medium heat. Stir constantly until heavy cream gives off a lot of steam and barely begins to rise in the pan; this is right before the boiling point. Immediately remove from heat.

While the cream is heating, beat 1 tablespoon sugar into egg yolk for about three minutes or until thick and pale lemon yellow in color. Slowly whisk a little hot cream into egg mixture. This is called *tempering*. Add the rest of the cream slowly so egg won't scramble.

Once all hot cream is added to egg, pour mixture back into pot and turn heat to low. Stir custard constantly with a wooden spoon, making sure it doesn't overcook. The custard is ready when it is thick enough to coat the back of a spoon; run your finger over the back of the spoon and if it leaves tracks, it's ready, about four minutes. Whatever you do, don't let the custard boil or it will scramble.

Whisk *candied ginger* into mixture and remove vanilla bean. Split vanilla bean in half, scrape seeds out from skin, and whisk them into the warm custard as well. Pour mixture into oven molds or ovenproof cups and place in a deep baking pan. Fill the baking pan halfway up the sides of the molds with hot water. Cover the baking pan lightly with foil (don't let the foil touch the custard) and pierce it in a couple places with a fork or knife so the steam can escape. Bake for 45 minutes. Remove the molds from the baking pan and let come to room temperature. When cool enough to handle, cover with plastic wrap and chill for three hours.

Preheat the broiler. Evenly sprinkle the surface of each custard with 1 tablespoon granulated sugar, and place them on a cookie sheet. Slide under the broiler until the sugar caramelizes. Watch it carefully; it can burn in the time it takes to sneeze. Serve immediately.

Recipes for Success

If you manage to scramble your custard (you'll know this by little flecks of solidified egg floating in it or by the simple fact that it has boiled), *immediately* pour the custard into a blender and add an ice cube. Blend for one minute and take a peek. If the custard isn't too far gone, it will reliquefy like magic.

Orient Expressions

Candied ginger (or crystallized ginger) is fresh peeled ginger that has been preserved in sugar syrup and rolled in sugar.

Ruby Crisp

Prep time: 20 minutes • Cook time: 20 minutes • Serves 2

1 cup sugar

9¹/₂ cups water

1 cup canned coconut milk

1 tsp. red food coloring

2 cups diced canned water chestnuts, drained

¹/₂ cup tapioca flour

1 cup crushed ice

Stir sugar and 1 cup water together in a 1-quart saucepan over high heat until liquid reduces by half in volume. Remove from heat. Stir in coconut milk and set aside to cool.

Combine ¹/₂ cup water with food coloring and add water chestnuts. Bring to a boil and cook for two minutes. Drain chestnuts and dredge them in tapioca flour with a large slotted spoon. Shake off any excess flour.

Bring a 3-quart saucepan with 6 cups water to a boil, add chestnuts, and cook for four minutes. Remove chestnuts and drop them into 2 cups cold water to stop the cooking. Place chestnuts in a pretty glass bowl that will hold about 6 cups. Pour coconut syrup over them. Top with crushed ice and serve immediately.

Thai Taro Custard

Prep time: 20 minutes • Cook time: 40 minutes • Serves 4

¹/₂ cup peeled and chopped taro root

1 TB. rice flour

1¹/₄ cups canned coconut milk

2 medium eggs

¹/₂ cup palm sugar

¹/₂ tsp. salt

Nonstick vegetable oil spray

Preheat oven to 350°F.

Place taro root into a food processor fitted with a metal blade and process until ground as finely as possible.

Orient Expressions
Palm sugar is the sugar made of the coconut palm. It's golden brown in color and has a distinctive flavor.

In a 2-quart saucepan, heat taro root, rice flour, and coconut milk over low heat. Raise the heat to medium and whisk in eggs, *palm sugar*, and salt until thick, about four minutes.

Spray a square 8 × 8-inch baking pan with vegetable spray and pour batter in. Bake for 35 minutes. Remove from oven and cool to room temperature. Cut into squares and serve cold or at room temperature.

Wapples

Prep time: 40 minutes • Cook time: 15 minutes • Serves 2

2 TB. unsalted butter

1 Fuji apple, peeled, cored, and diced

$^{1}/_{2}$ tsp. vanilla extract

1 TB. brown sugar

1 tsp. ground cinnamon

1 to 2 quarts canola oil

15 wonton wrappers

1 TB. powdered sugar

1 TB. cocoa powder

Heat a 1-quart saucepan over medium heat and add butter and apple. Stir to melt butter and stir in vanilla extract, brown sugar, and cinnamon. Bring to a boil, lower heat, and simmer for 10 minutes. Remove from heat and cool for 15 minutes.

Heat a wok over high heat, fill with oil a quarter of the way up the sides, and heat to 350°F. Place a teaspoon of apple mixture in center of a wonton wrapper. Moisten ends of wrapper with water. Bring all ends of wrapper together and pinch closed, sealing in apple filling. Fry wontons in small batches for about 45 seconds or until golden brown. Press down lightly on the wontons to make sure they are submerged in the oil. Drain on paper towels.

Arrange on a platter or individual plates, and sprinkle powdered sugar and cocoa powder on top of wapples. Serve hot with or without ice cream.

Chapter 17

Bodacious Asian Beverages

In This Chapter

- Sake: the divine drink of Japan
- Beer and wine will do just fine
- Cocktails with an Asian twist
- Coffee and tea made cold or hot

New Asian food is a willing partner to drinks of many persuasions, from traditional sippers like sake and tea to modern pairings of wine and food. And of course, don't forget a six-pack of zesty Asian beer that's a sure hit with many a hot dish.

The Sake Primer

Called the drink of the gods in Japan, sake at its most basic is a fermented rice beverage. But at its divine best it's one of the world's great drinks and an excellent partner for many Asian dishes.

Back in the stone ages, say the 1980s, we rarely saw anything in the United States but low-end sakes, the type served warm at Japanese restaurants. Now there are hundreds of brands available here. The best are served not heated to death but refreshingly chilled or over ice.

Although we think of sake as "rice wine," the brewing method is closer to the way beer is made. Special strains of sake rice are polished to remove 25 to 65 percent of the outer layer of the kernel and get to the little pearl of rice in the middle that's used for making sake. The more the rice is polished, the better the quality, and the higher the cost of the resulting brew.

After polishing, the rice is steamed to a semi-soft consistency. Now comes the multiple parallel fermentation process that sets sake apart from all other fermented beverages. A portion of the steamed rice is set aside and injected with the "koji" mold.

The mold is allowed to work on the steamed rice for a couple of days. After that, part of the koji rice, some steamed rice, yeast, and water are put together to make a starter for the rest of the batch. Over the next couple weeks, the starter, the rest of the steamed rice, and the water are combined in several stages to complete the fermentation. Some sakes have neutral grain alcohol added to them—in tiny amounts as an artistic expression of the sake maker, or in larger amounts to keep costs down. The final step is filtering out any bits of rice left in the sake before bottling.

Unlike some wines, there is virtually no sake made that is intended to be aged. When you buy sake, you want to buy the freshest stuff you can find, which can be a bit tricky. Good quality sake will have a freshness date on it, but deciphering that can be difficult if the date is written using a Japanese-style calendar based on the current emperor's reign. Your best bet is to find a store that carries a lot of sake, stores it away from the sunlight, and has someone on staff who can help you. This might sound like a hassle but it's worth it to get good-quality, fresh sake.

Sake Talkie

Impress your friends and annoy your enemies by casually dropping some of these sake terms.

General Terms

Kura is a brewery.

Toji is the master brewer.

Kanzake sakes are served warm.

Hiyazake sakes are not served warm, but at room temperature or chilled.

-shu is Japanese for wine or wine beverage and is added to the end of sake names.

Basic Sake Brewing Styles

Junmai sake is pure rice sake with no added alcohol.

Honjounceo sake has some added alcohol.

Ginjo sake is made from rice that has been polished to the nth degree and is the most delicate and fragrant of sakes.

Futsu sake is the workhorse of the sake world, with neither added alcohol nor extra special rice used.

Serving Sake

There is no one "correct" way to serve sake. Some are intended to be served warmed (not boiling hot, but warm) and others chilled; the serving temperature is determined by the style and quality of the sake. Generally, less-expensive sakes are served warm and upper-end ones are served chilled.

Fortune Cookies

When serving sake, always serve your guests first, starting with the most honored or eldest guest. And don't forget to offer a hearty toast of "Bonsai" (live 1,000 years) or "Kampei" (to your health) before drinking.

You can serve sake in almost any type of glass and enjoy it, but having your own traditional style vessels is a lot of fun. Serve warm from a *tokkuri*, a narrow-necked, small ceramic flask, and pour into the little ceramic sake cups called *ochoko*, *Guinomi*, or *sakazuki* cups in Japanese.

Traditionally, *masu* cups were little square boxes made from cedar. Because the cedar can add an unwelcome aroma to sake, they aren't used much anymore. However, they are a lot of fun and there are some made now that have a glass liner, or are made from something other than cedar—a different wood, ceramic, or lacquer ware. To serve, put the box on a small saucer and fill to overflowing as a gesture of generosity and hospitality. Drink from a corner of the box, otherwise you'll have sake all over your shirt. And be sure to pour the overflow back into your masu.

Sakes range in flavor from earthy and somewhat sweet to delicate, crisp, and dry. The sweeter styles work well with salty foods; crisp, acidic sakes work well with tempuras and seafood.

Sake Shenanigans

Sticklers for tradition might have a fit at the notion of using sake in a cocktail, but they'll just have to get over it. Obviously, you don't want to use a rare, expensive sake in a cocktail, but there's no reason not to play around with more reasonably priced ones.

Almost any rum or vodka concoction can be made with sake instead, with the added advantage that you've cut the alcohol content of your drink by more than half. In the recipes at the end of the chapter, we give you a few ideas to get you going.

Winning Wine Combos

Tomes have been written about matching food with wine, and when it comes to Asian food, they generally come up with the same idea: The no-brainer matches are Rieslings and gewürztraminers. These are wines that wine geeks describe as being "fruit forward" or "fruit driven" but that normal people think of as slightly sweet, especially when compared to a huge, oaky California chardonnay.

You might also try a sparkling wine with a little sweetness to it, like a Moscato d'Asti or Prosecco from Italy, or one of the many easy-to-drink, slightly sweet sparklers coming out of California.

Rieslings and gewürztraminers are a great place to start, and if you keep in mind that "fruit forward" notion, it will help you on your quest to find other wines that will work with Asian food. And get out of the cabernet, chardonnay, merlot rut—look for chenin blancs; fruity sauvignon blancs; spicy, fresh shiraz, pinot noir; or California's own red zinfandel.

But there's one wine that's usually forgotten, *ume-shu*, Japanese plum wine. Granted, it's not made from grapes, like "real wine," but it is a great match for spicy Asian dishes.

Though shopping for wine should be a lot of fun, uninformed or nonexistent salespeople can turn it into a chore. Find a wine shop where the staff not only understands your request for a "fruit-forward" wine to go with an Asian dish, but also understands that when you say you want to spend about $10 a bottle, they steer you to selections in the $8 to $12 range, not the $15 and up range.

Tea Time

Tea is the beverage of choice throughout much of Asia. It's drunk throughout the day, served in highly ritualized ceremonies, and believed to have great curative effects.

Tea comes from the *camellia sinensis* plant. It's how the leaves of the plant are processed that creates the different styles of tea. There are three basic styles—green, oolong, and black:

◆ Green tea is the least processed of the teas. Fresh tea leaves are picked, quickly steamed, and then rolled into various shapes, from long wiry bindles to little hand-rolled pellets. Then the tea is fired and dried until almost all the moisture is gone.

◆ Oolong tea is plucked and allowed to wither and ferment for several hours, until the edges begin to turn a ruddy reddish color. Then the tea is fired to stop the fermentation and dried before shipping.

◆ Black tea is laid out to dry until more than half of the moisture has evaporated. Then the leaves are rolled to break up the cell membranes, which starts the fermentation process. The leaves turn from green to red to black. Then the rolled leaves are fired to stop any further fermentation and the tea leaves are ready to ship.

Fortune Cookies

The phrase "orange pekoe" shows up on many teas, but it doesn't mean there's orange in the tea, nor does it tell you whether the tea is any good. The phrase refers to the size of the tea leaf used in the tea. The word *pekoe* comes from the Chinese for "white hair" and refers to the white down on the undersides and tips of tea leaves that is said to give tea its flavor. Orange pekoe is a size thing, not a quality thing.

To make a good cup of tea, the most important ingredient is water—pure, fresh, clean water. Even the best tea will taste like dirt if you don't use good water. If your tap water is tasty, use it. If not, filter tap water or buy bottled water for making tea.

Fill your teapot and cups with hot tap water, letting them warm while you put the kettle on.

Bring fresh water in the kettle to a boil.

Empty the tap water from the warmed teapot and cups. Add one ounce of tea per six ounces water to your teapot and add water from the kettle. Allow the tea to steep for about five minutes to allow the tea to release its aromas and flavors.

For black tea and oolong teas, you can pour boiling water directly into the teapot. For green tea, let the water cool down a bit before pouring into the teapot.

Chai

Chai isn't some obscure martial art. It's a style of tea-drinking created in India several centuries ago. Black tea is blended with milk and a variety of spices, milk, and sugar

Orient Expressions
Chai is the Hindi word for "tea." In the West we've gotten into the habit of referring to it as chai tea, which makes it a bit silly—you're asking for "tea tea, please."

or honey and served hot. Of course, now that it's gotten so popular in the rest of the world, iced, decaf, low fat, or fake sugar versions abound.

You can make chai from scratch or buy a chai masala, pre-mixed spice packs. Making chai from scratch takes a little time and effort but is well worth it. In the recipes that follow we offer a basic recipe and preparation method for brewing one cup of tea. Feel free to adjust the spice amounts to your tastes.

Beer

In the Asian timeline, beer is a relatively new addition, not having shown up until the colonial times of the 1800s. But like the chili pepper before it, once it got there, there was no stopping it. Especially when people realized that it was an awesome accompaniment to spicy and fried foods.

Today, there are hundreds of breweries throughout the countries of Asia. You'll find Asian beers almost anywhere that you can buy an assortment of beers from around the world. There are some black beers made, but most Asian beers are lightly malted, easy to drink, refreshing beers that are enjoyed by anyone who likes beer.

The Cocktail Hour

You'll have a lot of fun with our new Asian-inspired cocktails. Feel free to stick with cocktails throughout dinner—most new Asian dishes will hold up just fine when paired with spirits.

Booze-Free Beauties

Cruising the beverage aisle of an Asian supermarket is an adventure you don't want to miss. You'll find dozens of premixed iced coffees and teas, sodas, and juices from every fruit imaginable and, best of all, "bubble tea."

Bubble teas are a relatively new addition to the Asian drink market. First appearing in the early 1980s in Taiwan, bubble teas are made by combining fruits and flavoring syrups with tea, then shaking them vigorously to mix, which forms a foam or "bubbles" on the top of the drink. The grooviest of them all have little pearls of tapioca that drift through the drink when shaken and then pop in your mouth when drunk.

Thai Iced Coffee and Thai Iced Tea are deceptively simple, but very addicting, concoctions of either a spiced Thai powdered coffee, called oliang, or spiced Thai tea and condensed milk and sugar. If you can't find oliang, substitute espresso or a strong French roast coffee. For Thai tea you can substitute strongly brewed black tea.

Here's a basic recipe: Brew oliang or Thai tea as you would any other coffee or tea, and adjust sugar and milk to taste.

Lassi

Yogurt lovers might well fancy a glass of lassi, a yogurt drink that's very popular in India. Commercial brands are available at most Middle Eastern, Indian, or Pakistani markets. Lassi is made by combining yogurt and water with sugar and depending on whether you want a sweet or spicy version, a variety of spices such as nutmeg, cayenne, and cumin.

The Least You Need to Know

- Sake (Japanese rice wine), served warm or chilled, will go with almost any new Asian dish.
- Experiment with the incredible array of canned coffees, teas, and sodas at Asian markets.
- Think "fruit forward" when looking for wine matches.
- Beer is a favored beverage throughout Asia and is a great match for spicy and fried foods.

Saketini

3 oz. sake

$^{1}/_{2}$ to 1 oz. bianco vermouth

Wheel of peeled cucumber

Combine sake and vermouth in cocktail shaker with ice; shake and strain into a chilled martini glass. Garnish with cucumber wheel. Bianco vermouth is a white vermouth, but is not as dry as regular white/dry vermouth. Use white/dry vermouth if you can't find the bianco.

Sakerita

$1^{1}/_{2}$ oz. fresh lime juice

$1^{1}/_{2}$ oz. orange liqueur

3 oz. sake

Lime wedge

Pour lime juice, orange liqueur, and sake over ice in a tall glass, stir, and garnish with lime wedge.

Sakepolitan

$1^{1}/_{2}$ oz. sake

$^{1}/_{2}$ oz. orange liqueur

1 oz. cranberry juice

$^{1}/_{2}$ oz. lime juice

Combine sake, orange liqueur, and cranberry and lime juices in a cocktail shaker with ice; shake and strain into a chilled martini glass.

Sake Bomb

1 shot glass filled with sake (This is the bomb.)

1 mug beer, not quite full

Drop sake bomb in beer and chug.

Chai Tea

1 pod cardamom

1 tsp. grated fresh ginger

$^1/_8$ tsp. whole black peppercorns

1-inch section cinnamon stick

1 whole clove

1 tsp. loose or 1 tea bag black tea (Don't use green or leaf tea; it won't work!)

$^1/_2$ cup water

$^1/_2$ cup half-and-half or whole cream

Sugar or honey to taste

Coarsely crush all the spices together.

Heat cardamom, ginger, peppercorns, cinnamon, clove, tea, water, and half-and-half in a pan and bring almost to a boil; the mixture will start to foam. Reduce the heat and simmer for 10 to 15 minutes, stirring constantly.

Strain and serve. Add sugar or honey to taste.

Jade Martini

$^3/_4$ oz. vodka

1 oz. Apple Pucker apple liqueur

$^1/_2$ oz. Cointreau

Splash sweet-and-sour mix

Cherry for garnish

In a shaker with ice, combine vodka, Apple Pucker, Cointreau, and sweet-and-sour; shake; and strain into chilled martini glass. Garnish with a cherry.

Leap Year

1 oz. Absolut Citron

$^1/_2$ oz. Grand Marnier

$^1/_2$ oz. sweet vermouth

Splash sweet-and-sour mix

Pour vodka, Grand Marnier, and sweet vermouth in a shaker with ice and sweet-and-sour; strain into chilled martini glass.

Tiger's Milk

1¹/₂ oz. Absolut Mandarin

¹/₂ oz. Cointreau

¹/₂ oz. canned coconut milk

¹/₂ oz. orange juice

¹/₂ oz. pineapple juice

¹/₂ oz. heavy cream

Cherry for garnish

Pour vodka, Cointreau, coconut milk, orange and oineapple juices, and cream in a shaker with ice; strain into a glass with ice. Garnish with a cherry and serve with a black straw.

White China

1¹/₂ oz. vodka

1 oz. Bailey's Irish Cream

¹/₂ oz. white cream de cacao

Pour vodka, Irish cream, and cream de cacao in a shaker with ice; strain into chilled martini glass.

Liberty Mai Tai

1 oz. Captain Morgan's Spiced Rum

¹/₂ oz. light rum

¹/₂ oz. triple sec

¹/₂ oz. orange juice

¹/₂ oz. pineapple juice

Splash grenadine

Lemon, lime, and cherry for garnish

Combine spiced and light rums, triple sec, orange and pineapple juices, and grenadine over ice in a shaker, shake to mix, and strain into a tall glass filled with ice. Garnish with lemon, lime, and cherry.

Tokyo Tea

$^{1}/_{2}$ oz. vodka

$^{1}/_{2}$ oz. gin

$^{1}/_{2}$ oz. light rum

$^{1}/_{2}$ oz. silver tequila

$^{1}/_{2}$ oz. Razzmatazz raspberry liqueur

Splash Sprite

Lemon wedge

Combine vodka, gin, rum, tequila, raspberry liqueur, and Sprite on the rocks in a tall glass, garnish with lemon.

Blue Champagne

Granulated sugar

1 oz. vodka

1 oz. Blue Curacao

1 oz. champagne

Dash lime juice

Pour sugar into a shallow bowl. Wet the rim of the glass and dip it in sugar to coat. Pour vodka, Blue Curacao, and champagne in a shaker with ice and lime juice; strain into chilled and sugared martini glass.

Thai Iced Tea/Coffee

4 oz. brewed coffee or tea

$^{1}/_{2}$ TB. granulated sugar

1 oz. sweetened condensed milk

Pour coffee over ice in a tall glass, add sugar and condensed milk, and stir.

When serving to guests, float the condensed milk on top of the coffee or tea. It will make lovely swirls as it falls to the bottom of the glass, but be sure your guests give their glass a stir before drinking.

Part 4

Special Needs

It seems as though almost everyone is on some sort of diet these days. But with a little thought, you can adapt Asian food for everyone from very veggie vegans to massive meat-eating low-carb buffs. We'll look at some strategies for dealing with them all in the following chapters. And we'll take a look at adapting to fiery Asian peppers.

Chapter 18

For the Love of Veggies

In This Chapter

- ◆ Vegans—the total veg
- ◆ Lacto-ovo–style vegetarians
- ◆ The "mostly" vegetarian
- ◆ Some great vegetarian recipes

Although vegetarianism is now widely accepted as a healthful and for some, moral, way to live, in this country and in much of the West, until about 30 years ago, the practice of eating no meat was looked on as, well, eccentric. In Asia, however, vegetarianism has been a standard way of life for as long as anybody can remember. Buddhists abstain from meat for several days each month. Brahmins, the highest Hindu cast, as well as the Jains, eat no meat or animal byproducts. (And then there are those who abstain from certain kinds meat: Muslims and Jews eat no pork, while Hindus do not eat beef.) Finally, some in Asia go meatless because they can't afford it.

But most Asians who consider themselves vegetarians eat plenty of dairy products and/or eggs. The continent's cooks have, as a result, come up with countless delicious meatless cooking techniques and recipes. And so have we.

There's a great divide in the world of vegetarianism when it comes to the use of dairy products and eggs.

On one hand we've got *vegans*, those who eat no meat, fish, fowl, or animal by-product whatsoever. Then we've got the "lacto-ovo" vegetarians, who use both eggs and dairy in their cooking. Within that group are some who use dairy products but not eggs. And then there's that middle ground of people who eat what swims but not what walks.

Whether you're a vegan or vegetarian, or just cooking for one, here are some general guidelines for adapting many of the recipes in this book:

- Replace fish sauce and oyster sauce with soy sauce.
- Use tofu, tempeh, or mushrooms in place of meat, fowl, and fish products.
- Carefully check labels of any packaged food you buy. Gelatin, milk powders, meat stocks and flavorings, whey protein, and other animal products show up in all kinds of strange places. If you're still not sure if something is completely animal free, look for ones labeled meat and dairy free.
- Veganism and vegetarianism usually go hand in hand with avoiding artificial colorings and flavorings and preservatives. Again, carefully check labels of packaged foods. If you can't make it fresh, your best bet is buying sauces, condiments, and noodles in stores that cater to vegetarians rather than at Asian markets.

Whether you've chosen vegetarianism for your lifestyle or are just in a no-meat mood, these recipes will come in handy. Cooking these vegetarian recipes requires no special equipment or cooking techniques that you haven't already learned in this book.

The Least You Need to Know

- Vegans eat nothing with eyes, except potatoes.
- Some vegetarians eat dairy and/or eggs.
- Read food labels to make sure no animal products have crept into the vegetable patch.

Chow Thai Tofu

Prep time: 20 minutes • Cook time: 15 minutes • Serves 2

3 cups to 1 quart canola oil for frying

6 oz. firm tofu, cut into 1-inch cubes

1 large egg, beaten

1 tsp. chopped fresh garlic

2 cups fresh chow fun noodles, cut into 1-inch strips

3 TB. fish sauce

$^1/_2$ cup wet tamarind

2 TB. white vinegar

2 TB. granulated sugar

2 tsp. paprika

$^1/_4$ cup bean sprouts

$^1/_4$ cup shredded red cabbage

2 TB. crushed unsalted peanuts

Heat a wok over high heat. Add oil to fill it about a quarter full. Heat to 375°F. Fry tofu until golden brown, about three minutes. Remove tofu and blot with a paper towel to remove excess oil.

Pour off all but 2 tablespoons oil, add egg and garlic, and stir-fry for one minute. Add chow fun noodles and stir-fry until egg is firm, about one minute. Add tofu, fish sauce, tamarind, vinegar, sugar, and paprika. Toss together, add bean sprouts, cabbage, and peanuts, stir-frying for one minute more.

Remove from the heat and ladle onto two warmed serving plates. Serve hot.

Grilled Tofu Steaks

Prep time: 10 minutes • Marination time: 10 minutes • Cook time: 8 minutes • Serves 2

1 tsp. soy sauce

1 tsp. sweet soy sauce

$^1/_2$ tsp. honey

1 tsp. chopped cilantro

$^1/_2$ tsp. minced fresh garlic

$^1/_2$ tsp. freshly ground black pepper

1 pound firm tofu, cut lengthwise into 4 (1-inch thick) slices

Whisk soy sauce, sweet soy sauce, honey, cilantro, garlic, and black pepper together in a small, nonreactive bowl. Add the tofu and turn to coat. Refrigerate for 10 minutes.

Heat a grill to medium heat and grill tofu steaks for three minutes on each side. When turning tofu, be careful not to tear it as it is very fragile.

Serve hot with vegetables and steamed rice.

Sesame Noodles with Bean Sprouts

Prep time: 25 minutes • Cook time: 10 minutes • Serves 2

2 cups chantaboun rice sticks

3 TB. sesame oil (divided use)

1 tsp. minced fresh garlic

1 cup bean sprouts

¼ cup julienned carrot

½ cup chicken stock

1 TB. soy sauce

1 TB. fish sauce

½ tsp. red chili powder

2 tsp. chopped cilantro leaves

2 TB. sliced green onions

1 TB. toasted sesame seeds

Presoak rice sticks in water and cover for 20 minutes. Drain and set aside.

Heat a wok over high heat and add 2 tablespoons oil. When oil is smoking, add garlic and stir-fry for about 30 seconds. Add noodles, bean sprouts, and carrots, stir-frying for two minutes. Add chicken stock, soy sauce, fish sauce, and chili powder and continue to stir-fry for two more minutes.

Remove from heat, add remaining 1 tablespoon sesame oil, cilantro, and green onion, and toss.

Divide between two warm plates or bowls and sprinkle with sesame seeds. Serve hot.

Veggie Soba

Prep time: 20 minutes • Cook time: 12 minutes • Serves 2

8 oz. raw soba noodles	$1/4$ cup shredded red cabbage
$1/3$ cup peanut sauce	$1/4$ cup shredded green cabbage
1 TB. sesame oil	$1/4$ cup julienned carrot
$1/4$ tsp. salt	$1/4$ cup julienned yellow squash
2 cups canola oil	$1/4$ cup julienned seeded cucumber
4-oz. piece firm tofu	1 TB. chopped unsalted peanuts

Bring a 3-quart saucepan of water to a boil. Add soba noodles and boil for three to five minutes, or until they are fully cooked but not mushy.

In a large bowl, whisk together $1/4$ cup peanut sauce, sesame oil, and salt. Drain noodles, add to the bowl, and toss well with the sauce using a couple forks or your hands.

Preheat canola oil in a 2-quart pot to 350°F. Carefully place the tofu into the pot and fry until crisp on the outside, about three to four minutes or until it is golden brown. Remove from oil and briefly drain on paper towels. Cut tofu into $1/2$-inch strips.

Divide noodles between two bowls or plates. Place tofu on top of noodles and surround with little piles of red cabbage, green cabbage, carrots, squash, and cucumbers. Drizzle with remaining peanut sauce and sprinkle with chopped peanuts.

Recipes for Success

Simple recipes are the best. So now you've got a recipe that tastes great, is easy to make, and doesn't break the bank. What next? Well, kick it up a notch on the scale of perfection by creating contrasts in texture and temperature as in this recipe. The vegetables are cold and crisp and the noodles are warm and soft.

Chapter 19

Low-Fat Dishes

In This Chapter

- ◆ Cutting fat
- ◆ Keeping flavor
- ◆ Some great low-fat Asian recipes

Part of the appeal of Asian food is that most of it is fairly low in fat to begin with, falling well within the U.S. Department of Agriculture recommendation that fats make up less than 30 percent of your daily caloric intake.

But if you're on a low-fat diet, whether under doctor's orders or because you're seriously thinking about wearing that thong bikini somewhere besides the shower, most recipes in this book fall into the "easily adaptable to a low-fat diet" category. Use these tips to reduce fat even further:

Understand that fat plays a definite role in the way food tastes. There's a different chemical reaction when food is cooked in fat than when it is cooked in water or broth. But the great thing about cooking Asian-style low-fat food is that there are so many bold flavors—hot, piquant, salty and sweet—that mingle in Asian food, that you'll never feel deprived.

- ◆ Choose the leanest cuts of beef and pork.
- ◆ Remove the skin from chicken and duck.

- Replace meat or poultry with low-fat fish, such as red snapper, sea bass, trout, orange roughy, and sole.
- Use reduced-fat tofu.
- Substitute no-fat vegetable, chicken, or beef broth for all or part of the oil in a recipe.
- Use nonstick cooking sprays for stir-fry.
- Don't cook recipes that call for coconut milk. There is no real substitute for this ingredient as a lot of the flavor comes from fat.
- Even in tiny amounts, toasted sesame oil adds a lot of flavor.
- Sorry, but just forget deep-frying. Or save up your fat grams for an end-of-the-month splurge.

These recipes will help you trim the fat from meals without trimming the flavor. We've called in our own health and fitness expert Larry North, owner of Larry North Fitness, for a couple recipes. With Larry's great ideas for tasty and nutritious recipes, it will be hard to convince your guests that dinner is a low-fat extravaganza.

The Least You Need to Know

- Just say no to the deep-fryer.
- Get lean by buying lean.
- Use nonstick cooking sprays for stir-fry.

Ginger-Cilantro Grilled Chicken

Prep time: 10 minutes • Marination time: 20 minutes • Cook time: 15 minutes • Serves 2

1 TB. sesame oil

1 TB. oyster sauce

1 tsp. minced fresh garlic

1 TB. finely chopped fresh ginger

1 TB. chopped fresh cilantro

$^1/_2$ tsp. granulated sugar

1 lb. skinless, boneless chicken breasts

Vegetables of your choice and steamed rice for serving

Whisk sesame oil, oyster sauce, garlic, ginger, cilantro, and sugar together in a small bowl. Coat chicken with marinade. Cover and refrigerate for 20 minutes.

Heat the grill to medium heat and grill chicken for about six minutes on each side or until cooked through. To make sure chicken is fully cooked, cut a small incision in thickest part of breast. If the meat is white, it's ready. Serve with vegetables and steamed rice.

Grilled Tuna with Cucumber Chutney Noodle Salad

Prep time: 30 minutes • Cook time: 15 minutes • Serves 2

$^1/_4$ cup rice vinegar

1 TB. granulated sugar

$^1/_2$ tsp. wasabi paste

$^1/_4$ cup diced roma tomato

$^1/_2$ cucumber, sliced

1 tsp. salt (divided use)

2 tsp. sesame oil (divided use)

1 cup soba noodles

1 (8-oz.) tuna fillet, cut in half

$^1/_2$ tsp. freshly ground black pepper

2 tsp. toasted sesame seeds

Mix vinegar, sugar, and wasabi paste together in a medium-size bowl. Add tomato, cucumber, half the salt, and half the oil.

Cook noodles in 1 quart boiling water for six minutes and drain. Rinse under cold water to chill. Toss noodles with cucumber chutney. Cover and refrigerate.

Heat the grill to medium. While the grill is heating, season tuna by rubbing with remaining oil, salt, and pepper. Grill tuna for three minutes on each side.

Divide soba noodle salad between two serving plates and place tuna on top. Sprinkle with sesame seeds. Serve while tuna is hot.

Sake-Poached Salmon

Prep time: 20 minutes • Cook time: 20 minutes • Serves 2

$^1\!/_2$ bunch asparagus, woody stem removed and bottom part trimmed with a vegetable peeler

1 (10-oz.) salmon fillet cut in half

$^1\!/_4$ cup sake

$^1\!/_2$ cup fish stock

1 TB. fish sauce

1 tsp. pickled ginger

$^1\!/_2$ tsp. freshly ground black pepper

Place asparagus into a sauté pan and put salmon on top of asparagus.

Mix sake, fish stock, fish sauce, ginger, and black pepper in a small bowl and pour into the pan. Turn heat up to high and bring to a boil. When sauce boils, lower heat to simmer and cover.

Simmer salmon for eight minutes and remove from heat. Using a spatula, lift asparagus and salmon from the pan and place each fillet on a warm serving plate. Pour sauce over salmon and asparagus and serve hot.

Steamed Snapper in Banana Leaf

Prep time: 25 minutes • Cook time: 25 minutes • Serves 2

1 (10-oz.) Pacific red snapper fillet, cut in half

2 (8 × 10-inch) pieces banana leaf

¹/₄ cup sliced mushroom

¹/₄ cup julienne of carrot

¹/₄ cup sliced green onion

¹/₄ cup julienned red bell pepper

Juice of 1 lemon

1 TB. fish sauce

1 tsp. sesame oil

1 tsp. pickled ginger

¹/₂ tsp. minced fresh garlic

¹/₂ tsp. red chili powder

Steamed rice for serving

Place a half-fillet in center of each banana leaf.

Toss mushroom, carrot, green onion, and red bell pepper with lemon juice, fish sauce, sesame oil, pickled ginger, garlic, and chili powder. Spoon over snapper and wrap leaf around fish like an envelope. Secure with toothpicks. Set aside.

Place the steamer over a pot filled with water and bring to a boil. Place fish bundles into the steamer and cover. Steam for 12 to 14 minutes or until fish is cooked through. Take a peek by poking a hole in an inconspicuous spot of the package. If fish is white and flaky, it's done.

Recipes for Success

Sesame oil can contribute a great deal to the flavor of a dish. Keep the amount small and your body will barely feel the effect of the fat content.

Place each package on a warm serving plate, remove the toothpicks, and peel it open. Trim banana leaf if it's too big for the plate. Serve hot with some steamed rice placed on leaf.

Larry North's Thai Cucumber Salad

Prep time: 12 minutes • Cook time: 7 minutes • Chill time: 1 hour • Serves 2

1 Japanese or seedless cucumber, thinly sliced

1 cup boiling water

1/4 cup + 1 TB. granulated sugar

1/2 cup white vinegar

1 tsp. salt

1/2 tsp. red chili paste or 3 fresh red chilies, seeded and chopped

3 shallots, sliced or 1/4 red onion, thinly sliced

6 to 8 sprigs cilantro

Place cucumber into a small stainless-steel or glass bowl.

Pour boiling water into a heatproof bowl and stir in sugar until it's dissolved. Stir in white vinegar and salt. If you are using red chili paste, stir it in now. Pour over cucumbers while still hot.

Sprinkle cucumbers with shallots. If you are using chili peppers, sprinkle them on now. Cover and refrigerate for at least one hour. When ready to serve, garnish with cilantro. Serve cold.

Recipes for Success _____

This salad is a great hunger-pang quencher. You'll find yourself making it often. There are a lot of preservatives at work in this recipe, so it will keep for about five days in the refrigerator.

Larry North's Khal Bi

Prep time: 10 minutes • Marination time: 4 hours to overnight • Cook time: 40 minutes • Serves 4

¹/₄ cup soy sauce

1 TB. honey

1 TB. brown sugar

1 TB. minced fresh garlic

1 tsp. minced fresh ginger

¹/₄ tsp. freshly ground black pepper

2 lb. pork tenderloin (or boneless, skinless chicken breasts)

Combine soy sauce, honey, brown sugar, garlic, ginger, and black pepper in a plastic bag. Add pork and squeeze out as much air as possible as you seal the bag. Marinate at least four hours; preferably overnight.

When ready to cook, preheat the oven to 375°F. Remove pork from the bag and discard bag and marinade. Place pork into a shallow roasting pan. Bake uncovered for 25 minutes for pork or 20 minutes if you are using chicken breasts. Slice and serve warm.

Larry North's Spicy Shrimp Soup

Prep time: 20 minutes • Cook time: 15 minutes • Serves 2

4 cups water

1 stalk fresh lemongrass, peeled to the soft core and sliced

1 (8-oz.) can straw mushrooms, drained

¹/₂ lb. shrimp (16 to 20 count), peeled and deveined

1 to 2 TB. fish sauce

¹/₄ cup fresh lime juice

2 fresh tomatoes, seeded and diced

2 TB. sliced green onion

1 TB. chopped cilantro

1 to 4 red chili peppers, seeded and chopped (or ¹/₂ tsp. red chili paste)

Bring water to a boil in a 2-quart saucepan and add lemongrass and straw mushrooms. Reduce heat to medium low. Add shrimp and cook about three minutes. Stir in fish sauce, lime juice, and tomatoes and cook until heated through. Add green onions, cilantro, and red chili peppers or paste. If you are using red chili paste, stir to dissolve into soup.

Remove from heat and ladle into warm soup bowls.

Chapter 20

Low-Carb Dishes

In This Chapter

- ◆ Noodles and rice are not always nice
- ◆ If it walks or swims, go for it
- ◆ Some great low-carb Asian dishes

Noodles and rice play such a large part in Asian cooking that it's a little harder to adapt Asian food to a low-carbohydrate diet than it is a low-fat diet. Here are a few tips to help you on your quest to lower your intake of carbohydrates:

- ◆ Cut rice and noodle servings in half.
- ◆ Sashimi—it's the ultimate low-carb food.
- ◆ Use substantial or "meaty" vegetables such as green beans or portobello mushrooms for a filling and delicious alternative.
- ◆ Concentrate on grilled, roasted, baked, and steamed seafood, and meat and poultry dishes that don't rely on lots of noodles and rice. Think satay from Thailand or bulgogi from Korea.
- ◆ Use spaghetti squash "noodles" or long beans in place of regular noodles.

♦ Bulk up the meal with low-carb veggies like watercress, spinach, bok choy, asparagus, or bamboo shoots.

Fortune Cookies _____
Although Asian food often relies on rice and noodles as the filler for every meal, there are plenty of meat-heavy dishes, like bulgogi and satay, that are low-carb all-meat dishes.

♦ Careful with the sauces—many contain hidden carbs, such as sugar.

Science hasn't yet given a definitive answer on the benefits of any type of diet, but if you've chosen a low-carb, high-fat diet these recipes will be right up your alley. So while some of your friends are eagerly consuming the low-fat meals in the last chapter, you can munch on these tasty low-carb dishes.

The Least You Need to Know

♦ Cut rice and noodle servings in half.
♦ Read labels to check for hidden carbs.
♦ Look for recipes that aren't all about rice and noodles.

Baked Chicken Breast with Braised Bok Choy

Prep time: 20 minutes • Cook time: 25 minutes • Serves 2

2 (6-oz.) skinless, boneless chicken breasts

Salt and freshly ground black pepper

$\frac{1}{2}$ cup chicken stock

$\frac{1}{4}$ cup rice vinegar

1 tsp. fish sauce

1 tsp. brown sugar

1 tsp. canola oil

1 tsp. minced fresh garlic

$\frac{1}{4}$ cup thinly sliced red onion

1 cup bok choy, chopped into large pieces

Preheat the oven to 350°F.

Season chicken with salt and pepper.

Whisk together chicken stock, rice vinegar, fish sauce, and brown sugar in a small bowl. Reserve.

Heat a medium-size ovenproof sauté pan over medium heat and add oil. When oil is smoking, sear chicken breasts for two minutes on each side and remove from the pan. Keep warm.

Add garlic, onion, and bok choy to the sauté pan and sauté for two minutes. Place chicken on top of bok choy and add reserved chicken stock mixture to the pan. Place the pan in the oven and bake for 15 to 18 minutes or until chicken is cooked through.

To serve, mound bok choy on each serving plate and top with chicken. Ladle cooking liquid over chicken and serve.

Grilled Swordfish and Asparagus

Prep time: 30 minutes • Cook time: 20 minutes • Serves 2

$\frac{1}{2}$ bunch asparagus (about 12 to 16 stalks)	1 kaffir lime leaf
$\frac{1}{2}$ tsp. salt	1 TB. cold water
$\frac{1}{4}$ cup canned coconut milk	$\frac{1}{4}$ tsp. tapioca starch
1 tsp. red curry paste	1 (12-oz.) swordfish steak, cut in half
1 tsp. fish sauce	Salt and freshly ground black pepper to taste
$\frac{1}{4}$ tsp. granulated sugar	2 tsp. canola oil (divided use)
2 TB. fresh lime juice	

Trim asparagus by peeling bottom third of each stalk with a vegetable peeler.

Fill the wok halfway with water and bring to a boil over high heat. Lightly salt water and add asparagus. Boil uncovered for three minutes. Drain asparagus and cool.

Place a small saucepan over medium heat and add coconut milk, red curry paste, fish sauce, sugar, lime juice, and lime leaf. Whisk to combine and bring to a boil.

Meanwhile, mix water and tapioca starch together with a fork in a separate small bowl. Add this mixture to the saucepan and bring to a boil, stirring constantly. Remove from heat as soon as it comes to a boil.

Heat the grill to medium-high. While the grill is heating, rub swordfish with a little salt and pepper and 1 teaspoon oil. Place swordfish on the grill and cook for four minutes on each side.

While fish is cooking, sprinkle asparagus with remaining oil, place on the grill, and cook for about four minutes, turning as they brown.

Arrange fish and asparagus on each serving plate, spoon sauce over the top, and serve.

Poached Salmon with Asian Basil Sauce

Prep time: 15 minutes • Cook time: 20 minutes • Serves 2

1 cup chicken stock

1 TB. fish sauce

1 tsp. minced shallots

$^1/_2$ tsp. minced fresh garlic

$^1/_2$ tsp. freshly ground black pepper

2 TB. thinly sliced Asian basil

1 cup Chinese broccoli

2 (6-oz.) salmon fillets

$^1/_4$ cup sake

$^1/_4$ cup heavy cream or canned coconut milk

1 tsp. unsalted butter, room temperature

Combine chicken stock, fish sauce, shallots, garlic, black pepper, and basil in an 8-inch frying pan.

Place Chinese broccoli into pan and place salmon on top. Bring to a boil, lower heat to a simmer, cover, and simmer for 10 minutes. Remove fish and broccoli from liquid and keep warm.

Whisk in sake and heavy cream, bringing the mixture to a boil again. Remove from heat. Whisk in butter. Divide broccoli between two serving plates and top with the salmon. Ladle warm sauce over fish and serve.

21

Bring on the Heat: For Those Who Need the Peppers

In This Chapter

- ◆ Red Hot Mamas
- ◆ Peppering your palate
- ◆ Some spicy recipes

If you've ever bitten into a dish so fiery you thought your ears might start bleeding, then you went back and took another bite, this chapter is for you.

Travelers to Asia always come back with tales of dishes so hot it took them days to get over them. And they aren't joking. We're talking recipes calling for peppers 5, 6, or even 30 times as hot as jalapeños, and then adding fiery chili paste to the mix. Ouch!

To give you an idea of what we're talking about, peppers are measured in Scoville heat units. Jalapeños max out at 5,000 units, while some habaneros measure a blistering 300,000 units.

There are hundreds of varieties of peppers and regional variations on the names of each, so trying to figure out what's what can drive you crazy.

When we call for chili peppers in this book, we're talking bird's-eye chili peppers or Thai red chili peppers, Latin name *capsicum glabiriscum frutescens*—thin, pointed peppers around two inches long, which turn from green to red as they mature. They measure 50,000 to 100,000 Scoville heat units.

Another common Asian pepper is the Japone pepper, *Capsicum frutescens*. They are those deep red little critters that show up in lots of Szechuan dishes. They measure around 25,000 Scoville heat units.

Don't blow off the instructions to deseed peppers before using. Seeds add pure heat and can give a bitter taste to food.

Intensity of store-bought chili pastes can vary by manufacturer, so try a little before you casually toss in the amount called for in a recipe.

> **Lucky Treasures**
> Red hot chili lovers have always sworn that the only way to build up a taste for these little suckers is to keep on eating them. Some research suggests that you're really killing off pain receptors in the mouth by bombarding them with capsicum.

Two key things to remember:

- You can always add more heat to a dish, but there's nothing you can do to cool it down.
- Don't be fooled by an early taste from the pot—the peppers get hotter as they cook.

Go ahead, be a wimp. If you're not ready to ignite your buds, ease off on the quantities of chili peppers called for in these recipes, or forge ahead to the next chapter.

The Least You Need to Know

- Jalapeños are babies compared to Thai red chili peppers.
- Deseeding peppers cuts down on bitterness and heat.
- If you're new to hot peppers, start out easy, using more and hotter peppers as you build your buds.

Pepper in a Pepper

Prep time: 35 minutes • Cook time: 40 minutes • Serves 2

2 large red bell peppers

1 TB. canola oil

1 tsp. minced fresh garlic

1 tsp. chili paste made with soybean oil

4 oz. lean ground beef

1 jalapeño, seeded and minced

1 bird's-eye chili pepper, minced

2 TB. julienned shiitake mushroom caps

$^1/_2$ tsp. Szechuan peppercorn powder

1 TB. soy sauce

$^1/_4$ cup sweet corn kernels, fresh or frozen

1 TB. chopped fresh cilantro

2 TB. tomato ketchup

1 TB. sweet soy sauce

$^1/_2$ cup steamed jasmine rice

Preheat the oven to 350°F.

Rinse and dry bell peppers. Make a horizontal slice about one inch from top of pepper, leaving it whole. Remove seeds and pith with your fingers. Reserve the tops.

Heat a wok over high heat and add oil. When oil is smoking, add garlic, chili paste, and ground beef. Stir-fry for one minute. Add jalapeño, bird's-eye pepper, mushrooms, Szechuan pepper, and soy sauce. Stir-fry for one minute and then add corn, cilantro, ketchup, and sweet soy sauce. Bring to a boil and add rice.

Remove from heat. Stuff mixture into red bell peppers. Fill peppers to top and place tops back on loosely.

Bake for 35 minutes. Serve at once.

Thai Curry Chicken

Prep time: 15 minutes • Cook time: 30 minutes • Serves 2

1 TB. canola oil

1 TB. green curry paste

8 oz. skinless, boneless chicken breasts, thinly sliced

$^{1}/_{2}$ cup chicken stock

2 TB. fish sauce

2 TB. granulated sugar

1 jalapeño pepper, quartered

$^{1}/_{4}$ cup julienned green bell pepper

$^{1}/_{4}$ cup julienned red bell pepper

$^{1}/_{2}$ cup canned bamboo shoots, drained

1 cup canned coconut milk

1 cup steamed jasmine rice

Thai basil sprigs for garnish

Heat a wok over high heat and add oil. When oil is smoking, add curry paste and stir-fry for 30 seconds. Add chicken and mix to coat. Immediately add chicken stock, fish sauce, and sugar and bring to a boil. Add jalapeño, green and red bell peppers, bamboo shoots, and coconut milk. Return to a boil. Cook for three minutes more and remove from heat.

Divide rice between two warm soup bowls and ladle chicken curry mixture over rice. Garnish with basil sprig and serve hot.

Tomsam

Prep time: 20 minutes • Cook time: 15 minutes • Serves 2

5 cups chicken stock	$^1/_4$ cup snow peas
4 kaffir lime leaves	$^1/_4$ cup straw mushrooms
12 oz. shrimp (16 to 20 count), peeled and deveined	2 TB. fish sauce
	2 cups fresh egg noodles
$^1/_2$ stalk fresh lemongrass, trimmed and peeled to the soft core and roughly chopped	1 TB. sliced green onions
	1 TB. chopped fresh cilantro
1 TB. lite soy sauce	$^1/_2$ tsp. freshly ground black pepper
1 TB. red chili powder	
4 TB. fresh lime juice	

Heat a wok over high heat and add chicken stock, lime leaves, shrimp, lemongrass, soy sauce, and chili powder. Bring to a boil and add lime juice, snow peas, straw mushrooms, and fish sauce.

While soup is simmering, cook egg noodles in 2 quarts boiling water for 5 minutes and drain.

Divide noodles between two warm soup bowls; ladle soup over noodles and sprinkle with green onions, cilantro, and black pepper. Serve immediately.

Part **5**

Entertaining

After college, Jeffrey went to New York City to make his mark in the fiercely competitive world of high fashion. He joined Fairchild Publications, publisher of the fashion bible *Women's Wear Daily.* Jet-setting between Los Angeles and New York City and entertaining powerful clients and fashion celebrities meant Yarbrough got firsthand experience in wining, dining, and event-planning for some of the world's most eccentric characters. In this part, he will expose you to some helpful tips for hosting a party and some great theme ideas.

Whether you're planning a major shindig or a cozy get together, using your noodle to plan an Asian-inspired evening is a sure way to spice up your soirée.

22

Cooking for Parties

In This Chapter

- A dash of the East
- A crash course in party planning
- A Chinese New Year party
- Some great party recipes

Whether you're planning a major shindig or a cozy get-together, using your noodle to plan an Asian-inspired evening is a sure way to spice up your soirée.

Asian Chic on the Cheap

You don't have to invest in Ming dynasty vases to add a dash of the east to your party. Asian-style dinnerware, serving pieces, and decorative bits can be found at reasonable prices in Asian supermarkets and restaurant supply stores. Thanks to the popularity of Asian-influenced design in everything from cars to cups, Asian-inspired pieces abound in the kitchen section of department and discount stores.

And remember, this is pan-Asian dining, so don't get hung up on only using the right thing in the right way—mix and match as you see fit. We've come up with some ideas to get you started adding an Asian flair to your party.

- Think outside the box—the bento box, that is. High-gloss, lacquered little boxes with compartments, bento boxes are intended to hold different elements of a Japanese meal. But we use them for a stylish presentation of dipping sauces, nuts, and condiments.

- Smooth, cool, black river rocks immediately conjure up thoughts of a serene Zen garden. Which might be just what you need in the final moments before your guests arrive! Scatter the rocks about the buffet table or use them as chopstick rests. Write on them with a silver metallic pen to make place cards.

- Curled or straight stalks of fresh, luscious green lucky bamboo are an inexpensive way to add a dramatic touch to your house. You'll find ready-made arrangements of curled and straight bamboo sold in Asian markets as well as many flower markets. Short of tossing them down the disposal, even the blackest thumb can't kill these beauties.

- Lacquered chopsticks are far more elegant than plain wood. Buy a couple dozen in various colors and patterns, and let your guests mix and match as they see fit.

Lucky Treasures

Ancient Chinese folklore has it that the number of bamboo stalks you have portends different types of luck. For instance, three stalks is said to bring on happiness, wealth, and longevity, but you'll need seven to guarantee good health.

- Celadon is more than just that luxuriant shade of green somewhere between sea foam and jade. It also refers to a type of pottery with a celadon-colored glaze that first appeared around the fourth century in China. The real stuff will set you back more than a few pennies. Luckily the color celadon is a popular shade of green for dishes, glasses, tea cups, and serving platters whether in an East Asian market or a department store. Celadon accents add an Asian feel to any room.

- It's hip to be square, at least for your plates. Taking a cue from Japanese sushi restaurants, look for footed square plates and platters to mix in with your own stuff.

- Use big, bold banana leaves as place mats, plates, or serving platters, to line large bowls or as a decorative part of your centerpiece. Just don't try to cut a steak on them—you might end up cutting through to the table.

- Inexpensive paper lanterns and paper fans instantly transform even the simplest rooms into a Shanghai salon.

- Traditional Indian and Malaysian textiles make great table linens.

- Send your guests home with a Chinese takeout box full of fortune cookies.

- Rare is the person who makes his or her own potato chips, so don't feel like you have to cook absolutely every morsel your guests will ingest. Check out the snack aisle of the Asian grocery store for spicy wasabi-flavored peas, flavored rice, seaweed crackers, Asian "trail mix," or whatever strikes your fancy.

Recipes for Success

You want your party to be remembered, but not because someone had to go to the hospital.

Food allergies are a problem for many people. Peanuts and shellfish are two of the most common and potentially lethal allergies. They are also two common ingredients in Asian cooking. So it's a good idea to ask your guests when you invite them whether they are allergic to either.

If that's not possible, and to be on the safe side, don't use peanut oil for cooking or in any sauces. If peanuts are used in any dish, serve them on the side in a separate dish.

Scallops, lobsters, prawns, crabs, clams, mussels, crawfish, shrimp, and anything else with a shell are shellfish. If you're cooking for a crowd, have at least one dish that is completely shellfish free.

When to Wok and When to Not

Let's get real here, people—when it comes to party planning, our efforts usually look more like an episode of *I Love Lucy* than *Dinner at Eight.* But so what? Entertaining is about being with your friends, not driving yourself insane trying to make everything perfect.

Planning a new Asian party is not much different from planning any other party, so let's do a crash course in basic party planning and then move on to specifics for new Asian parties.

- Realistically assess your abilities and your kitchen's. If you have the patience to carve four dozen radish roses, go right ahead. If not, just keep it simple, fresh, and lively.

- Prepare as much food as possible in advance. It's no fun if you're stuck in the kitchen all night while your guests are sipping sake on the sofa.

- Do as much of your grocery shopping the day before the party as possible. This leaves you at least 20 hours to remember the stuff you forgot to get, like ice, which you can never have too much of.

- At least the day before, make sure you have all the napkins, serving pieces, and dishes you'll need.

- The day of the party run the dishwasher, clean up the kitchen, and take out the garbage before you even so much as put on a pot of water to boil.

- Dim the lights and bring out the *unscented* candles. Nothing makes a room more inviting, and makes your friends look at least five years younger, than a softly lit room.

- Do we have to say this? Clean the cat box.

Now for some specific secrets to successful new Asian parties:

- Think about your noodles. Some noodles take well to being prepared in advance and then reheated; others don't. Check out the noodle chart in Chapter 4 for which ones are which. Once you've figured out which noodle to use, go ahead and cook them early in the day.

- Make the rice ahead of time.

- Make dumplings ahead of time. To reheat, place them in a plastic bag and pop them in the microwave for one minute on medium-high or 70 percent power.

- Get as much of your slicing, dicing, and chopping out of the way as possible before your guests arrive.

- Wokking and rolling stir-fry might not be a feasible approach if you're cooking for the whole gang. If it's a more manageable group of six to eight, a little planning makes it possible.

- Remember that overfilling a wok is a sure recipe for disaster; better to get two woks rolling than one overflowing.

- If you have enough space at the stove, enlist a friend to man the second wok. You'll be so good at it by now that you can teach him what to do in a couple of minutes.

- Try a do-it-yourself approach. Set out all the ingredients and, under your kind tutelage, let each guest stir-fry their own combination.

- Chill with the chilies. Not everyone enjoys a mouth-blistering meal. Put out fresh chopped chilies and chili-sauce for those who want to turn up the heat.

Chinese New Year

Chinese New Year is a great excuse for a party wherever you are.

The two-week Spring Festival celebration of Chinese New Year begins with the second new moon after the winter solstice and ends 15 days later on the full moon with the Lantern Festival, a night of feasting celebration, red lantern displays, and lantern parades. It's the time of year for cleaning out the house to make a fresh start for the New Year.

Think red when putting together your party. Red paper lanterns and strips of red paper with handwritten wishes for good fortune are hung on the walls as decorations for the Chinese New Year. Look for red serving platters, bowls, and chopsticks for the occasion.

Flowers are a must for the evening as they are considered essential to bringing happiness in the New Year. Extra lucky are the households whose potted plants flower at the New Year.

Orient Expressions

Be sure to wish your guests "Gung Hey Fat Choy," the traditional wish for prosperity and wealth in the coming year.

Chinese New Year is a family occasion, so we've put together a festive family-style feast for six with recipes that can easily be put together ahead of time.

The Least You Need to Know

◆ Prepare as much of the food as possible in advance.

◆ Take a field trip to the Asian stores in your area to pick up party supplies and snacks.

◆ Mix and match for a festive tabletop.

◆ Chill out! They're your friends, not restaurant critics.

Crab Dim Sum

Prep time: 40 minutes • Cook time: 40 minutes • Serves 6

12 oz. lump crabmeat, picked over to remove any shell fragments

1 TB. minced fresh ginger

1 TB. minced fresh garlic

1/4 cup thinly sliced shiitake mushroom caps

1/4 cup chopped green onion

1/4 cup minced red bell pepper

1 TB. sriracha sauce

2 TB. soybean sauce

2 TB. chopped fresh cilantro

18 wonton wrappers

Nonstick vegetable spray, as needed

Sprigs of cilantro for garnish

Dipping sauce:

2/3 cup soy sauce

1/4 cup soybean sauce

1/4 cup sweet soy sauce

1 tsp. toasted sesame seeds

1/2 tsp. tapioca starch

2 TB. water

Place crab in a large nonreactive mixing bowl and add ginger, garlic, shiitake mushrooms, green onion, red pepper, sriracha sauce, soybean sauce, and cilantro. Toss with a spoon, being careful not to break up lumps of crab too much. Set aside.

Recipes for Success

These delicious little morsels can be cooked ahead of time, frozen, and reheated the evening of your party. Serve the dim sum on a platter and put dipping sauce at each place setting in little Chinese teacups. To freeze, place the cooked dim sum on a cookie tray and put in freezer. When the dim sum are frozen, remove them from the tray, place them in a freezer bag and return to the freezer. To warm, simply do the steamer ritual from the following recipe, steaming for about 10 minutes. Even though they are frozen, they're already cooked so the steam time will be less than the original cook time.

Place a wonton wrapper in the palm of one hand and spoon about 1 tablespoon crab mixture into the middle. Pinch the ends with the other hand while turning wrapper clockwise. The final pinch seals the dumpling closed. This takes practice, but the result is an edible work of art. Repeat with the remaining wontons and crab mixture.

Boil water in the pot or wok for your steamer, making sure the water is deep enough to produce steam but does not touch the steamer. Spray the steamer rack with nonstick vegetable spray. Place dumplings on the rack about one inch apart. Cover the steamer. Place the filled steamer on the pot of boiling water and steam for 13 minutes. Dumplings should feel firm when ready.

Meanwhile, stir soy sauce, soybean sauce, sweet soy sauce, and sesame seeds together in a 1-quart saucepan. Bring to a boil. Mix tapioca starch and water together in a small bowl and stir into sauce. Return mixture to a boil and immediately remove from heat. To serve, ladle some sauce into each serving plate and place three dumplings on each plate. Garnish with a sprig or two of cilantro. Serve at once.

Roasted Garlic Cashew Chicken

Prep time: 35 minutes • Cook time: 20 minutes • Serves 6

$^1/_2$ cup garlic cloves, peeled

$^1/_2$ cup canola oil

4 quarts water

2 lb. skinless, boneless chicken breasts, diced

1 cup broccoli florets

$^1/_2$ cup pineapple chunks

$^1/_2$ cup whole cashews

$^1/_2$ cup chicken stock

$1^1/_2$ cups oyster sauce

Steamed rice for serving

Preheat the oven to 400°F.

Place garlic cloves into a small ovenproof pan or pie tin and drizzle with oil. Cover the pan with foil and roast in the oven for 25 minutes. Remove garlic and reserve oil.

Bring a 4-quart pot filled with water to a boil. Add chicken and bring to a boil again. Reduce heat to low and simmer for three minutes. Remove from heat and drain chicken. Keep warm.

Heat a wok over high heat and add $^1/_4$ cup garlic-flavored oil. When oil begins to smoke, add chicken and stir-fry for two minutes. Add broccoli, pineapple chunks, cashews, and garlic cloves. Stir-fry for three minutes, add chicken stock, and bring to a boil. Add the oyster sauce, simmer for two minutes longer, and remove from heat. Spoon onto a large, heated platter and serve with lots of steamed rice.

Fuji Apple Crisp

Prep time: 30 minutes • Cook time: 30 minutes • Serves 6

4 Fuji apples

2 tsp. fresh lemon juice

1 TB. unsalted butter, chilled

2 TB. packed brown sugar

1 cinnamon stick

$^1/_2$ tsp. tapioca starch

2 TB. water

For the streusel topping:

2 TB. unsalted butter, chilled and diced

$^1/_2$ cup all-purpose flour

$^1/_2$ cup granulated sugar

1 tsp. Chinese five-spice powder

Preheat the broiler.

Peel, core, and slice apples $^1/_2$-inch thick. Sprinkle apples with lemon juice. Heat a 4-quart ovenproof sauté pan over medium heat and add butter, brown sugar, cinnamon stick, and sliced apples. Sauté for five minutes, tossing the apples.

Mix tapioca with water in a small bowl. Sprinkle over apples and stir gently to distribute the tapioca. Bring this mixture to a boil and reduce heat to low, simmering for three minutes. Remove cinnamon stick at this point or spoon around it when serving.

Fortune Cookies

If you're making this one in advance, keep the filling and topping separate until you're ready to broil. Reheat the apple filling on the stovetop followed by broiling as in the recipe. If you can't find Fuji apples, Galas are a good substitute. For a tart crisp, try Granny Smith apples.

Make streusel topping by mixing butter, flour, sugar, and five-spice powder in a bowl, cutting into it with a whisk or pastry cutter until you have lumps about the size of small peas. Crumble streusel over apples and broil until streusel turns golden brown, about three to four minutes. Remove at once and serve warm.

Show your flair for the unusual by presenting this dessert family-style in the cooking pan hot from the oven. If you like, add vanilla bean ice cream to the pan as you're bringing it to the table, so it won't be totally melted by the time you get there.

Chapter 23

Big Hurrahs for a Cast of Many

In This Chapter

- ◆ Party Production 101
- ◆ Easing those opening-night jitters
- ◆ Some great party ideas

Now you're ready to debut in your new role as an old hand at new Asian cooking. With a little pre-show planning and some audience participation on opening night, you'll be guaranteed rave reviews.

Your Party Production Schedule

Because you'll be acting as producer, director, casting director, prop manager, music master, and all-around gopher, it's essential that you have your act together. Here's our production schedule for a smooth opening night.

Three Weeks Out

Send invitations to the cast. Be sure the RSVP on the invitation includes your first and last name, telephone number, and full address.

Make arrangements to hire servers or bartenders and rent any equipment you'll need. During the holiday season, you'll need to book even earlier, six or more weeks out. If you've never hired help before, ask for recommendations from friends who have, ask the manager at your favorite restaurant if any of the wait staff wants a one-night job, or hire someone through a catering company.

All sorts of great rentals are available, ranging from large chafing dishes, flatware, dishes, glasses, fondue pots, and serving platters to tents, elaborate candelabras, and frozen drink machines that can make large-scale entertaining much easier. Look in the Yellow Pages under "rentals" or "party rentals" for companies in your area.

Begin to plan your menu and start a shopping list for food, flowers, props, and drinks. Brilliant ideas often happen in the middle of the night, so keep your list handy.

One Week Out

Refine your shopping list and buy all the nonperishables.

Run a prop inventory. Now is the time to get extra napkins, plates, and serving pieces as well as decorations and party favors.

Go ahead and make any foods that can be frozen and reheated the day of the party.

Shop for wine, beer, spirits, mixers, and other beverages.

Start your tech rehearsals. Walk through your house imagining it filled with guests. Visualize where bottlenecks will happen and figure out what you can do to keep the traffic flowing. Try not to put the bar, buffet, and all the chairs in one big clump; otherwise you'll end up with a clumpy party.

If you're setting up the buffet on the dining table, check to see whether simply moving it over a couple of feet will ease congestion and keep traffic moving through and around the dining room.

If a major cleaning is in order, start it now!

Keep opening-night jitters to a minimum by having your costume ready to go. Figure out what you're going to wear and get it cleaned. If your outfit requires losing five pounds to look good in, pick another outfit—you want to be comfortable when you entertain.

The Day Before

Do the rest of the food shopping. Pick up flowers and ice.

Give the house a once over, arrange flowers and decorations. Make sure all the necessaries are in the powder room.

Set up the bar area with glasses, ice bucket, tongs, corkscrew, cocktail shaker, mixers, spirits, and red wines. Chill white wines and beer.

Arrange furniture for maximum traffic flow.

Lucky Treasures

Short on bar space, or worse yet, no bar at all? Flip open the top of the washing machine, fill it with ice, and sink the beverages inside. Oh yeah, we forgot one thing—unplug it first.

Opening Night

The big day is here and it's time to put the show on stage.

Hire someone to help you in the kitchen and to serve. A great resource is your favorite restaurant. Most waitstaff work catered parties and can use the extra cash.

As early in the day as you can manage, cook everything that can be easily reheated when the guests arrive.

Run the dishwasher and clean up the kitchen. Take the garbage out.

An hour before the show, calm your opening-night jitters with a warm shower, then slip into your costume.

Light the candles, dim the lights, put on the music, and sit down and relax for a few minutes before the curtain rises.

Post Production

This is where the hired waiter or kitchen helper really comes in handy. Show them where the trash bags are and let them have at it. Add an additional $1^{1}/_{2}$ hours for this and tell them up front.

No matter how tired you are after the last guest leaves, clean up the mess before you go to bed.

Seasonal Themes

We've come up with a few fun, seasonal themes for your big hurrahs. Recipe quantities are adaptable for a party of 12 to 16 and can easily be doubled or tripled as needed.

Spring Roll Party

Everyone roll up your sleeves! This party requires group participation! Start the new season with a Spring Roll Party where guests pitch in to help make the food.

For this party we've included the following recipes:

◆ Fresh Vegetable Spring Rolls

◆ Lobster Mango Rolls

◆ Stir-Fry Chicken Wrap

◆ Rock Shrimp Wrap

◆ Mango Sticky Rice

Too bad you can't have a Spring Cleaning Party, too!

Summer Satay and Sake Social

Chilled sake is a refreshing summer delight. Revisit Chapter 18 for a review of the different kinds of sake to help you make the best selection. Or purchase several kinds of sake and serve in unlabeled sake carafes. This is called a "blind tasting." It will be like the chocolate scene in *Forrest Gump:* "You never know what you are going to get …" Be sure to make a list of what's what, or the unlabeled sake thing is moot.

For this party we've included the following recipes:

◆ Chicken Satay

◆ Beef Satay

◆ Shrimp Satay

◆ Grilled Tofu Satay

◆ Fruit Satay

Fall Mussel Party

A true eyebrow raiser, the party name itself can make someone blush! Maybe guests won't be using weights, but they will be exercising their jaws, lifting their forks, and stretching their bellies.

For this party we've included the following recipes:

- Green Papaya Salad
- Prince Edward Mussels
- Ginger Pumpkin Pie

Braise Yourself—Winter's Here!

Winter is here and so are savory, bracing, cozy dishes that will keep you and your guests warm all through the season.

For this party we've included the following recipes:

- Braised Beef with Seasonal Vegetables
- Coconut Cheese Cake

The Least You Need to Know

- Asian food makes feeding a crowd a breeze.
- Plan ahead and don't get in over your head, call in for help if you need it.
- Pick a theme for your party and let the good times roll.

Fresh Vegetable Spring Rolls

Prep time: 1 hour, 15 minutes • Cook time: 45 minutes • Makes 16 rolls

1 cup rice vermicelli noodles, soaked in water for 20 minutes and drained

1 cup shredded iceberg lettuce

1 cup julienned ($\frac{1}{2}$-inch) carrot

1 cup bean sprouts

$\frac{1}{4}$ cup roughly chopped Asian basil

16 rice paper wrappers

2 cups peanut sauce

Cook noodles in boiling water for 20 seconds. Drain noodles and chill. In a medium-size mixing bowl, thoroughly toss together lettuce, carrots, bean sprouts, and basil. Submerge one rice paper wrapper in simmering water for 45 seconds. Remove from water and hang on a corner of a counter by its edge to dry for about 20 seconds. This will make it easy to roll.

Place the softened rice paper on work surface. Place 1 tablespoon or so of lettuce mixture on lower third of sheet. Place about 2 tablespoons noodles on top of lettuce. Pull bottom edge of rice paper up over lettuce and noodles using thumb and forefinger of each hand while holding stuffing at bay with middle fingers. Keep rice paper tight as you roll, but not too tight, or it will tear. Once you have covered filling, fold sides of rice paper in and continue to roll until you have made a cylinder. Repeat the process with remaining wrappers and filling. If the rolls will not be served immediately, cover with damp paper towel and keep at room temperature until ready to serve. Serve with peanut sauce for dipping.

Recipes for Success

These rolls do not keep well. Make them no more than $1\frac{1}{2}$ hours before you plan to serve them, covering the dish with a damp paper towel. *Do not* put them in the refrigerator where they will quickly lose their moisture. If you have leftover filling, go ahead and keep that in the fridge. You can roll whenever you get the craving.

Lobster Mango Rolls

Prep time: 2 hours • Cook time: 1 hour • Makes 16 rolls

$^1/_4$ cup fresh lemon juice

1 cup soy sauce

$^1/_4$ cup pickled ginger

1 tsp. minced fresh garlic

2 TB. minced jalapeño

3 quarts water

Salt to taste

1 lb. frozen lobster meat, thawed, or fresh lobster tail meat

16 rice paper wrappers

2 mangoes, peeled and cut into $^1/_2 \times 3$-inch strips

2 red bell peppers, cut into $^1/_2 \times 3$-inch strips

1 cup Asian basil leaves

1 lb. arugula

1 cup vermicelli noodles, soaked in water for 20 minutes and drained

Whisk together lemon juice, soy sauce, ginger, garlic, and jalapeño in a nonreactive bowl. Transfer to a serving bowl with a ladle and set aside.

Bring 3 quarts salted water to a boil in a 4-quart saucepan, add lobster, and reduce heat to medium or low. Simmer for eight minutes, or just until opaque. Remove lobster from pot, drain, and cut into large bite-size pieces. Cover lobster with slightly damp paper towels and refrigerate.

Submerge one rice paper wrapper into simmering water for 45 seconds. Remove from water and hang on a corner of a counter by its edge to dry for about 20 seconds. This will make it easy to roll.

Place the softened rice paper on work surface. Place a strip or two of mango and bell pepper on lower third of sheet. Top with some lobster, one basil leaf, three or four arugula leaves, and noodles. Pull bottom edge of rice paper up over filling using the thumb and forefinger of each hand while holding stuffing with the middle fingers. Keep rice paper tight as you roll, but not too tight or it will tear. Once you have completely covered the filling, fold sides of rice paper in, and continue to roll until you have made a cylinder. Repeat the process with remaining wrappers and filling. Serve immediately with dipping sauce or cover with damp paper towel and keep at room temperature until ready to serve.

Fortune Cookies

If you are lucky enough to find frozen shelled lobster, use it for this recipe. This can usually be found at most Asian markets. If that's unavailable, fresh lobster tail is an obvious, pricier substitute.

Stir-Fry Chicken Wrap

Prep time: 1 hour • Cook time: 1 hour • Serves 12 to 16

2 lb. skinless, boneless chicken breasts	2 TB. coconut milk
1/2 cup peeled and diced raw baking potatoes	2 tsp. yellow curry powder
1 quart water	3 TB. fish sauce
Salt to taste	2 TB. oyster sauce
3 heads curly leaf lettuce, rinsed and trimmed	1/2 cup chopped cilantro leaves
2 TB. canola oil	1 tsp. freshly ground black pepper
2 TB. garlic, minced	1/2 cup green peas
1/2 cup onion, diced	1/4 cup fried garlic

Cut chicken into large pieces and place them into a food processor fitted with a metal blade. Pulse machine on and off quickly several times to process chicken roughly into a thick paste.

Place potatoes into a 1-quart saucepan of lightly salted water set over high heat and bring to a boil. Reduce heat to medium-high, and cook for three minutes. Drain potatoes and cool to room temperature.

Meanwhile, tear about 30 leaves off the lettuce. Each leaf should be big enough to form a hand-held cup. Stack leaves, wrap with a damp paper towel, and refrigerate.

Fortune Cookies _____
Wraps cut your time down in the kitchen and put your guests to work—but easy, tasty work! The etiquette is easy. Remember that if your guests are confused about how to make this, they will look to see what you do, so don't be in the kitchen when this dish goes to the table.

Heat a wok over high heat and add oil. When oil is smoking, add garlic, onion, and chicken. Stir-fry for two minutes. Add potatoes and continue to cook for three minutes more. Toss this mixture with coconut milk, curry powder, fish sauce, and oyster sauce and bring to a boil. Stir-fry for three minutes and stir in cilantro, black pepper, and peas. Remove from heat.

To serve, mound warm chicken mixture into a medium-size bowl. Place the bowl on a large, round platter and arrange lettuce leaves all around. Have your guests assemble the wraps themselves. Show them how to spoon some chicken mixture into lettuce, sprinkle with fried garlic, and wrap lettuce around chicken. Plan to serve two wraps per person.

Rock Shrimp Wrap

Prep time: 1 hour, 30 minutes • Cook time: 1 hour • Serves 12 to 16

3 heads curly red leaf lettuce, rinsed and trimmed

3 TB. sesame oil

2 lb. rock shrimp (if unavailable, use small salad or popcorn shrimp)

2 TB. minced fresh garlic

$^{1}/_{2}$ cup minced red bell pepper

$^{1}/_{2}$ cup minced white onion

$^{1}/_{4}$ cup minced jalapeños

2 TB. fish sauce

$^{1}/_{2}$ cup chopped fresh cilantro leaves

$^{1}/_{2}$ cup oyster sauce

2 TB. toasted sesame seeds

Tear about 30 leaves off lettuce. Each leaf should be big enough to form a handheld cup. Stack leaves, wrap with a damp paper towel, and refrigerate.

Heat a wok over medium heat and when hot, add oil. When oil is hot, add rock shrimp and stir-fry for two minutes. Add garlic, red bell peppers, onions, and jalapeños, and stir-fry for three minutes more. Add fish sauce and cilantro, and toss thoroughly to coat shrimp. Stir in oyster sauce and cook for one more minute. Immediately remove from heat.

To serve, mound warm shrimp mixture into a medium-size bowl. Place bowl on a large, round platter and arrange cold lettuce leaves all around. Have your guests assemble the wraps themselves. Show them how to spoon some shrimp mixture into lettuce, sprinkle with toasted sesame seeds, and wrap lettuce around shrimp. Plan to serve two wraps per person.

 Lucky Treasures
This is a particularly nice dish. The warmth of the shrimp gives good contrast to the cold, crisp lettuce.

Mango Sticky Rice

Soak time: 12 hours • Prep time: 1 hour • Cook time: 1 hour, 30 minutes • Serves 12 to 16

3 cups uncooked glutinous rice

12 to 16 lettuce leaves

2 cups canned coconut milk

1 cup palm sugar

2 vanilla beans

$1/4$ tsp. salt

4 mangoes, pitted, peeled, and sliced

Soak rice in water to cover overnight.

Line the rack of a steamer with lettuce leaves, pour rice in, and spread it out evenly. Set steamer over pot or wok of boiling water, being careful that water does not touch the steamer. Steam rice for 35 minutes or until rice is tender. Transfer to a large serving platter, arranging rice on one side, leaving a little room for the bowl of sauce. Cover with damp paper towel and refrigerate.

Bring coconut milk, sugar, vanilla beans, and salt to a simmer in a 2-quart sauce pan set over medium heat; cook for 25 minutes. Remove vanilla beans, rinse them, and refrigerate, reserving them for another use. Pour coconut sauce into a large serving bowl, cover, and chill in the refrigerator.

When ready to serve, place the sauce bowl on the platter next to rice. Fan sliced mango around rice. Pop a ladle into the coconut sauce. Alongside the platter, stack some small plates and chopsticks. Show your guests how to spoon some rice and mango on their plates and ladle a little (or a lot of) coconut sauce over rice.

Chicken Satay

Prep time: 35 minute • Marination time: 1 hour • Cook time: 45 minutes • Serves 12 to 16

2 lb. skinless, boneless, chicken breasts	$^1/_2$ tsp. salt
$^1/_2$ cup canned coconut milk	1 tsp. freshly ground black pepper
2 TB. oyster sauce	30 bamboo skewers
1 tsp. yellow curry powder	1 cup peanut sauce
$^1/_4$ cup chopped cilantro leaves	1 cup chopped unsalted peanuts

Cut chicken into 1-inch strips across the grain and set aside.

Whisk coconut milk, oyster sauce, curry powder, cilantro, salt, and pepper together in a medium-size bowl. Add chicken, tossing well to coat. Cover and refrigerate for one hour.

Soak the skewers in water for at least 20 minutes. Remove chicken from marinade and discard remaining marinade. Heat a grill to medium-high. Thread chicken onto skewers. Grill chicken for four minutes on each side. Place cooked chicken satay skewers on a large platter and pour peanut sauce over them, avoiding the grip end of the skewers. Sprinkle with chopped peanuts. Serve hot. Plan to serve two skewers per person.

Fortune Cookies

Devotion to the motion of skewering chicken can be tricky. If you impale a piece on a skewer straight on, it will just twirl around on the skewer like a pinwheel, making it bit difficult to grill. To get it tight, hold the chicken strip at a slight angle to the skewer and insert the skewer about an inch or so; then turn the chicken strip the opposite way and insert the skewer a little bit more. Do this one more time. It's kind of like a lazy "z" motion.

Beef Satay

Prep time: 1 hour • Marination time: 30 minutes • Cook time: 45 minutes • Serves 12 to 16

2 lbs. beef flank steak

1 tsp. sesame oil

2 TB. oyster sauce

1 TB. soybean sauce (Golden Mountain brand)

2 tsp. granulated sugar

$^1/_2$ tsp. freshly ground black pepper

2 TB. sesame seeds

1 cup shiitake mushroom caps

30 bamboo skewers, soaked in water for 20 minutes

Dipping Sauce:

1 cup soy sauce

2 TB. sweet soy sauce

1 tsp. minced fresh garlic

2 tsp. minced fresh ginger

$^1/_2$ tsp. tapioca starch

1 TB. cold water

Trim fat from beef and cut into one-inch strips across grain. Set aside.

Whisk sesame oil, oyster sauce, soybean sauce, sugar, black pepper, and sesame seeds together in a medium-size nonreactive mixing bowl. Add beef and shiitake mushrooms, cover, and refrigerate for 30 minutes.

Heat a grill to medium. Thread one piece of beef and one mushroom cap on each skewer and discard remaining marinade. Set aside.

To make dipping sauce, whisk together soy sauce, sweet soy sauce, garlic, and ginger and simmer in a medium-size saucepan for five minutes. Mix tapioca starch and water together and add to sauce. Bring to a boil and immediately remove from the heat.

Grill beef for three minutes on each side for medium doneness. Arrange the skewers on a platter and pour sauce over them, avoiding the grip end of the skewers. Serve hot. Plan to serve two skewers per person.

Shrimp Satay

Prep time: 1 hour • Cook time: 45 minutes • Makes 30 skewers

1 cup cherry tomatoes

$1^1/_2$ lb. shrimp (16 to 20 count), peeled and deveined

1 cup pineapple chunks

30 bamboo skewers, soaked in water for about 20 minutes

$1^1/_2$ cup sweet chili sauce

Heat the grill to medium. Thread one tomato, one shrimp, and one pineapple chunk on each skewer. Grill the skewers for four minutes on each side, turning once.

Baste shrimp with sweet chili sauce while grilling. The chili sauce adds a nice caramelized color and flavor.

Artfully arrange shrimp satay on a serving platter and pour remaining chili sauce over it. Plan to serve two skewers per person.

Grilled Tofu Satay

Prep time: 25 minutes • Marination time: 20 minutes • Cook time: 20 minutes • Serves 12 to 16

1 cup soy sauce

3 TB. sweet soy sauce

2 TB. sesame oil

1 TB. minced fresh ginger

2 TB. honey

2 lb. firm tofu, cut into 1-inch cubes

$1/_4$ tsp. tapioca starch

2 TB. cold water

30 bamboo skewers, soaked in water for at least 20 minutes

1 tsp. freshly ground black pepper

2 TB. toasted sesame seeds

In a large bowl, mix soy sauce, sweet soy sauce, sesame oil, ginger, and honey. Add tofu, toss to coat, and marinate for 20 minutes. Using a flat strainer, remove tofu from the bowl, being careful not to break tofu. Pour excess marinade into a 1-quart saucepan. Over medium heat, warm the marinade.

Meanwhile, mix tapioca starch and water together in a small bowl. Stir mixture into marinade and bring to a boil. Once mixture boils, remove from heat and reserve.

Thread cubes of tofu onto each skewer, leaving enough room for a handle.

Heat grill to medium-high and cook tofu for three minutes on each side. Remove to a large platter. Ladle sauce over tofu and sprinkle with pepper and sesame seeds. Serve hot.

Fruit Satay

Prep time: 1 hour, 30 minutes • Serves 12 to 16

3 Asian pears, peeled, cored, and cut into bite-size pieces

Juice of 2 lemons

2 pints strawberries, wiped clean and hulled

1 pineapple, peeled, cored, and cut into bite-size pieces

30 bamboo skewers

1 cup heavy cream

¹/₄ cup confectioners' sugar

1 tsp. vanilla extract

Recipes for Success

Strawberries are like sponges and absorb liquids rather quickly, which can dilute the flavor of the berry. If you must rinse them, do it quickly and pat them dry with paper towels.

After cutting pears, drizzle them with lemon juice to keep them from turning brown.

Thread one piece pear, strawberry, and pineapple onto each skewer. Set them on a large platter covered with a damp paper towel and refrigerate.

In a medium-size mixing bowl, whisk cream until it begins to thicken. Add sugar and vanilla extract. Whisk until cream is stiffly whipped. Place whipped cream into a bowl and serve with cold skewered fruit. Plan to serve two skewers per person.

Green Papaya Salad

Prep time: 25 minutes • Marination time: 20 minutes • Serves 12 to 16

4 green papayas, medium-firm to the touch

¹/₂ cup fish sauce

¹/₂ cup fresh lime juice

2 TB. granulated sugar

¹/₂ cup minced fresh garlic

¹/₂ cup minced shallots

2 tsp. red pepper flakes

2 cups halved cherry tomatoes

1 cup julienned carrot

¹/₂ lb. fresh green beans, cut into ¹/₂-inch pieces

Peel papayas. Scoop out seeds and discard. Soak papaya under cold water for five minutes to help tone down the bitterness and acidity.

Whisk together fish sauce, lime juice, sugar, garlic, shallots, and red pepper flakes in a large nonreactive bowl. Add papaya, tomatoes, carrots, and green beans. Toss well and marinate for 20 minutes in the refrigerator. Serve cold.

Prince Edward Mussels

Prep time: 1 hour, 30 minutes • Cook time: 7 to 20 minutes • Serves 12 to 16

15 lb. Prince Edward black mussels

2 quarts tomato juice

2 cups chicken stock

1/4 cup chili paste with soybean oil

1/2 cup fish sauce

1/2 cup fresh lime juice

1/3 cup minced fresh garlic

2 TB. red pepper flakes

2 cups dry sherry

10 kaffir lime leaves

5 stalks lemongrass, peeled and trimmed to the soft core

3 bunches fresh cilantro

1 lb. butter, at room temperature, cut into chunks

5 baguettes, sliced or broken into pieces and toasted

Place mussels into a large bowl. Discard any open mussels. Remove "beards" (hairlike fibers that connect the mussel to rocks and piers and collect dirt and debris). To debeard, gently pull on beard with a side-to-side motion; some mussels might require a mild tug. Check for mud clinging to shells and remove with a soft brush; then give them a final rinse in fresh water.

In a 3- to 4-quart bowl, whisk together tomato juice, chicken stock, chili paste, fish sauce, lime juice, garlic, and red pepper flakes. Heat a 5-gallon stockpot over high heat. When hot, add mussels and pour in sherry. Cover immediately and steam for one minute. Add tomato juice mixture, lime leaves, lemongrass, and cilantro. Stir lightly to combine. Bring to a boil, lower heat, and continue to cook, covered, for three minutes. Take a peek. At this point, mussels should be almost fully opened. Add butter, cover, and simmer until mussels are completely opened, about three more minutes. Remove mussels from the heat immediately; continuing to cook them will make them dry and rubbery. Discard any mussels do not open.

This recipe will serve at least 15 people. The mussels can be presented in cooking pot with tongs and a ladle, which will keep them warm longer, or they can be transferred to a large serving bowl with liquid. Offer small bowls and forks. You can always use chopsticks to eat mussels, but unless you are knowledgeable in the Tao of chopsticks, they will become missiles instead of mussels. Serve with warm baguette slices on the side.

 **Fortune Cookies**

This recipe requires the use of a 3- to 5-gallon stockpot to cook the mussels. If you don't have one, plan to cook the mussels in smaller batches. Three pounds of mussels will require a 1- to 2-gallon stockpot.

Ginger Pumpkin Pie

Prep time: 1 hour, 15 minutes • Chill time: 6 hours • Cook time: 1 hour, 30 minutes • Serves 12 to 16

Scant $1/2$ cup granulated sugar

$1/4$ cup brown sugar, packed

$1/2$ tsp. ground cinnamon

2 TB. powdered ginger

$1/4$ tsp. ground nutmeg

1 TB. tapioca starch

$1/4$ tsp. salt

$1\,1/4$ cups canned pumpkin

$3/4$ cups whole milk

2 TB. light corn syrup

4 large eggs, beaten well with a fork

1 cup graham cracker crumbs

1 medium egg white

2 oz. unsalted butter, melted

Whipped cream for garnish

Using an electric mixer set on low speed, combine 2 tablespoons granulated sugar, brown sugar, cinnamon, ginger, nutmeg, tapioca starch, and salt. Mix until completely incorporated. Add pumpkin, milk, and corn syrup. Cover and rest in the refrigerator for two hours.

Preheat oven to 350°F. Beat eggs into batter on low speed. Cover and allow to rest in the refrigerator for two more hours. While batter is resting, stir graham cracker crumbs, egg white, melted butter, and $1/4$ cup sugar together in a large bowl with a wooden spoon until graham cracker crumbs feel a bit moist. Line an 8-inch pie pan with crust and pat down evenly. Pour pie batter into pan and bake for 50 minutes. Remove from oven and cool to room temperature. Chill in the refrigerator for at least two hours. Serve cold, garnished with whipped cream.

Braised Beef with Seasonal Vegetables

Prep time: 1 hour, 30 minutes • Cook time: 2 hours, 30 minutes • Serves 12 to 16

10 lbs. boned beef chuck roast

$^1/_4$ cup salt

2 TB. sesame oil

$^1/_2$ cup garlic cloves, peeled and left whole

2 cups chopped onion

2 cups chopped carrot

$^1/_2$ cup shredded fresh ginger

2 cups chopped shiitake mushroom caps

1 cup red wine

$^1/_2$ cup soy sauce

$^1/_2$ cup sweet soy sauce

$2^1/_2$ quarts chicken stock

2 quarts chicken broth

3 TB. red pepper flakes

4 Asian pears, cut into a $^3/_4$-inch chunks

3 TB. tapioca starch

$^1/_2$ cup water

1 cup chopped fresh cilantro leaves

$3^3/_4$ quarts (15 cups) steamed jasmine rice

Season beef on all sides with salt.

Heat a large stockpot over high heat and add oil. When the oil is smoking, add beef and sear it on all sides (about four minutes on each side). Remove beef from pot and keep warm.

Add garlic, onions, carrots, ginger, and mushrooms and cook for five minutes over high heat, stirring constantly. Stir in red wine. Bring to a boil and reduce in volume by half. Using two sets of tongs, place beef back into the pot and add soy sauce, sweet soy sauce, chicken stock, chicken broth, and red pepper flakes. Bring to a boil and reduce heat to low. When liquid is at a simmer (when tiny bubbles rise to the surface), add pears and cover. Simmer for 90 minutes. Beef should be fork-tender at this point. Remove beef from pot, transfer to a cutting board, and cut into two-inch chunks. Keep warm.

Whisk tapioca starch and water together in a small bowl or cup and stir it into the pot. Turn heat to medium high. While stirring constantly, bring contents of pot to a boil; immediately remove the pot from the heat. Stir in cilantro. Remove from heat and return beef to pot. Ladle stew into a large serving bowl. Serve with hot steamed rice. Have each guest put some rice on the bottom of his or her bowl, ladle stew over it.

Fortune Cookies

This is a great party dish incorporating a guaranteed, never-fail method that assures moist and flavorful beef every time. After the initial preparation, all you have to do is cover it and work on other party stuff. This, my friends, is the magic of braising.

Coconut Cheese Cake

Prep time: 40 minutes • Cook time: 2 hours • Chill time: 2 hours • Serves 6 to 8 (one cake)

Nonstick vegetable spray

1 cup graham cracker crumbs

1 egg white

2 oz. unsalted butter, melted

1 cup granulated sugar (divided use)

2 TB. tapioca starch

Zest of $1/2$ lemon

$1^1/4$ lb. cream cheese, room temperature

2 medium eggs

1 medium egg yolk

$1/2$ cup canned coconut milk

1 TB. coconut extract

$1/2$ cup shredded coconut

Preheat the oven to 350°F.

Spray one 8-inch spring-form baking pan with nonstick vegetable spray.

In a large bowl, stir graham cracker crumbs, egg white, melted butter, and $1/4$ cup sugar together with a wooden spoon until graham cracker crumbs feel a bit moist. Line the bottom of the pan with cake crust and pat down evenly.

Using an electric mixer set on low speed, combine tapioca starch, lemon zest, and remaining sugar in a medium-size mixing bowl. Mix for one minute. Set the mixer to medium speed and add softened cream cheese a little at a time, mixing until smooth. This should take about five minutes. Add eggs and yolk, one at a time, and mix for three minutes. Turn the speed down to low and slowly add extract milk and coconut extract. Mix for five minutes longer. Pour cake batter into prepared pan. Sprinkle shredded coconut evenly over top of cake.

Now you'll make a water bath, which will help keep the cake moist during baking. Place cake pan into a larger pan that has at least a $1^1/2$-inch lip. A roasting pan is ideal. Slide the pans into the oven and pour enough hot water into the outer pan to come up the sides of the spring-form pan by at least $3/4$ inch. Bake cake for 90 minutes or until coconut is a dark golden brown. Cool cake in the refrigerator for at least two hours.

Fortune Cookies

Short of buying a laser, it can be difficult to neatly cut a cheesecake. The edgiest and easiest way is to cut the cheesecake with a piece of fishing line. Holding the line taut, simply place it on top of the cake and push all the way to the bottom. To remove it, let one hand go and pull out the side. Repeat until you have the desired number of cuts. If you can't be bothered with such worldly items as fishing line, get real with a knife. Any knife will do, as long as you have plenty of hot water to dip it into between each cut.

Chapter 24

Dinner for Six

In This Chapter

- ◆ A last-minute feast
- ◆ Laid-back TV nights
- ◆ Budget dining
- ◆ A toast for any occasion

Now's your chance to really show off your new Asian cooking skills. Small dinner parties are an ideal excuse to pull out all the stops and really test your mettle.

Entertaining in Asian countries is all about making your guests feel welcome, offering the best you can, and honoring your host when you are the guest. Elaborate rituals for introductions, seating, and eating are the norm, but don't feel like you need to attend diplomatic school just to have an Asian dinner party. But there is one thing you can add that's fun for all, and always an icebreaker if one is needed: the right toast.

Toasts

Toasts are a part of entertaining in many Asian countries, especially in Japan and China.

Write out toasts for each guest to offer during the meal on small slips of paper, but don't let them know what you're up to until it's toast time. Hide the toasts on the table in tiny white Chinese take-out containers, or fold them in each guest's napkin, or slide them under the plates. At the start of the meal, astound your friends with the ease in which you offer up an exquisite toast (don't tell them it took you days to memorize it) and then ask them to offer the toasts you've strategically placed for each guest.

Fortune Cookies

In most Asian countries, a drink, like a business card, is offered and held with two hands. And it's the host's job to offer the first toast.

Here are some all-occasion toasts that your guests will surely enjoy:

- ◆ "Here's to cold nights, warm friends, and a good drink to give them."
- ◆ "Here's to a long life and a merry one. A quick death and an easy one. A pretty girl and an honest one. A cold beer—and another one!"
- ◆ "May your troubles be less, and your blessings be more. And nothing but happiness come through your door."
- ◆ "Forsake not an old friend, for the new is not comparable to him. A new friend is a new wine: When it is old, thou shalt drink it with pleasure."
- ◆ "Here's to beauty, wit, and wine."
- ◆ "Happy to share with you, such as we got, the leaks in the roof, the soup in the pot. You don't have to thank us, or laugh at our jokes; sit deep and come often, you're one of the folks."
- ◆ "To the chef: Good food, good meat, good God, let's eat!"

Sound like a multilingual expert by memorizing these Asian-inspired toasts:

- ◆ Chinese: *Yum sen!* ("Drink to victory!")
- ◆ Chinese: *Kan pei!* ("Bottoms up!")
- ◆ Korean: *Gung bai!* ("Bottoms up!")
- ◆ Korean: *Chu-kha-ham-ni-da!* ("Congratulations!")
- ◆ Thai: *Chai yo!* ("To your health and well-being!")

Last-Minute Dinners ("Uh-Oh, the Boss Is Coming!")

If you end up having to do something at the last minute, what could be more impressive than whipping up a quick, new Asian dinner? No one needs to know that these incredible dishes take little time to prepare. And now that your pantry has plenty of

Asian basics in it at all times, you can zip over to your local grocery store for the fresh veggies and meat or fish and you're ready to "wok" out.

Our recipes for last-minute dinners include Asian Paella, Jasmine Meat Loaf, Mixed Greens Salad, and Peanut Salad.

Must-See TV: Dishing It Up for the Academy Awards or a Rerun of *I Love Lucy*

Dishing on the stars' outfits during the Academy Awards or those oh-so-realistic plot lines of our favorite nighttime dramas is all the more fun when you have a few friends over.

We offer some delicious treats (Edamame; Red Curry Chicken Wings; and Crab, Corn, and Cream Cheese Wontons) that will spice up the evening even further. This trio of knife-and-fork-free morsels makes it easy to concentrate on just how high Carrie's heels are or whether Lucy will last more than five minutes in that chocolate factory.

If You're Broke, Fix It—If You Can't Afford to Go Out, Stay Home!

Just because the rent's due, the car broke down, and you are now officially "rethinking your employment options" doesn't mean you can't gather a few of your nearest and dearest together for an evening of cheap eats and priceless conversation. Delectable, richly flavored dishes that celebrate the versatility of those very inexpensive staples of the Asian diet, rice and noodles, will satisfy the tummy and the soul. Try our recipes for Sriracha Fried Rice, Asian Bolognese, Dan Dan Noodles, and Green Curry Fried Rice.

And who knows, maybe tomorrow you will win the lottery!

The Least You Need to Know

- Whether it's an intimate evening for two or a quick dinner for a couple friends, Asian is the way to go.
- Keep Asian basics in the pantry, and you'll always be ready to prepare a fine meal.
- Don't bust the budget, think Asian food when the cash is low.
- Always raise your glass with a warm-hearted toast to friends and family.

Asian Paella

Prep time: 15 minutes • Cook time: 35 minutes • Serves 6

2 TB. canola oil

1 lb. chicken legs and thighs

2 TB. diced yellow onion

1 tsp. minced garlic

1 tsp. yellow curry paste

1 TB. yellow curry powder

$^1/_4$ cup jalapeño chili pepper, minced

3 cups uncooked jasmine rice

$^1/_2$ cup diced roma tomato

$^1/_2$ cup diced red bell pepper

3 TB. fish sauce

6 cups chicken stock

1 lb. shrimp (26 to 30 count), peeled and deveined

1 lb. black mussels

$^1/_2$ cup green peas

$^1/_2$ cup ($^1/_2$ lb.) thinly sliced Chinese sausage

$^1/_2$ cup sliced green onion

3 limes, cut in half

Preheat the oven to 400°F.

Heat a large roasting pan (that has a lid) over high heat and add oil. When oil is smoking, sear chicken pieces on all sides until golden brown, about five minutes. Add onion, garlic, curry paste, curry powder, and jalapeño, and sauté for three minutes. Add rice, tomato, and red bell pepper, tossing in the pan to coat thoroughly; continue to cook for two minutes. Stir in fish sauce and chicken stock and bring to a boil. Immediately cover with a lid and place in the oven. Cook for 15 minutes.

Remove the pan from the oven, add shrimp, mussels, green peas, and Chinese sausage, cover, and return to oven for 10 minutes longer. Remove from the oven, uncover, and let rest for five minutes. Serve in the pan sprinkled with sliced green onion and garnished with lime halves.

Lucky Treasures

This is a fun take on the Spanish favorite, paella. When presented in the baking pan, it's a stunning presentation studded with all the seafood, chicken, and sausage. If you can, use only the Chinese sausage—the flavorful effect is fabulous in this dish.

Jasmine Meat Loaf

Prep time: 20 minutes • Cook time: 1 hour, 10 minutes • Serves 6

1 TB. canola oil

^{1}/$_4$ cup diced yellow onion

1 TB. minced fresh garlic

2 slices white bread, cut into small cubes

^{1}/$_2$ cup whole milk

2 lb. ground beef

2 TB. soy sauce

1 TB. fish sauce

1 TB. sweet soy sauce

^{1}/$_2$ cup tomato ketchup

^{1}/$_2$ cup chopped canned water chestnuts

^{1}/$_2$ cup steamed jasmine rice, plus more for serving

^{1}/$_2$ cup Panko (Japanese breadcrumbs)

^{1}/$_4$ tsp. chili powder

1 tsp. yellow curry powder

2 TB. freshly chopped cilantro leaves

2 TB. chopped Asian basil

2 large eggs

Preheat the oven to 350°F.

Heat a wok over high heat and add oil. When oil is smoking, stir-fry onion and garlic for three minutes, stirring frequently. When tender and translucent, place onion and garlic into a large mixing bowl.

Soak bread cubes in milk for five minutes. Squeeze to drain excess milk and place bread into the bowl. Add ground beef, soy sauce, fish sauce, sweet soy sauce, ketchup, water chestnuts, rice, Panko, chili powder, curry powder, cilantro, basil, and eggs to the bowl. Work mixture with your hands until all ingredients are thoroughly mixed.

Place meat onto a 13 × 9 × 2-inch baking pan and form it into a loaf, patting down firmly. Place the pan into the oven and bake for one hour. Serve hot with steamed rice and plenty of sweet soy sauce on the side.

Mixed Greens Salad

Prep time: 20 minutes • Chill time: 10 minutes • Serves 6

6 cups mixed baby salad greens

1/2 cup rice vinegar

1 tsp. honey

1 tsp. minced fresh garlic

1 TB. minced fresh ginger

1 tsp. chili paste made with soybean oil

1/4 tsp. red chili powder

1 TB. toasted sesame seeds

1 cup sesame oil

1 cup cherry tomatoes, halved

1 Asian pear (Any firm, flavorful pear can be substituted.)

Wash greens under cold water and blot dry with paper towels. Set aside.

Whisk vinegar, honey, garlic, ginger, chili paste, chili powder, and sesame seeds together in a nonreactive bowl. Start an emulsion by pouring sesame oil into vinaigrette drop by drop until the dressing starts to hold together. After this happens, pour oil in a slow, steady stream, whisking until all oil is incorporated. Chill for 10 minutes.

Put tomatoes in the bowl with greens. Remove core from pear and slice thinly. Add to the salad bowl. Immediately pour dressing onto salad and toss gently with a plastic spoon, covering pears with the vinaigrette yet being careful not to bruise lettuce. Serve in the salad bowl or put salad on a large chilled platter. Serve cold with chilled salad plates.

Dan Dan Noodles

Prep time: 15 minutes • Cook time: 12 minutes • Serves 6

1 1/2 lb. egg noodles

2 TB. sesame oil

3 TB. peanut oil

1/3 cup soy sauce or to taste

3 TB. rice vinegar

3 TB. dark Chinese vinegar

2 TB. chili paste made with soybean oil

2 TB. shredded fresh ginger

1 tsp. minced fresh garlic

1/2 cup sliced green onion

1 tsp. red pepper flakes

2 TB. chopped fresh cilantro leaves

Boil water in a large stockpot and add noodles. Cook for five minutes. Transfer noodles to a colander and rinse under cold water to wash off any starch, which makes noodles sticky. Drain well. Place noodles into a bowl and toss with sesame oil. Whisk peanut oil, soy sauce, rice and dark Chinese vinegars, chili paste, ginger, garlic, green onion, red pepper flakes, and cilantro together in a large bowl. Add noodles to the bowl and toss to coat. Serve at room temperature or cold.

Peanut Salad

Prep time: 20 minutes • Serves 6

1 large head iceberg lettuce, rinsed and drained

1 cup thinly sliced cucumber

1 cup thinly sliced plum tomatoes

$^1/_2$ cup shredded red cabbage

$^1/_2$ cup thinly sliced red onion

$1^1/_2$ cups peanut sauce

$^1/_2$ cup crushed unsalted peanuts

$^1/_4$ tsp. salt

1 tsp. freshly ground black pepper

Cut lettuce into bite-size pieces and place in a large mixing bowl. Toss with cucumber, tomatoes, red cabbage, and onion. When you are ready to serve, add peanut sauce, peanuts, salt, and pepper to salad and toss to coat.

Fortune Cookies

This is an easy salad to prep for a party or an everyday dinner. Just remember to toss the lettuce with the dressing at the last minute and you'll have crisp lettuce every time.

Red Curry Chicken Wings

Prep time: 10 minutes • Cook time: 15 minutes • Serves 6

2 lb. all-purpose shortening

3 lb. chicken wings

$^1/_2$ to 1 cup tapioca starch

3 TB. butter, at room temperature

1 TB. red curry paste

1 TB. fish sauce

2 tsp. paprika

1 TB. honey

2 TB. chopped cilantro leaves

Fill a frying pan halfway up the sides with shortening and heat to 350°F.

Dredge chicken wings in tapioca starch, shaking off any excess. Submerge wings in shortening in a single layer, working in batches if necessary. Wings should just fit into the pan, but not touch. Fry chicken for 8 to 10 minutes. Drain on paper towels and keep wings warm in a large stainless-steel bowl placed in a 150°F oven until all batches are cooked.

Heat butter, curry paste, fish sauce, paprika, and honey in a small saucepan set over low heat. Whisk just until butter is melted. Pour red curry sauce over wings and toss to coat. Top with cilantro, toss again, and serve in individual bowls with lots of paper towels.

Edamame

Prep time: 2 minutes • Cook time: 6 minutes • Serves 6

4 cups water

2 lb. frozen edamame

Sea salt to taste

$^1\!/_2$ tsp. freshly ground black pepper

Bring a 2-quart pot filled with water to a boil. Add edamame and boil for five minutes. Drain pods and place into large serving bowls. Toss with sea salt and pepper. Serve at once.

To eat edamame, hold a pod to your mouth and squeeze, popping beans in. While removing pod from your mouth, gently graze your lips over the pod, picking up a little of the seasoning.

Lucky Treasures

Edamame can be found frozen in most Asian or health food markets. There simply is no substitute for these addictive pods. Once you try them, you'll want to stock up; they make a fast, tasty impromptu snack or appetizer.

Although traditionally served warm, edamame can also be served cold. After draining the water off, throw the pods into a bowl filled with ice water, tossing until they chill. Strain again and serve with salt and pepper.

Crab, Corn, and Cream Cheese Wontons

Prep time: 25 minutes • Cook time: 20 minutes • Serves 6

$^1/_2$ cup cream cheese, softened

2 TB. chopped green onion

$^1/_4$ cup frozen sweet corn

2 TB. diced red bell pepper

$^1/_2$ tsp. salt

$^1/_4$ tsp. freshly ground black pepper

8 oz. lump crabmeat, picked over for shell fragments

1 egg yolk

2 TB. water

30 wonton wrappers

2 quarts canola oil

1 cup sweet chili sauce

Place cream cheese into an electric mixer fitted with the paddle attachment and mix for three minutes on low speed. Add green onion, corn, red bell pepper, salt, and pepper, mixing on low for one minute or until thoroughly mixed. Add crab and briefly mix at low speed just until crab is incorporated into the mixture.

In a small bowl or cup, beat egg yolk and water together with a fork. Place a wonton wrapper in front of you and brush two adjacent sides of wrapper with egg wash. Place a rounded tea-spoon crab-cheese mixture onto center of wonton and fold in half creating a triangle, pressing at edges to create a tight seal. Repeat the process with remaining wontons and filling.

Heat oil to 350°F in a 1-gallon heavy pot and fry wontons in three or four batches until they are golden brown, about 1 to 2 minutes per batch. Heat chili sauce in a small saucepan. When warmed through, pour into small dipping bowls and serve with wontons.

Sriracha Fried Rice

Prep time: 15 minutes • Cook time: 15 minutes • Serves 6

1 lb. skinless, boneless chicken breasts, sliced against the grain

3 TB. canola oil

4 eggs, beaten with a fork

1/3 cup sriracha sauce

2 TB. soy sauce (Golden Mountain brand)

3 TB. fish sauce

2 TB. granulated sugar

6 cups steamed jasmine rice

1 cup chopped pineapple chunks

1/2 cup chopped green onion

3 roma tomatoes, quartered

2 limes, quartered

Bring a 2-quart saucepan filled with water to a boil. Add chicken and boil for three minutes, remove from the pot, and drain on paper towels.

Heat a wok over high heat and add oil. When oil begins to smoke, add eggs and chicken. Stir-fry just until eggs start to scramble. Add sriracha sauce, soy sauce, fish sauce, sugar, and rice. Continue to stir-fry for three minutes. Add pineapple, green onion, and tomato. Toss together in the wok and arrange on a large platter. Serve hot, garnished with lime wedges.

Green Curry Fried Rice

Prep time: 15 minutes • Cook time: 40 minutes • Serves 6

1 lb. boneless, skinless chicken breast, sliced

3 TB. canola oil

3 tsp. green curry paste

1 cup chopped (1-inch cubes) eggplant

1/2 cup chopped carrot

1/4 cup canned coconut milk

2 TB. granulated sugar

3 TB. fish sauce

6 cups jasmine rice, steamed

2 TB. soy sauce (Golden Mountain brand)

1/4 cup chopped Asian basil

Boil a 2-quart saucepan filled with water over high heat. Add the chicken. Cook in the boiling water for three minutes, remove chicken from water, and drain on paper towels.

Heat a wok over high heat and add oil and curry paste. Stir-fry for two minutes. Add eggplant and carrot, stir-frying for two minutes. Stir in coconut milk and bring to a boil. Add chicken to the wok with sugar and fish sauce; stir-fry for two more minutes. Toss in rice and soy sauce. Stir-fry until rice has turned green from curry. Sprinkle with basil and toss everything one last time. Place fried rice in a warmed large bowl and serve hot.

Asian Bolognese

Prep time: 20 minutes • Cook time: 45 minutes • Serves 6

1 TB. canola oil	1 cup plain tomato sauce
$\frac{1}{2}$ cup diced yellow onion	3 TB. fish sauce
$\frac{1}{4}$ cup minced fresh garlic	2 TB. tomato purée
$\frac{1}{2}$ cup diced carrot	1 TB. granulated sugar
1 lb. ground chuck	$\frac{1}{2}$ cup canned coconut milk
8 oz. lean ground pork	$\frac{1}{4}$ cup chopped Asian basil
1 TB. Panang curry paste	$\frac{1}{2}$ lb. egg noodles (or fettuccine)

Heat wok over high heat and add oil. When oil begins to smoke, add onion, garlic, and carrot and stir-fry for two minutes. Add ground chuck and pork and stir-fry for three minutes. Stir in curry paste and cook for another two minutes. Add tomato sauce, fish sauce, tomato purée, and sugar. Reduce heat to low and simmer sauce for 30 minutes. Turn heat to high on sauce and stir in coconut milk and basil. Bring to a boil and simmer for three minutes.

During the last 15 minutes of simmering, boil noodles in a 3-gallon pot filled with 8 quarts lightly salted water for six minutes or until tender. Drain well. Divide noodles among six warm soup bowls using a pair of tongs. Remove sauce from heat and generously ladle it over the noodles. Serve hot.

Chapter 25

Dinner for Two

In This Chapter

- ◆ A spectacular menu for a special someone
- ◆ Couch potatoes, Asian-style
- ◆ Wok quickie
- ◆ Asian al fresco dining
- ◆ Sharing in the kitchen

Too often we find ourselves just popping something in the microwave for dinner, more as a way to avoid starvation than to achieve any sort of gastronomic delight.

Start using your new Asian cooking skills to bring even a Monday night up to "night on the town" standards. We've put together menus to cover occasions ranging from a grand celebration to a last-minute meal.

Special Occasion

We've provided a distinctive "Special Occasion" menu for a celebratory evening, be it an anniversary, birthday, or the first time you cook for a potential love interest. Splurge on some first-rate sake and make it an evening to remember.

Dinner and a Movie

Big bowls of steaming noodles and easy-to-grab popcorn with an Asian twist are the perfect partners for an evening at home, nestled in front of the TV to watch the latest release of an old favorite. Our recommendation is *Tampopo,* an Asian "cowboy" classic that portrays the true essence of the royalty of noodle soup.

> **Orient Expressions**
> Hanami, cherry blossom time, is a very popular time for picnics in Japan. Masses of people gather to eat sushi, drink sake, dance, and do the karaoke thing under trees ablaze with white and pink blossoms.

Picnic

Our "Picnic" menu is an elegant assortment of Asian fruits and Old World cheese, followed by a Vietnamese version of an American standard, the club sandwich, with paté standing in for the bacon and a lovely jicama slaw-style dressing. All you need to add is the meadow and a rippling brook.

A Quickie–Last-Minute Dinner

Our "Quickie" menu is a spur-of-the-moment dinner that will leave your guest thinking you've slaved all day to prepare this elegant, enticing meal.

"I Cook. You Cook. We All Cook ..."

Cooking together can be lots of fun, even if one of you is, shall we say, somewhat "culinarily challenged." One can grill the pineapple and string the snow peas, while the other gets the crab cakes together.

The Least You Need to Know

- Whether lounging in front of the TV or beside a babbling brook, an Asian meal is always appropriate
- Think of sharing kitchen duty as a great way to bond with a friend.
- Celebrate important dates with an Asian meal.

Wasabi Caesar Salad–Special Occasion

Prep time: 20 minutes   •   Chill time: 30 minutes   •   Serves 2

1 egg yolk

1 tsp. Worcestershire sauce

$^1/_2$ cup vegetable oil

2 TB. lime juice (divided use)

$^1/_2$ tsp. minced fresh garlic

1 tsp. wasabi paste

1 tsp. minced fresh ginger

Salt to taste

1 quart canola oil

$^1/_2$ cup fresh egg noodles, divided in half

1 head romaine lettuce, washed and trimmed

$^1/_4$ cup shaved Parmesan cheese

Freshly ground pepper to taste

Beat egg yolk in a small nonreactive bowl. Whisk in Worcestershire sauce. Slowly whisk in oil in a very slow, steady stream. As dressing begins to emulsify (thicken), add 1 tablespoon lime juice, garlic, wasabi, ginger, and a pinch of salt to the bowl. When oil is fully incorporated, stir in remaining lime juice. Dressing should coat the back of a spoon. Refrigerate for 30 minutes.

Heat canola oil in a 2-quart saucepan to 350°F. Fry noodles for 15 seconds on each side, or until they are golden brown and crispy. Drain on paper towels. Season noodles with salt while they are hot.

Chop romaine into one-inch pieces with a sharp knife, place it into a salad bowl, and pour dressing over it. Toss salad gently and add cheese. Toss again. Season to taste with salt and pepper. Divide salad between two chilled dinner plates and top with fried noodles.

Fortune Cookies

This recipe seems like it has a lot of wasted tossing, doesn't it? Besides an impeccable dressing, the secret to a good Caesar salad is that every bump and cranny of the lettuce is lightly coated with the dressing; then the flavor melds nicely with the cheese—taste it—then salt and pepper. Gentle repetitive tossing ensures success.

Five-Spice Pecan Truffles—Special Occasion

Prep time: 30 minutes • Chill time: 2 hours • Cook time: 10 minutes • Serves 2

2 tsp. granulated sugar

$^1/_2$ tsp. butter

$^1/_4$ cup heavy cream

$^1/_2$ cup chocolate chips

$^1/_2$ tsp. Chinese five-spice powder

$^1/_4$ cup chopped pecans

Heat a small saucepan over low heat and add sugar, butter, and heavy cream. Bring to a boil. Stir in chocolate chips with a wooden spoon until chips are completely melted. Remove from heat and transfer chocolate mixture to a container, cover, and refrigerate for two hours. Chocolate should be pliable, but not too hard or soft, like a very thick icing.

Preheat the oven to 350°F. Mix five-spice powder and pecans together and toast in the oven for five minutes. Cool the nuts.

At this point, you need to work very quickly, because the heat from your hands will melt chocolate. Take a teaspoon-size scoop of mixture in the palm of your hand and quickly roll it into a ball. Place on a baking sheet lined with waxed paper. Keep making truffles until all the mixture is used. Place the cookie sheet in the refrigerator for 10 minutes to set surface of balls. Remove from the refrigerator and roll them in the pecan mixture. Serve at room temperature.

These truffles can stay out for several hours. Store them in an airtight container in the refrigerator, but always serve them at room temperature for the best flavor and texture.

Ginger Crab Stuffed Lobster—Special Occasion

Prep time: 25 minutes • Cook time: 20 minutes • Serves 2

Salt to taste

2 (1- to 1¹/₂-lb.) lobsters

¹/₄ cup lump crabmeat, picked over for shells

¹/₄ cup panko (Japanese bread crumbs)

¹/₂ tsp. minced jalapeño

¹/₂ tsp. minced fresh garlic

1 large egg

1 TB. soy sauce

1 TB. chopped cilantro leaves

2 tsp. minced fresh ginger

¹/₄ cup dry sherry

2 stalks lemongrass, trimmed, peeled to the soft core, and chopped

¹/₄ cup heavy cream

3 TB. unsalted butter, cut into 6 pieces

Preheat the oven to 375°F.

Bring a 4-gallon pot of water to a boil and add salt to taste. Place lobsters into pot and boil for three minutes. Remove lobsters from pot and plunge them into cold water to stop the cooking. Remove them from water and with a sharp knife, cut the underside of the lobsters in half length-wise from head to tail.

To make stuffing, combine crabmeat, panko, jalapeño, garlic, egg, soy sauce, cilantro, and ginger, with your hands, making sure it's moist enough to hold together when you give it a little squeeze. Set aside.

Pry lobster apart where you made the cut. Sure, you'll hear cracking, but that's a good thing. Don't pull so hard that you pull lobster into two pieces; that's a bad thing. Remove the *tomalley* (green substance) from cavity just above tail. Fill cavity with crab mixture and set lobsters in a roasting pan, crab side up. Bake lobsters for 10 minutes. Remove from the oven and keep warm.

Boil sherry and lemongrass together in a small saucepan over high heat. Reduce this by half and add heavy cream. Reduce by half again and turn heat down to low. Cut butter into large pieces and slowly whisk it into sauce piece by piece until all is incorporated. Season sauce with salt to taste and strain. Place each lobster on a warm serving plate and serve with sauce on the side in a small dish or cup for dipping.

Orient Expressions

Just what is all that green stuff? It's called **tomalley,** which is the liver or digestive tract of the lobster. Considered by some to be a delicacy, it's usually whisked into a butter sauce to serve with the lobster. It can be quite tasty, but because lobsters are bottom feeders, it's a good idea not to make a steady diet of it.

Chicken Ramen Noodles—Dinner and a Movie

Prep time: 15 minutes • Marinate time: 1 hour • Cook time: 15 minutes • Serves 2

3 TB. sweet soy sauce

1/4 cup sake

3 TB. mirin

1 tsp. granulated sugar

1 TB. chopped cilantro leaves

2 (3/4 lb.) chicken breasts

1/4 cup thinly sliced bamboo shoots

2 TB. distilled white vinegar

5 cups chicken stock

2 TB. fish sauce

1 cup ramen noodles

1 cup fresh spinach, stemmed

1/4 cup minced green onion

Mix sweet soy sauce, sake, mirin, sugar, and cilantro in a medium-size nonreactive bowl. Add chicken, turn to coat, and marinate in the refrigerator for one hour.

Mix bamboo shoots and vinegar together.

When ready to cook, remove the chicken from the marinade and discard the marinade. Heat a grill to medium-high heat. Grill chicken for five minutes on each side, remove, and let rest, keeping it warm.

Heat a wok over high heat and pour in chicken stock, fish sauce, and noodles. Bring to a boil, and continue to boil for five minutes. Remove noodles from soup using a large flat strainer and divide between two large warm soup bowls. Reserve the soup in the wok.

Add spinach to the wok and bring to a boil again. Remove from heat. Remove spinach from soup. Ladle hot soup over noodles and slice chicken. Pick up chicken slices with your knife and slide them off to top of noodles. Place spinach on top next to chicken, remove bamboo shoots from vinegar, and place them next to spinach. Sprinkle with minced green onion. Serve hot with a soupspoon and chopsticks.

Orient Expressions

You know ramen, those cellophane-wrapped folded curly noodles you've stumbled across in the soup aisle at the market? *Ramen* is the Japanese pronunciation of the Chinese *lo mein*, which means "boiled noodles." Buy ramen noodles at Asian markets where you will find noodles that are fresh or frozen. The ramen noodles found in American supermarkets are, unfortunately, not very good for you. Each package contains more than 1,500 mg of sodium; they are deep-fried in palm oil, one of the worst oils you can ingest.

Popcorn with Lemongrass Butter— Dinner and a Movie

Prep time: 5 minutes　•　Cook time: 10 minutes　•　Serves 2

2 TB. sake

1 stalk lemongrass, trimmed, peeled to the soft core and chopped

1 kaffir lime leaf

2 TB. unsalted butter

1 package microwave popcorn, containing no butter or salt

$^{1}/_{4}$ tsp. kosher salt

Combine sake, lemongrass, and lime leaf in a small saucepan, and bring to a boil. Reduce in volume by half and melt in butter. Pop corn in the microwave. Strain sauce to remove any lemongrass and lime leaf pieces and pour over hot popcorn. Sprinkle with salt and toss to coat.

Popcorn with Curry Dust—Dinner and a Movie

Prep time: 5 minutes　•　Cook time: 4 minutes　•　Serves 2

$^{1}/_{2}$ tsp. kosher salt

$^{1}/_{4}$ tsp. yellow curry powder

1 package microwave popcorn, unsalted

Mix salt with curry powder. Pop popcorn in the microwave. Sprinkle popcorn with curry dust and toss.

Asian Fruit and Cheese—Picnic

Prep time: 15 minutes • Cook time: 5 minutes • Serves 2

2 TB. walnut pieces	1 Fuji apple
$1/4$ tsp. Chinese five-spice powder	1 Asian pear
2 oz. goat cheese	1 star fruit
2 oz. Roquefort cheese	2 TB. white truffle oil
2 oz. ripe Brie cheese	$1/2$ tsp. freshly ground black pepper

Preheat the oven to 350°F.

Toss walnuts with five-spice powder and toast in the oven for five minutes or until fragrant and lightly browned. Make bite-size balls of goat cheese by using a wet teaspoon and rolling each ball with slightly damp hands. Roll balls in the spiced walnut mixture. Crumble Roquefort cheese into small pieces and place on one side the platter. Slice Brie and place next to Roquefort along with the walnut crusted goat cheese. Core apple and pear; cut into bite-size pieces. Slice star fruit. Arrange fruit on other side of platter. Finish presentation by drizzling truffle oil over fruit and cheese. Grind fresh black pepper over all. Serve at room temperature.

Recipes for Success

Cheese is served best slightly warmer than the 40°F straight from the refrigerator. To get it to this temperature, pull out the platter about 15 to 20 minutes before you plan to serve it. If your picnic is on the road, pack the fruit and cheese in plastic containers, place them in a basket or cooler, and plan to serve about an hour later. The temperature should be about right.

Vietnamese Sandwich–Picnic

Prep time: 10 minutes　•　Marinate time: 1 hour　•　Cook time: 10 minutes　•　Serves 2

¹/₂ cup distilled white vinegar

2 TB. granulated sugar

1 jalapeño chili pepper, cut in (2-inch) julienne

¹/₂ cup julienned (2-inch) jicama

¹/₄ cup julienned (2-inch) carrot

1 baguette French bread

2 TB. pork paté

3 oz. deli ham, thinly sliced

3 oz. deli turkey breast, thinly sliced

¹/₄ cup whole cilantro leaves

Boil vinegar and sugar in a small saucepan set over high heat for five minutes. Remove from heat and cool.

Add jajapeño, jicama, and carrot to sweet vinegar and marinate for one hour.

Preheat the oven to 350°F. Toast baguette in the oven for five minutes or until crisp. Cut baguette in half and slice each half lengthwise. Spread paté evenly on one side. Top with ham, turkey, and pickled vegetables and scatter cilantro leaves on top. Replace top of baguette and serve with Thai Cucumber Salad.

Lucky Treasures

There are as many varieties of the Vietnamese sandwich as there are Vietnamese. This is just one of them. Other types include sliced Chinese sausage, sliced fresh serrano chiles, grilled pork ... but we digress. Time to make the sandwich!

Baked Halibut in Banana Leaf—the Quickie

Prep time: 20 minutes • Cook time: 35 minutes • Serves 2

2 halibut fillets (about 1 lb.), rinsed and dried with paper towels

2 tsp. sesame oil

$^1/_2$ tsp. salt

$^1/_2$ tsp. freshly cracked black pepper

2 sheets banana leaf

2 lemons

$^1/_4$ cup julienned (2-inch) carrot

$^1/_4$ cup sliced green onion

1 tsp. sliced fresh garlic

1 tsp. minced fresh ginger

2 kaffir lime leaves

2 TB. chopped fresh cilantro

2 cups steamed jasmine rice

Heat the oven to 375°F.

Rub halibut fillets with sesame oil and season with salt and pepper. Lay a banana leaf out flat on a work surface and place fish in center. Squeeze juice of one lemon on each fillet. Scatter half the carrots, green onion, garlic, ginger, lime leaves, and cilantro over each fillet. Wrap banana leaf around fish to make an envelope and seal with a couple toothpicks.

Place halibut on a roasting pan and bake for 25 minutes or until fish flakes. Check for doneness by poking a hole in leaf and taking a peek. Remove from banana leaf and serve on a large plate with steamed rice.

Ginger Snow Peas—We All Cook

Prep time: 10 minutes • Cook time: 5 minutes • Serves 2

$^3/_4$ cup fresh snow peas

1 TB. unsalted butter

2 tsp. shredded pickled ginger

2 TB. chicken stock

$^1/_4$ tsp. red pepper flakes

$^1/_4$ tsp. salt

Rinse snow peas, leaving them whole. If ends are brown, snap them off.

Heat a wok over medium-high heat. Add butter, ginger, and snow peas and stir-fry for one minute. Add chicken stock, red pepper flakes, and salt. Stir-fry for two minutes longer and spoon onto a large, warm serving plate. Serve hot.

Garlic Chinese Long Beans—the Quickie

Prep time: 2 minutes • Cook time: 5 minutes • Serves 2

1 TB. sesame oil	$^1/_4$ cup chicken stock
2 tsp. minced fresh garlic	2 TB. oyster sauce
$^1/_2$ lb. Chinese long beans	$^1/_2$ tsp. freshly ground black pepper

Heat a wok over medium heat and add oil. When oil begins to ripple, add garlic. Stir-fry for one minute, tossing frequently to prevent garlic from burning. Add long beans. Stir-fry for three minutes and add chicken stock. Bring to a boil and add oyster sauce. Stir-fry for two more minutes and remove from heat. Season with black pepper. Serve hot as a side dish on a warm serving plate.

> **Lucky Treasures**
>
> Chinese long beans are just that—l-o-n-g. When buying them at the Asian market, they might be marked as *long beans* or *Chinese long beans*. Their flavor is comparable to that of green beans, which you can substitute for them. What you can't substitute is the delight with which people will eat them.

Grilled Pineapple—We All Cook

Prep time: 10 minutes • Cook time: 10 minutes • Serves 2

1 small pineapple, skinned and cut in half lengthwise

2 TB. brown sugar

$^1/_2$ cup water

Cut pineapple in $^1/_2$-inch slices (creating half-moon shapes). Place into a medium-size bowl.

Bring brown sugar and water to a boil in a small saucepan set over high heat and cook for three minutes or until syrupy. Pour over pineapple.

Heat the grill to high heat. Remove pineapple from sugar sauce, shaking off excess. Place pineapple slices on the grill, basting with extra sauce. Grill pineapple for two minutes on each side or until each piece has a nice caramel glaze. Serve warm or at room temperature.

Crispy Noodle Crab Cakes—We All Cook

Prep time: 45 minutes • Chill time: 20 minutes • Cook time: 15 minutes • Serves 2

$^1/_2$ cup panko (Japanese breadcrumbs)

1 medium egg, beaten

2 TB. mayonnaise

2 tsp. minced fresh ginger

1 tsp. minced fresh garlic

2 TB. thinly sliced green onion

$^1/_4$ cup minced red bell pepper

$^1/_4$ tsp. red pepper flakes

$^1/_2$ tsp. salt

2 TB. fresh cilantro leaves, chopped

8 oz. lump crabmeat, picked over to remove shell fragments

$^1/_2$ cup thin, fresh egg noodles

$^1/_4$ cup buttermilk

$^1/_2$ cup sour cream

2 tsp. yellow curry powder, or to taste

2 tsp. fresh lime juice

$^1/_2$ tsp. salt

1 quart canola oil

Mix breadcrumbs, egg, mayonnaise, ginger, garlic, green onion, red bell pepper, red pepper flakes, salt, and cilantro together in a medium-size stainless-steel or glass bowl. Gently fold in crab, taking care not to break crab up too much. You should be able to see lumps of crab in the mix. Refrigerate for 20 minutes so mixture will set up, making it easier to form crab cakes.

Divide crab into six portions. Pick up one portion and roll it lightly into a ball. The goal here is to make a puck-shape crab cake, so with a ball of crab in the palm of one hand, press down with the other, making two flat sides. While your hand is still over crab cake, wrap your thumb around side and press in lightly. Rotate crab cake around with your top hand, making the edges even. Place uncooked noodles on a flat surface and divide into six portions. Pick up one crab cake and wrap some noodles all around it. Roll remaining crab cakes in the noodles and set them aside.

Whisk buttermilk, sour cream, curry powder, lime juice, and salt in a stainless-steel or glass bowl. Pour canola oil into a medium-size sauté pan to come halfway up the sides. Oil should come up around crab cakes halfway, so add more oil if necessary. Heat oil over medium-high heat. When oil is 350°F, place half of the crab cakes into the pan in a single layer and fry for two minutes on each side until noodles expand and have a golden brown color. Repeat with remaining crab cakes. Drain on paper towels. Place cakes on individual warm serving plates, spoon sauce on top and around cakes, and serve hot.

>—<⊖>—<

Glossary

apple, Fuji   Red, crisp, and juicy, the Fuji is more aromatic and subtler than most apples. As the name implies, this variety originated in Fuji.

asparagus   Asparagus is sold in bunches that weigh in at about 1 to 1½ pounds. The younger the stalk, the more tender—although older, thicker stalks, if not too woody at the bottom, usually provide the most flavor.

baby corn   You can find fresh baby corn in some markets, but usually you'll find these little ears of pickled corn sold in cans and jars. Though Tom Hanks did try to eat them like corn on the cob to rather hysterical results in the movie *Big*, they are completely edible, cob and all.

bamboo shoots   The delicate young shoots of bamboo plants harvested when they are less than two weeks old. Fresh bamboo shoots must be peeled, sliced, and cooked in boiling water before eating. Canned bamboo shoots are ready to eat.

bamboo skewers   These all-purpose skewers are made of bamboo (obviously) and are used to make satays and just about anything that requires skewering. Always soak in water for at least 30 minutes before skewering and they won't burn when they are put on the broiler or grilled.

banana leaves   Big, fresh banana leaves are sold at Asian markets and used as wraps for cooking much like foil but with far more aesthetically pleasing results. Frozen leaves can be bought and stored in the freezer until you're ready to use them.

basil   Thai or Asian basils are small-leafed, often purple tinged, very aromatic basils that have the distinct scent of anise to them. Chop the leaves and add them just before serving as they don't stand up well to cooking.

bean curd   *See* tofu.

bean sprouts   There are all sorts of bean sprouts, but in Asian cooking mung bean sprouts are most often called for. They are crispy, slim, two- to three-inch-long white sprouts that are usually sold in bulk. Store in cold water in the refrigerator to preserve freshness.

beef paste   A beef concentrate used to make soups and light years beyond powdered soup mixes and canned broth, beef paste can be found in the soup section next to the bouillon cubes in most grocery stores.

black bean sauce   Black bean sauce is made from fermented black beans and soy sauce. Closer to a paste in texture than a sauce, it's very salty and usually used in small quantities, often with a dab of sugar for balance.

black vinegar   Slightly similar to balsamic vinegar, black vinegar is a mild, slightly sweet vinegar made from glutinous rice. It has a somewhat smoky flavor, but the degree of smokiness depends on the brand.

blue crab   A variety of crab found in the Atlantic Ocean on both coasts of Europe and the USA. It is also found in the Gulf of Mexico. Blue crab is just that, blue; the body has a dark blue to emerald hue and blue claws and has a rich flavor with a hint of sweetness. The most popular crab eaten in the USA by far, the blue crab is available in hard or soft shell (in season) and fresh or frozen.

bok choy   This versatile and widely used Chinese cabbage has a long, thick, white, bulbous stem and deep green leaves. It's closer in shape to celery than the round heads we call cabbage.

button mushrooms   Cultivated worldwide, button mushrooms are available in practically every food market across the country. They are dense, white, and round with thick stems and come in sizes from small to jumbo. The flavor is mild and earthy. For the mildest flavor, purchase button mushrooms while the caps are still covering the "gills" (where the cap meets the stem) and for a fuller, earthier flavor buy them when the gills are exposed.

calamari   Calamari is the Italian word for "squid." This romantic term has become so widely used in the USA that both are virtually interchangeable. Calamari is available fresh, frozen, whole, cleaned, sliced, and stuffed.

cardamom   These aromatic seeds come from a member of the ginger family that is native to India but is now grown throughout the tropical world. Its distinctive flavor is reminiscent of eucalyptus, rosemary, and ginger. Best to buy it in pod form and pop them open for the seeds as needed.

chicken stock   *See* stock.

chili flakes   Coarsely crushed dried red chilies that come in many varieties. The most widely available is that of the cayenne pepper, which is usually just marked "red pepper flakes."

chili oil   Usually a deep orange color, this very spicy hot oil, made from ground chilies steeped in oil, is used in many dishes, especially in Szechuan fare. Use sparingly—its intense heat can take over a dish if you're not careful. Will last several months when stored in a cool, dry place.

chili paste   Coarsely ground chilies mixed with vinegar, and garlic, oil, or other spices. *Sambal oelek* is one of the most common varieties. The heat varies from brand to brand. Refrigerate after opening and it will keep for several months.

chili peppers   Chili peppers are the fruit of various plants of the *capsicum* or pepper family, which ranges from peppercorns to the fleshy bell pepper to the tiny ultra hot pequin chili pepper. Flavors span mild to hot and skins are usually orange, red, yellow, and green colored. Also available dried, they usually go by a different name than their fresh counterparts. Dried chilies cannot be substituted for fresh.

chili sauce   Well-puréed chilies are mixed with water and seasoned with salt, garlic, sugar, and vinegar and usually packaged in squeeze bottle. Sriracha is the most commonly found variety. Heat varies from brand to brand, so try a little before you use a lot!

chilies, bird's-eye   Bird's-eye chilies are native to Thailand and are shaped like a teardrop, hence the reference to a "bird's eye." These chiles can be fiery hot to medium hot, so taste them first to gauge how much should go in a dish. The more plentiful chili pequin, which is available in Mexican markets, is a good substitute if you can't find the rarer bird's-eye.

chili sauce, pineapple   Usually found as a condiment in Asian markets. If you can't find it, combine 2 tablespoons oyster sauce, 5 tablespoons sweet chili sauce, 5 tablespoons water, $1/4$ cup crushed or diced pineapple, and $1/4$ teaspoon cornstarch in a saucepan. Bring to a boil, remove from the heat, and cool.

Chinese broccoli   The stalk looks like a slender, mini version of regular broccoli, but the heads are small and flowerlike. The stems are more tender and the broad leaves and tiny flower buds on the ends of the stems have a more pronounced and somewhat more bitter flavor than regular broccoli. Great in stir-fry and may be steamed or boiled. Can substitute with broccoli rabe.

Chinese cabbage   *See* bok choy.

Chinese or Asian celery   This is a descendent of the wild celery of Asia and differs from our celery in that it has a hollow stem, a much stronger flavor, and is rarely eaten raw. Ranging in color from almost white to deep green, it's great in soups and stir-frys.

cilantro   The fresh green leaves of the coriander herb, cilantro is widely used in Asian cooking and its tangy flavor is also the key to Mexican salsas. Sprinkle chopped leaves on soups, curries, salads, and seafood dishes. The stems are often added to Asian dishes to lend extra flavor. The seeds of the cilantro plant are called coriander, a flavor which is not interchangeable with cilantro.

cinnamon   Sri Lanka and Myanmar (formerly Burma) are home to real cinnamon. Made from the inner bark of an evergreen of the laurel family, it's been prized for centuries for its culinary and medicinal uses. Cassia, or Chinese cinnamon, is grown in many countries and is less expensive and less aromatic than true cinnamon. Powdered cinnamon is mostly cassia, maybe with a little true cinnamon added.

cloves   Cloves are made from the dried flower buds of a myrtle tree native to Southeast Asia. Usually used whole, little spikes of cloves add a spicy, perfumed flavor to many dishes. The head of the bud may be ground to make a powder. Do not eat whole cloves as they are indigestible; be sure to remove them before serving.

coconut   Fresh coconut is a delightful addition to many dishes, especially Indian and Thai curries, and is far more aromatic than the dried version. When shopping, look for coconuts that are mold and moisture free on the outside and, when shaken, sound like they are full of water. Which they are! The milky white water in the center of a coconut is used as a drink and in many recipes. It's not to be confused with coconut milk, which is cooked down from the white flesh of the coconut and water. Coconut cream is a sweeter, more condensed version of coconut milk. "Cream of coconut" is an entirely different animal, used in desserts and drinks. You can buy canned coconut milk, but making your own is simple: Combine the grated flesh of 1 coconut with 1 cup hot water, stir, then let stand and cool, squeeze and strain through cheesecloth to extract as much liquid as possible, then refrigerate.

coriander   The seeds of the coriander (or cilantro) plant, which are available whole or ground and used in curries, stews, and soups throughout Asia. *See* cilantro.

cucumber, Japanese/Korean/Chinese   Asian cucumbers are generally longer and thinner than our cucumbers with smaller or no seeds, more prickly skins, and a sweeter flavor. American cucumbers that have had the seeds scraped out can be substituted.

cumin   These pale brown seeds are used in spice mixtures throughout Asia, particularly in India. Though the shape of the seed is similar to its cousin, caraway, the flavor is more intense. Pale green and black varieties can also be found.

curry leaf   Small, dark green leaves of the curry leaf tree are used extensively in India and Southeast Asia much the way we use bay leaves. Indian grocers carry fresh leaves which will keep for a couple of weeks in an airtight container. Dried curry leaves are milder but a more satisfactory substitute than bay leaves.

curry, Musman   Musman means Muslim. Traditionally combined with cilantro, lemongrass, and garlic, this Malaysian paste makes a creamy, medium curry with a vibrant flavor.

curry paste   Curry paste is a blend of clarified butter, curry powder, vinegar, and other seasonings. It is available as yellow, red, green, and panang curry, each with its own individual flavor.

curry powder   Curry powder is not made from the curry leaf. Rather, it's a blend of various spices ground together to form curry powder. Almost always there is some cumin, coriander, and chili pepper in the mix, with other spices added according to whether it's a surf, turf, or vegetarian dish.

curry powder, Madras   Madras curry is a distinctively pungent curry powder that is medium hot and named after the Indian state of Madras, where it originated. In India, there is no such thing as prepackaged powdered curry mixes. Each household blends their own daily. Madras usually contains a blend of curry leaves, turmeric, coriander, cumin, cinnamon, cloves, chile pepper, bay leaves, fenugreek, allspice, and black pepper.

daikon   A long, large cylindrical radish native only to Asia, with white or black skin. Daikon is eaten raw or cooked and used either way, and has a crisp fresh flavor that can be hotter than American radishes.

dashi   Japanese soup stock made with *kombu* (dried kelp) and *katsuobushi* (dried bonito fish). It's the basis for almost all Japanese soups, and gives them a flavor profile unlike soups from the rest of Asia.

dungeness crab   Dungeness crab is found all along the Pacific Ocean from Alaska to Mexico. It has a sweet flavor and is available fresh or frozen in its hard shell only. Incidentally, the only legal dungeness crabs available for sale are male.

edamame   *See* soybeans.

eggplant   Ranging in color from white to deep purple, eggplants are native to the tropical areas of Asia. Most are longer and slimmer than ours, some over a foot long and only a couple of inches in diameter. There are also some small, bite-size pebble-shaped versions that are worth seeking out.

fennel   Only the seeds of the fennel plant are used in Asian cooking. Its distinctive aroma of anise makes is easy to recognize.

fish fumet or **fish stock**   *See* stock.

fish sauce   Called *nam pla* in Thailand and *nuac mam* in Vietnam, this distinctive sauce made of fermented fish is light golden brown in color and is used in marinades, dressings, and dipping sauces and as a seasoning. Don't be deterred by the aroma fresh out of the bottle, this flavor plays a key part in Asian dishes.

fish stock or **fish fumet** *See* stocks.

five-spice powder A strong combination of star anise, Szechuan peppercorns, fennel, cloves, and cinnamon used in Chinese cooking. Use sparingly until you get the hang of cooking with it.

galangal (Thai ginger) This pungent, aromatic member of the ginger family is used liberally in Asian cooking. Fresh galangal is available in Asian markets and is far preferable to the dried or powdered versions. Peel off the tough skin before pounding or slicing.

garam masala There are many varieties of garam masala, but the dry-roasted, aromatic, and flavorful blend usually contains black pepper, nutmeg, turmeric, and/or fennel seeds and can include up to 15 spices. *Garam* is the Indian word for "warm" or "hot," and *masala* means "spice." Garam masala may be purchased in Indian markets and in the gourmet section of some supermarkets. It's also easily prepared at home, but should be made in small batches to retain its freshness. Garam masala is usually used at the end of cooking or sprinkled over the final preparation.

garlic Another member of the lily family (*see* asparagus); the highly aromatic and spicy bulb is covered in a papery layer that is peeled off to reveal the cloves, which are used individually. Garlic is a universal vegetable that is used in just about every cuisine around the world.

ginger Quintessential flavoring for hundreds of Asian dishes, this rhizome, erroneously thought of as a root, adds spirit, liveliness, and verve to a dish. Scrape or trim off the tough outer skin before slicing or grating the yellowish, pulpy flesh used in cooking. Never use powdered or ground ginger as a substitute for fresh ginger; save that for cookies.

ginger, pickled Pickled ginger is preserved in a brine of rice vinegar or red wine and salt. It is available thinly sliced and in shoots. This pinkish condiment is a standard on sushi bars everywhere.

ginseng Ginseng root resembles ginger in appearance, but that's where the similarity ends. Highly aromatic, it is used in soups, lending a slight fennel flavor. Ginseng is also believed in most Asian cultures to be a healthful restorative and an aphrodisiac.

glutinous rice Glutinous rice is a white or dark brown rice used in sweet and savory Asian dishes and snacks. This rice contains more starch, accounting for the "stickiness" and its milky, chalky color. The best to buy is called "Sanpathong" from northern Asia.

Golden Mountain Sauce   Golden Mountain Sauce contains soybeans, water, sugar, salt, disodium-inosinate, and no preservatives. Slightly sweet, its contribution to Asian food and the food in this book makes it worth finding.

hoisin sauce   Dark, thick, spicy, and sweet, hoisin sauce is a mix of soybeans, sesame seeds, chili peppers, and sugar. It's used in hundreds of recipes for meat, noodles, and vegetables and as a dipping sauce.

horseradish, Japanese   *See* wasabi.

hot mustard powder   This is the yellow hot stuff they serve with eggrolls in your favorite Chinese restaurant. It can be purchased in little packets (which we throw away) or made fresh at home. Just mix a small amount with a little hot water for a killer heat each time you need it. It doesn't store well, so make in small batches of a tablespoon at a time.

jasmine rice   Jasmine rice is a young, tender rice with a strong flower-like aroma when raw that transforms into a subtle delicate flavor when cooked. Jasmine is Thai rice of the highest quality and it is the preferred rice by many around the world. It is available in most grocery stores and in Asian markets in big bulk bags.

jicama   Looks like a round version of its fellow member of the tuber family, the potato. It may be eaten raw or cooked and is particularly useful in stir-fry as it doesn't lose its crunch when cooked. Just be sure to peel it before eating or cooking.

juniper berries   The blue-black, aromatic berry of an evergreen bush, juniper berries are used to flavor gin and game dishes, particularly duck.

kaffir lime   The kaffir lime looks like a very bumpy, little green grapefruit with a knot on its head. The zest of the rind and the leaves have a flavor and aroma like no other citrus fruit. The leaves have a figure-eight shape and are available fresh, frozen, and in dried powder form (the latter not a great option) in Asian markets. If you can't find fresh kaffir limes for the zest, regular limes can be used, but the flavor will not be as intense.

kim chee   Kim chee is an extraordinarily spicy Korean pickled cabbage that is served as a condiment at the Korean table. It is usually made of Chinese cabbage and/or turnips that are heavily seasoned with garlic, chili peppers, green onions, ginger, and other spices and aged. Also known as Korean cabbage pickles.

kohlrabi   A member of the cabbage family. The bulbous, turnip-shaped root part that lies on the ground is used in cooking. Raw, it works as a crudités when thinly sliced. The leaves of very young plants may be used as you would spinach or mustard greens. Smaller bulbs are more tender and tasty.

leeks   Part of the onion family, the leek looks like a scallion on steroids. Sweet and milder than onion, the entire plant can be used in cooking. Leeks attract gritty dirt the way honey attracts flies. Wash well before using, especially between the blades where the white base meets the green stalks.

lemongrass   A lemon-scented grass-like plant that grows in thick clumps. Sold in stalks about a foot and a half long, it's only the bottom third that is used in cooking. For soups and long-cooking dishes, peel off the tough outer layer and pound the stalk slightly, leaving it in a long strand for easy removal before serving.

Chinese long beans   A long bean is an exceptionally long legume that grows as long as one yard, although most you will find are 18 to 24 inches long. It resembles a green bean that is easily bent and tastes similar as well, albeit not as sweet. It is also known as the asparagus bean.

lotus   Lotus flowers floating on the water are pretty to look at as well as good for cooking. The fat, tube-shaped root has a crunchy texture and is used in all sorts of Chinese dishes, while the leaves are used as a wrap. Its seeds are used fresh or dried in a variety of dishes both savory and sweet.

mango   Luscious, sweet, orange-fleshed, and juicy, mangos are a delicious tropical fruit used in drinks, salads, sweets, and other Asian treats. Green-skinned when young, ripe mangos are reddish yellow and yield slightly to the touch.

mirin   A sweet rice wine that's often referred to as sweet sake. Used extensively in Japanese cooking, it adds a little touch of sweetness to a dish. Aji-mirin is the most typical type found; it has some salt added, so taste before using.

miso   Miso is a mixture of soybeans and rice that has been salted, fermented, inoculated with yeast, and then aged. Used mainly in Japan, it is used as a flavoring and coloring agent, but is also used as a marinade and to make soup. Miso paste is available in more than 150 varieties, but just remember this: the lighter the color, the more subtle and sweeter the flavor.

mung beans   Most often used in stews and soups, dried mung beans are a staple item throughout much of Asia. Mung bean sprouts are the long, white, crunchy sprouts used in stir-fries and salads. Bean paste noodles are made from mung bean starch.

mushrooms   Thousands of varieties of mushrooms are grown in Asia and hundreds of them are used in cooking. Two of the most common and easiest to find are *shiitake* and *enoki* or golden mushrooms. With their elegant texture and nutty, earthy flavor, shiitake mushrooms are particularly popular. Available fresh or dried, the dried ones need to be soaked in warm water for 15 to 20 minutes before using. The fibrous stems are better reserved for the stockpot than the wok. Enoki or golden mushrooms look like a collection of little straws with hats on them. These soft, lightly flavored mushrooms are mostly eaten raw. When cooking with them, add at the last minute to retain the texture and flavor.

mussels   Mussels are found in most shallow waters of the Atlantic and Pacific oceans and the Mediterranean Sea. Many varieties are available, but the most common have a dark blue/black shell and average about two inches long. Green Tipped Mussels are named for the vibrant emerald green that lines the lip of the shell and come from New Zealand. They are only available frozen in the United States.

mustard, Chinese   *See* hot mustard powder.

pickled mustard cabbage   Pickled mustard cabbage is an Asian condiment. It's available in small tins, but if you can't find it you can make it at home by combining $^1/_2$ pound blanched, coarsely chopped mustard cabbage, $^1/_2$ cup soy sauce, $^1/_4$ cup grated ginger, and $^1/_4$ cup water. Refrigerate overnight for the flavors to blend.

mustard powder   *See* hot mustard powder.

nam pla   *See* fish sauce.

nori   *See* seaweed.

nuoc mam   *See* fish sauce.

nutmeg   Nutmeg is the kernel of a fleshy, apricot-like fruit native to parts of Indonesia. It's an essential spice in curries and has many medicinal uses. Buy fresh nutmeg and grate as needed as it loses its flavor very quickly after grating.

onion, fried   Fried onions are already prepared for you packed in cellophane bags. They can be found in the condiment aisle of the Asian market.

oyster sauce   A thick, rich sauce made from ground oysters, water, and salt, it's used to flavor a variety of dishes. It has a smoky, sweet flavor that masks the taste of the oysters.

palm sugar   Similar to maple sugar in method only, palm sugar is a coarse brown sugar that is made from the sap of the palm tree. It is available in syrup and in a sticky granular form.

pandan leaves   Pandan is a fragrant leaf used to wrap meats and sweets in Asia. You can also find a bottled "essence" that is used to flavor desserts and some main dishes.

panko   Panko are Japanese breadcrumbs that are flaked instead of ground. They lend a greater degree of crispness when used as a breading.

pear, Asian   These lumpy, round, juicy, crunchy, firm pears range from light brown to green and from small to large. They are also called Chinese Pear.

pine nut   These tiny, ivory-colored, wedge-shaped nuts come from several varieties of pine tree and offer a rich, distinctive, nutty flavor.

plum sauce   Plum sauce is a jam-like combination of plums, vinegar, sugar, and chilies. In the United States, we've taken to mistakenly calling it "duck sauce." It's that orange-hued sauce in the little plastic packet that comes with your egg rolls.

portobello mushrooms   Portobellos are actually very large, overgrown criminis (a brown button mushroom) that offer a rich mushroom experience. Use the tops and save the stems for soup.

prawns   Prawns are shrimp-like creatures that stand taller than a shrimp, with a narrower, crustier body and are usually about five to six inches long. The flesh is firm and white and the flavor is sweet and nut-like.

rice paper   Made from a mixture of rice flour, water, and salt, rolled out in thin sheets, steamed, and dried. Used as wrap for spring rolls. Be sure to dampen them with a little lukewarm water before rolling and folding.

rice vinegar   Made from rice wine, rice vinegar has a clear to straw color and is less acidic than the American counterparts.

rice wine   *See* sake.

saffron   Why is saffron the world's most expensive spice? Because it takes 70,000, hand harvested, *Crocus sativus* flowers to produce about a pound of saffron threads. Luckily it takes only a couple of the dark red threads to flavor a dish and add that gorgeous deep yellow color. For cooking, soak whole strands in hot (not boiling) milk for about 15 minutes and then add to the dish. Or lightly toast in a dry pan over low heat until they are crisp, crush, and add to the dish. Store fresh saffron threads in the freezer as they will quickly lose their fragrance if left at room temperature.

sake   A fermented rice beverage made in Japan. It's often referred to as rice wine, though the production method is closer to beer. See Chapter 19 for more information.

seaweed   Packed with nutrients and protein, seaweed in its various forms is a mainstay of the Asian diet. Dried sheets of dark green *nori* are used for sushi rolls in Japan. Fresh, green strands of seaweed called *wakame* are used in salads and soups. Dried wakame is also available; be sure to soak before using. *Kombu*, a brown to grayish black seaweed, is dried and folded into sheets, and is used as one of the basic seasonings for Japanese soups. *Laver* is dried and pressed into sheets. Deep purple or green in color, it's got a great zesty flavor. Must be soaked for at least an hour before using. *Mozuku* are hairlike strands sold in small squares.

sesame oil   Made from the oil of sesame seeds, sesame oil comes in toasted and untoasted varieties. The toasted variety is deep brown in color with a deep, rich, concentrated nutty flavor. Used more as a condiment than as a cooking oil, it's excellent in salad dressings. Untoasted, or cold-pressed, sesame oil is almost clear and has none of the flavor of the toasted oil; don't try to use it in place of the toasted variety.

sesame seeds   Toasted, white sesame seeds show up in everything from hamburger buns around the world to sticky, sweet sesame balls in Asian bakeries. But seek out black sesame seeds for a richer, nuttier flavor than their white cousins.

shrimp paste   Known by a variety of names such as *gkapbi*, *trasi*, and *belacon*, it's made of fermented, dried, and ground shrimp with an intense aroma that can blow you away the first time you smell it. The color and style vary from a pinkish color sold in jars to blackish brown bricks of paste. If a recipe does not add the shrimp paste prior to cooking, you must be sure to cook it separately before eating. To cook, wrap in foil and either broil or dry-fry in a heavy skillet for a couple of minutes.

soybeans   Soybeans are pea shaped, yellow-green beans packed with protein, fiber, amino acids, and vitamins. They are a key part of the Asian diet, whether ground for flour or made into a sauce, tofu, milk, or the ubiquitous soy sauce. The trendy way to eat them is as *edamame*, which is made from a variety of soybeans that have a larger, sweeter, and more nutty tasting bean than regular soybeans. The green pods are boiled whole in salty water. Serve whole and perfect the art of shooting the beans out of the pod into your mouth. Or remove the beans and toss in salads, stir-frys, or soups.

soy sauce   The most common seasoning used in Asian cooking for 3,000 years. Soy sauce is made from fermented soybeans, flour, salt, and water which is then aged. A somewhat thicker and more intense version is made with added mushrooms.

sriracha sauce   *See* chili sauce.

star fruit   Thin, mouth-puckering, star-shaped slivers of the star fruit are lovely as a garnish and are a nice balance to fried dishes.

stock   As in western cooking, stock is made by long and slow simmering of a variety of vegetables, either with or without meat, to extract their aromas and flavors to make a base for literally thousands of dishes. Chicken stock and fish stock are most commonly used in Asian cooking. Fish fumet is a more intense type of fish stock. Making stock at home is fairly simple and what's not used immediately can be frozen for future use. A variety of stocks are available to buy; some are sold as reductions that are reconstituted with water before using, whereas others are closer to a paste in consistency.

straw mushrooms   Looking like something out of Disney's movie, *Fantasia*, these mushrooms have a long, graceful, conical cap over a bulbous stem. The texture is silky and they have a mild flavor. Very hard to find fresh, but plentifully available canned.

sugarcane   Peel the tough outer layer of the sugarcane to reveal the white, sweet meat in the middle. Used in numerous recipes, sugarcane stalks also make a great garnish for drinks and skewers for satay.

tamarind   Brown pods of tamarind grow on evergreen trees soaring up to 80 feet tall. The tangy acidic pulp of the pods is used in drinks, curries, soups, chutneys, and sauces, most famously in Worcestershire sauce. Usually sold in packets of dried powder, it can sometimes be found fresh at Asian markets.

taro   The barrel-shaped root with its brown skin and white flesh is used like potatoes in southeast Asian cooking. The green leaves can be eaten, but, like the roots, must be cooked before eating, as the fresh sap contains crystals of calcium oxalate that can really tear up the mucus membranes in your mouth and throat.

tofu (soybean curd)   Produced from soymilk much the way cheese is from cow's milk. Though it's rather bland on its own, it readily absorbs flavors when cooked. Available in most grocery stores, it's sold in white blocks of various firmness. Extra-firm and firm are best for stir-fry. Silken is smoother in texture and great for salads and is used in Japanese soups. Deep-fried and grilled versions are also available. Store in cold water to preserve after opening.

wasabi   Often referred to as Japanese horseradish, this pungent condiment is a member of the cabbage family to which both mustard and horseradish belong. Native to Japan, the freshly grated rhizome of the wasabi is a great delicacy rarely found outside Japan. More common to us is the powdered form, which is reconstituted with water to make the green paste found on every plate of sushi. Also available in tubes, but it's not as flavorful as the dried version.

water chestnuts   Peel away the dark brown skin of fresh water chestnuts to reveal the crunchy, delicately flavored center. Used in salads, soups, and stir-fry. Canned water chestnuts are available at most grocery stores, but it's worth the effort to seek out fresh ones.

wood ear mushroom   Wood ear mushrooms have a wonderful crunchy, silky quality to them that is irreplaceable in Asian cooking. Used mostly for texture, the flavor can be quite bland. Available mostly in dried form and should be reconstituted according to recipe directions. If you find fresh, lucky you.

Index